CANCELLED

Fritz

The Story of a
Political Assassin
by
RONALD FLORENCE

THE DIAL PRESS   NEW YORK 1971

Fritz
The Story of a Political Assassin

Copyright © 1971 by Ronald Florence

Library of Congress Catalog Card Number: 72–150402

Printed in the United States of America

First Printing

"*Es ist passiert*"—"It just sort of
happened," people said there when other
people in other lands thought heavens know
what great events had taken place.

Robert Musil, *The Man Without Qualities*

"Beg to report, sir, I'm glad as I
can be," replied the Good Soldier Schweik.
"It'll be a grand thing if you and me
was to fall together fighting for the
Emperor and his family."

Jaroslav Hašek, *The Good Soldier Schweik*

Contents

CONTENTS

Fritz

1

At the Hotel Meissl
& Schadn

Count Karl Stürgkh, the Prime Minister of Austria, ate lunch every day at the Hotel Meissl & Schadn. Even in the midst of a world war, when the destiny of fifty million people depended upon the daily decisions of the Prime Minister, Count Stürgkh rarely varied his daily ritual. He would arrive at the great gold-and-white rococo dining room around twelve thirty. There he would sit at the reserved corner table from which he could survey both the entrance to the dining room and the floor-to-ceiling windows overlooking the Kärntnerstrasse (in peacetime the busiest and most fashionable street in Vienna) and dine on some variation of the beefsteak for which the hotel was deservedly famous. After he had eaten, he would carefully choose a liqueur and a cigar to go with his coffee, slowly savoring the brief leisure that both afforded. The few friends and many colleagues with whom he dined knew well how much Count Stürgkh enjoyed this ritual—understandably, since these lunches and the few hours he spent each evening at the

FRITZ

Café Pucher were his only respites from a life of awesome responsibility.

On October 21, 1916, a Saturday, Count Stürgkh lunched with the Governor of the Tirol, Count Friedrich von Toggenberg, who was in Vienna for a one-day business trip, and with a close friend with whom he often dined, Baron Felix von Aeherenthal, brother of the late Minister for Foreign Affairs. At the table nearest to them a German general sat with two staff officers. At the next table, separated from the tables of the Prime Minister and the general by the row of columns which divided the room, a lady sat alone. She was not a regular customer, and afterward no one remembered her very well. Other tables in the dining room were filled with the usual complement of politicians, financiers, diplomats, artists, and writers: the very rich and the very influential of Vienna who came daily to mix cabal with their coffee at the Hotel Meissl & Schadn.

Two tables away from Count Stürgkh, a slightly built man in his thirties sat alone facing the Prime Minister. He was dressed like a civil servant—stern black suit, plain white shirt, stiff collar, plain black tie—although he was somewhat more rumpled in appearance than a conscientious bureaucrat might permit. His more distinguishing features, which most of the other diners later remembered, were a full head of wavy hair, a bushy blond mustache, and small gold-rimmed glasses. Several of the guests who noticed him thought him somewhat out of place; he looked too donnish to be eating at the Hotel Meissl & Schadn.

The man with the gold-rimmed glasses ordered a large lunch of several courses, including plum pastry and coffee. He ate quickly, and paid his bill immediately (rather unusual in Vienna, where a popular expression says that *Herrenschaften haben Zeit,* "Gentlemen have time"). Then, for about forty-five minutes after he paid, he sat nervously, trying with apparent difficulty to concentrate on reading a newspaper he had brought with him.

A few minutes past two thirty, just after Count Stürgkh

had selected and lit a cigar, the man with the gold-rimmed glasses got up from his table, and with his right hand in his coat pocket, walked quickly toward the Prime Minister's table. He almost ran the last three steps. Count Toggenberg, who saw him coming, thought that he was headed for another table, since from his appearance he obviously had no business with anyone at the Prime Minister's table.

As the man passed Count Stürgkh, he turned sharply to the left and pulled a pistol from his coat pocket. Holding the weapon only a few inches from the Prime Minister's head, he rapidly fired three shots. After he had fired, he half mumbled, half shouted: "Down with tyranny! We want peace!"

Count Stürgkh slumped to the side, falling from his chair onto the floor. Blood streamed over his face and clothes, and as he fell he left a trail of blood on the tablecloth and on a menu that lay on the table.

The three shots came as such a surprise in the calm of the dining room that one diner thought he had heard loud handclaps until he saw the light cloud of powder floating over one corner of the room. After a few seconds of shocked silence, Count Toggenberg picked up a chair to use as a weapon against the assailant. The German general who had been sitting near the Prime Minister's table drew his saber and lunged, swinging the weapon madly above his head. Finally, amid much shouting and confusion, the headwaiter, with the help of the wine steward, a wiry man who had once belonged to an athletic club in America, succeeded in disarming the assailant, although in the scuffling someone had torn off his glasses and another shot had gone off, lightly wounding the headwaiter in the face before finally lodging in Baron Aeherenthal's foot.

When the assailant was apprehended and held immobile by the frenetic crowd of guests and waiters, he shouted, loudly enough for everyone in the dining room to hear: "I want to be tried in a court. I am Doctor Friedrich Adler."

FRITZ

Someone had gone to summon a physician immediately after the shots were fired. The physician, an emergency specialist named Dr. Lindenbaum, realized as soon as he saw the head wounds that the situation was hopeless. He nonetheless gave the Prime Minister an injection and listened in vain for a heartbeat. Finally he covered the body with a clean tablecloth and turned to attend the wounds of the headwaiter and Baron Aeherenthal.

Outside the entrance to the hotel, a crowd had begun to gather even before the physician arrived. The news of the assassination, mixed with sordid rumors about the identity and motives of the assassin, traveled quickly through the city, the empire, and the world. That evening Vienna was buzzing with hearsay. From the street in front of the Hotel Meissl & Schadn to Schönbrunn Palace, everyone had a favorite explanation of what happened. No one knew too much about the assassin, except that he was the son of Victor Adler, the most famous (the police would say infamous) leader of the Austrian labor movement, but in the third year of the world war, that connection alone was enough to "prove" what many would have suspected anyway—that the "Reds" were behind the assassination.

By morning, newspapers all over the world carried the headline: AUSTRIAN PRIME MINISTER ASSASSINATED. In Vienna it was the first time in more than two years that battle reports and other war news had been crowded off the front pages of the newspapers.

2

Fritz

While the Viennese public and the press were busy with their trial of the assassin, at police headquarters on the Elisabeth-promenade, in the Alsergrund district of Vienna, detectives took down what they called the "particulars" of the assassin. His name was Dr. Friedrich Adler. He was born in Vienna on July 9, 1879, was married, had three children (aged five, ten, and twelve), listed his religion as atheist, and gave his address as Sonnenhofgasse 6/7, in the Margareten district of Vienna, an area of cheap rooming houses and apartments. Looking up his criminal record the detectives found only two minor violations of the press censorship laws, in 1912 and 1913, for which he had been fined twenty and forty crowns respectively.

That evening Adler was placed in a cell. His necktie and belt were removed, and special guards were posted in his cell. In the middle of the night he asked one of the guards: "What do you

---

5

want? You do not believe that I would attempt suicide? I want to be tried."

The next morning Adler was arraigned before a magistrate and questioned.

He readily confessed: "Yesterday, at two thirty, I fired three or four shots from a Browning automatic pistol at Prime Minister Count Stürgkh with the intention of killing him . . ." He went on to explain that he had planned the assassination for six days.

"What did you expect from the success of the assassination?" asked the magistrate.

Adler answered: "I wanted to draw the attention of the European public to conditions in Austria, to explain that the situation, which is worse than in Russia, must necessarily have the same consequences that Russian Tsarism has brought about through its system."

After a few more questions and answers, the magistrate asked: "What was the connection between what you shouted in the restaurant and the murder of Count Stürgkh?"

Adler answered: "I considered the demonstration through assassination as an action in the struggle against tyranny and for peace. I did not believe that I would do away with tyranny through this demonstration, nor that I would bring about peace. Rather, I considered and I consider it only a small contribution in the struggle for these goals."

Adler denied that he had acted as part of a conspiracy, but on the direct orders of the Minister of Justice a formal inquiry was launched. For an ordinary murder the confession of the accused and the testimony of witnesses would have been more than enough evidence to proceed to trial. But this was no ordinary murder, and no corners were cut in the investigation.

On Monday, October 23, a court investigator, Dr. Jacobs, began the systematic interrogation of the accused. For two weeks Dr. Jacobs questioned Adler once or twice every day, except

Sundays. He was an expert interrogator, and he ranged over much of Adler's life and activities, allowing him extraordinary leeway to ramble in his answers. It was a good technique, for the freedom to speak often tripped suspects into revealing far more than they intended. Adler, somewhat unsure in his first answers, soon fell into the pattern of the interrogation. After the first morning Dr. Jacobs only occasionally had to interrupt Adler's long autobiographical statements with specific questions.

They began with Adler's medical history.

I was born on the ninth of July 1879, the son of the physician Doctor Victor Adler and his wife, Emma, née Braun. I have a sister, Marie, and a brother, Karl, born in 1880 and 1885, respectively. My sister has been ill for many years and is at present in the Steinhof Sanatorium. She has never had any vocation, and since 1897 she has suffered from severe melancholia. My brother is a journalist; at present he is serving in the army at the front. My mother too was struck once with melancholia, for three years, from 1890 to 1893, and during that period she spent several months in the Svetlin Sanatorium. My father and my brother are healthy. A brother of my mother suffered from melancholia, especially when he was a student in the eighteen-eighties. My father's sister, who died eight or ten years ago, had frequent attacks of depression. Whether she was treated in an institution, I do not know. I know of no other mental illness in my family.

As for me, I often had severe angina as a child, and twice I had German measles. In October 1911 I was stricken with a very bad case of fish poisoning. I thought nothing of the episode and afterward I took an extended hiking trip in the mountains, which resulted in incredible heart pains and other symptoms. When I returned, on the orders of a physician I was confined to bed for three months. In the following two years I went several times to Bad Neuheim to take the cure for my condition (myocarditis). Whenever I overwork I have mild heart attacks, consisting of a severe slackening of the pulse and general weakness. I had one such attack in April 1915, and for my holiday that year I went in May to the spa at Edlach. The last attack was in December 1915, as I was recovering from influenza. I have had no nervous diseases of any kind, and the heart condition has had no consequences, except to keep me from participating in sports and to exempt me from military service. I have had no other illnesses, especially no diseases of the nervous system and no venereal diseases.

By the middle of the first morning of interrogation, without any prompting by Dr. Jacobs, Adler was reminiscing about his early political development.

The strongest, and I believe most decisive influences on my political development occurred in my early childhood. My father first became active in politics in 1885. From that time on, so to speak, I was raised in a political milieu, which surrounded me in every possible way. Every day at lunch I heard from my father about episodes of his activities, especially about the repressive measures the authorities had taken toward the labor movement.

When I was only seven years old, my father took me with him to the March Demonstration in the Schmelzer Cemetery. On the way there, in the carriage, he told me how much parliamentary institutions meant to him. The demonstration that day was attended by about two hundred fifty people, and almost as many police, who forbade any speeches or proclamations. It all made an extraordinary impression on me, especially when some men were arrested for shouting something, and my father took me with him to the police station where he tried to obtain the release of the men.

The March Demonstrations were held every year in Vienna on the anniversary of the Revolution of 1848. In the only public demonstration of the labor movement that was at all tolerated by the government, the workers would gather quietly for a few hours at the base of the obelisk that had been built to commemorate the martyrs of the revolution. Little Fritz began to go to these demonstrations with his father each year after 1886. By the age of ten, he had seen the police viciously disperse a crowd of workers who were peacefully marching toward the cemetery along the tram tracks.

He had also been at home when three police agents burst into the Adler home at six thirty in the morning to search for "illegal materials." The house was ransacked, drawers and cupboards were broken open, their contents strewn over the floor. When the police approached the children's playroom, one of the agents asked Fritz if the room had also been used as a workroom. Fritz, aged eight, answered ingenuously, "No, please, this is only a playroom," and the police, after giving him a pat on the head, went on their way. But Fritz remembered the episode and the impunity with which the police could harass his father.

Even at the age of ten, Fritz told Dr. Jacobs, he was convinced that "quite simply, the struggle against the police and the government authorities was an obvious duty." He had no clear idea of the specific program of the Social Democratic party, but in the activities of his father, whom he "worshiped," he saw the personification of the struggle for righteousness and against oppression.

On the second day of the interrogation, Fritz continued with episodes out of his youth. When he was eight years old, he was up late one night waiting with his mother for his father to return from the Wienerberg Brickworks, where he had gone incognito to study the atrocious conditions under which the brickworkers lived. As Victor described what he had seen at the brickworks—appalling scenes of eighty men, women, and children sleeping in rooms big enough for four, crowded around open stoves to keep from freezing to death—little Fritz began to cry. Victor, with tears in his own eyes, tried to reassure the boy. "You will help to change all of that," he said. "When you grow up."

From that day on, Fritz believed that he would take part in the struggles of the Social Democratic party. He would distribute newspapers, join in demonstrations, and participate in meetings.

> I thought the party was revolutionary. I thought that it would take up the goals of the Revolution of 1848, about which an old servant in our house, who had lived through that year, had told me. I thought that when the party was strong enough, it would lead a powerful uprising against the ruling system, after the model of the earlier revolution, and that I would work in that uprising.

> Dr. Jacobs asked: "Did you think of street fighting?"

> I thought of that, among other things. I remember clearly that once, when I was about eight, I imagined in great detail a barricade battle near the Hofburg, which ended with the Hofburg being blown to pieces. I described it all to a boy I had befriended. It was associated with a specific demonstration, but I cannot remember which.

Fritz's father had also been interested in radical politics since he was a student, but out of respect for and fear of his own father, a prominent and wealthy businessman who abhorred any mention of the "murderers, thieves, and tramps" of the labor movement, he had kept out of public meetings and demonstrations for many years. As a medical student at the University of Vienna, and during the first years of his practice as a psychiatrist, he had been active in several radical political movements, including the founding of the German nationalist movement in Vienna. But it was not until the death of his father, in January 1886, that Victor Adler committed his life to the labor movement. By the end of the year he had all but abandoned his medical practice to work full-time trying to unite the bickering factions within the labor movement into a single effective party.

Until Victor Adler's intervention, the factions of the Austrian labor movement expended most of their energies, not against the government, but against each other. The radicals, advocates of direct action, branded the moderates as "sellouts" and "police agents." The moderates, advocates of gradual growth and parliamentary pressure, called the radicals "anarchists," and accused them of jeopardizing the entire movement by their provocative tactics. Both sides could quote from the rich Scripture of Marxism to prove the other heretical, and by their constant internecine warfare they assured that the government had little to fear from the Left.

With the substantial inheritance left him by his father, Victor Adler founded a weekly newspaper, *Gleichheit,* which challenged the limits of government censorship to reach an eager audience of workers in the industrial areas around Vienna and in Bohemia and Moravia. The earlier newspapers of the labor movement had been irregular and secretive; *Gleichheit* proudly proclaimed on its masthead: "Social Democratic Weekly." Crown Prince Rudolph still sent lackeys to pick up copies of the newspaper each week, but the authorities had grown so lax that they failed to ban the paper.

The Adler home and the tiny editorial offices of the newspaper were soon filled with workers and with leaders of the labor movement. After three years of furtive meetings in smoke-filled pubs, Victor Adler succeeded in uniting the different factions of the labor movement into the Austrian Social Democratic party. Although his own political positions hardly differed from those of the moderates, as an outsider he had been able to thread his way through the maze of rhetoric and personal squabbles that had kept the movement in shambles for so many years. The new party was proclaimed on New Year's Day, 1889, and Victor was named chairman, a position he held until his death.

FRITZ

As the factions of the Austrian labor movement grew closer together, Victor Adler's activities attracted the attention of the leaders of international socialism, who until then had regarded the Austrian labor movement with disdain and distrust. Men like Friedrich Engels, Karl Kautsky, August Bebel, and Eduard Bernstein became regular visitors to the Adler home. These were the men whom little Fritz learned to call "Uncle," on whose knees he played, who told him tales of socialist heroics far more exciting than any children's stories.

For Fritz, the newspaper was the most important activity in the world. He and his brother and sister folded the first editions, and every time he was allowed to run an errand down to the editorial offices on the Gumpendorfstrasse, he considered it "a major mission in service of the cause." Being allowed to listen to discussions of party matters was a special treat, and even as he was still learning to read, Fritz read *Gleichheit* from cover to cover with an attention and diligence seldom given his schoolwork.

In 1889, when Fritz was ten, the tram drivers of Vienna went out on strike. Although horses worked only four-hour shifts, the men had been working up to sixteen hours a day, and for miserable wages. When they struck, the municipal government brought in crews of scab drivers, each escorted by four mounted hussars with drawn sabers. Weeks of bloody street fights and demonstrations followed, until finally the government called in police and cavalry to put an end to both the strike and the demonstrations.

At home, Fritz heard from his parents about the bloody battles between the workers and the police, and in *Gleichheit* Victor Adler wrote several editorials supporting the strike and condemning the excesses of the police intervention. On the basis of these articles he was arrested as a severe violator of the press laws, convicted of anarchism, and sentenced to four months' imprisonment.

12

I was at that trial and I was very proud of my father [Fritz told Dr. Jacobs]. I remember that when my parents came home from the court in the evening and spoke about the sentence, I ran out into the courtyard beaming with joy to tell a cab driver who was working there. A woman who lived on the courtyard said, "Well, that's something children should not know about." I remember all of this very well, because what she said was completely incomprehensible to me. I saw in the trial and the sentence only that my father was fulfilling his self-evident duty. As always, I saw in him a great fighter for the righteous, for whom it was obvious that such consequences were to be suffered.

On another occasion Victor Adler was being tried for various political "crimes" he had allegedly committed in the course of an election campaign. Fritz, who had carefully read the penal code, "especially the sections which applied to the labor movement," calculated that his father would be sentenced to twenty years' imprisonment. When he told his sister, prompting her into uncontrolled tears, she ran to their mother and protested. Fritz's answer to the inquiries of his mother and his uncle was that he saw in the sentence "only a consequence of the struggle for righteousness, which one ought not shirk." His father was acquitted.

After the tram strike, *Gleichheit* was disallowed by the government. Victor established a new paper, the *Arbeiter-Zeitung,* which after 1895 became a daily newspaper. By the 1890s the Social Democratic party was rapidly growing in Austria. Fear of the activities of the party prompted some mild anti-socialist legislation, but the continued agitation of the party did much to persuade the government in 1893 to expand the suffrage to include many people who had previously been without the vote.

The constant campaigns of the Social Democrats—for equal suffrage, the right to demonstrate, better working conditions in the factories, the right to strike, the right to distribute party newspapers without censorship—involved Victor Adler in continuous organizing and demonstrations, all of which were carefully discussed in the Adler home in interminable debates over tactics. Often, Victor's organizing activities went further than the rigid laws would allow. Dozens of times he was arrested for such crimes as "disparaging public officials" and "distributing censored publications." He was convicted for seventeen different counts of various offenses, and eight different times he found himself serving jail sentences of anywhere from a few days to a few months.

Whenever he could, Fritz would visit his father in jail, coming home with an overwhelming feeling of satisfaction about everything his father had done and had suffered. "I saw in those jail sentences only the confirmation that the activities of the Social Democrats were right," he told Dr. Jacobs, "and I told my schoolmates about my father's prison record with great pride. I have never seen in imprisonment an instrument of the law, but always a tool of authority of the ruling classes, which they have used to oppress the people."

In 1890, when the Austrian Social Democratic party was scarcely a year old, Victor Adler decided that the party should lead the workers of Vienna in a parade to celebrate May Day as a workers' holiday. The plan was in total defiance of the authorities, and the government accepted the challenge, bringing additional troops into Vienna, moving fences in the Prater to give the cavalry room to maneuver, and issuing arms to militia units which had not been called up since 1848. An article in the *Neue Freie Presse, The New York Times* of Vienna, painted the imminent dangers of the approaching day in vivid colors: "The soldiers are in readiness, the doors of the houses are locked, in homes provisions have been prepared as if for a siege, shops are completely shut down, women and children dare not venture outside, in all hearts a heavy concern weighs its load." Parents forbade their children going out on the day which might see Vienna in flames, and clubs called off meetings lest men have to leave their wives alone.

In the Adler household, the talk for weeks was nothing except the preparations that the police and the army were making in anticipation of the demonstrations, and the preparations that the workers were making in turn. For Fritz, Vienna seemed on the verge of the great revolution. "People told us children that the houses in the Praterstrasse were completely sealed up in expectation of the hordes of workers. Two police stood in the doorway of every house, . . ." With the excitement of any eleven-year-old at the expectation of a super-parade, Fritz counted off the days and hours until the first of May, the glorious day.

When the great day came, the workers marched four abreast through the Prater, each with a red carnation in his buttonhole, singing revolutionary songs. The police and soldiers either smiled at the workers like comrades or turned away, unable and unwilling to disperse the demonstration. It was a great victory for the Social Democratic party.

Victor was in prison that day, serving a four months' sentence. As he explained it, the authorities had adjusted his sentence to prevent him from participating in the workers' parade. Little Fritz, anxious to fill in for his father, woke up on May Day with a sore throat. His mother made him stay in bed for the day, an act for which he never really forgave her, because, as he put it, "I belonged at the demonstration."

3

Zurich

Fritz spoke freely with Dr. Jacobs, but there was much he would not tell. Whatever he told was somehow related to politics —to his political education, his involvement with politics, his political values. He rarely mentioned his wife, his children, or his mother, and he never mentioned the many episodes of family life that were not "political"—even those which may have left traumatic scars.

For three years, from 1890 to 1893, while his mother was in and out of various sanitoriums and mental hospitals, Fritz, Karl, and Marie lived with the family of his father's close friend Engelbert Pernerstorfer. Victor would visit on weekends, sometimes bringing Emma.

Emma's condition had been diagnosed as melancholia, or what the contemporary psychiatrist would call depression. She also suffered delusions that her children were menaced. When she was with them she became so overly protective that Marie was often frightened into tears. Emma also seemed concerned that her illness was ruining her husband's political career. In her notes to Victor she would sometimes sign herself as "your millstone," ostensibly as a joke, but painfully revealing of her fears.

By the age of sixteen, Fritz had become accustomed to spending long hours alone with his books. His favorite readings were rather heavy fare: Köhler, *The Creation and Destruction of the World;* Aveling, *Darwin's Theory;* Kautsky, *The Erfurt Program and Marx's Economic Teaching;* and especially three books by his father's friend Friedrich Engels, *The Origins of the Family, Private Property and the State, The Conditions of the Working Class in England,* and *Anti-Dühring:* He read *Neue Zeit,* the weekly theoretical journal of the German Social Democracy, regularly, and he could follow easily the discussions of materialistic interpretations of history written by Belfort-Bax for a Vienna weekly.

Indeed, as a sixteen-year-old, Fritz's knowledge of political theory was advanced enough for him to get into serious arguments over the merits of Marxism and other doctrines with friends of his father, such as Pernerstorfer, who was a member of parliament. By the time of his graduation from high school in 1897, Fritz felt that his political development was fully mature: "I agreed fully with the goals and tactics of the Austrian Social Democratic party, and my theoretical position was that of Marxism. . . . I wanted already to dedicate my life to the labor movement, and to that end I wanted to organize my studies to be of the best possible use for that purpose." For Fritz, that meant further study of history, philosophy, and political economy—subjects which could lead into theoretical studies of Marxism and social theory relevant to the labor movement.

When Fritz articulated these plans to his father during his last year of high school, Victor was dismayed. Since Fritz's earliest childhood, Victor had been wary of the boy's passionate interest in politics. As a child Fritz had never been strong, and his father had diagnosed the frequent angina attacks as a potentially serious condition. Wary as he was of the record of mental illness that had long plagued the family, Victor was afraid that a strenuous life could easily cause a nervous condition. He thus went out of his way to protect Fritz. Instead of going to an elementary school, Fritz was instructed at home by a private tutor. And when he did enter school, at the age of eleven, his father insisted that he elect the easier scientific curriculum instead of what was regarded as the more rigorous classical curriculum. Thus Fritz studied French instead of Greek, and took intensive courses in mathematics and science instead of history and philosophy.

Fritz always considered his studies far less important than his "political activities" and those few favorite books which he read and reread. Nonetheless, he was an excellent student, almost always at or near the head of his class. He would have qualified with ease for any of the famous gymnasiums in the city, including the Schottengymnasium, the Eton of Vienna, which his father had attended. But at Victor's insistence Fritz attended instead the newer and less prestigious Mariahilfer Realschule (Scientific High School), where he continued his scientific and technical curriculum.

In *Anti-Dühring*, Engels champions the humanities, including the study of those very subjects—ancient languages, poetry, art—that Victor thought too demanding and too irrelevant for Fritz. In contrast to both the early materialists whom they criticized, and the later Marxists who were quick to ignore this aspect of their thought, Marx and Engels were firm believers in the Renaissance ideal of the man who was both thinker and doer. One of their arguments for communism was that it would once again produce "complete" men.

Even when denied the possibility of the broad humanistic education that his father had followed, Fritz was eager to mold himself into the "complete" man idealized by Marx and Engels. His facility in his school work left him the time to pursue a broad pattern of reading in poetry and the popular literature of the day, as well as music and opera. Later, when his scientific and political work expanded to fill working days of fourteen hours or more, he still managed somehow to squeeze in a steady diet of literature and music—as if he were satisfying a sweet tooth upon the once forbidden fruits.

Victor wanted Fritz to go into a technical field. His reasoning was that if Fritz were to be trained as a technician or an engineer, or even as a professor, he would be spared the exhausting rigors of the political life toward which he leaned. Fritz, of course, continued to argue for politics, and for studies at the university in fields that would prepare him for service to the labor movement.

Father and son, both strong willed, argued the question throughout Fritz's last year of high school. Victor would contend that even if Fritz were ultimately to work for the labor movement, he would need an independent source of income. Fritz would answer that any work not directly "in service of the cause" was wasted. By temperament Fritz was no compromiser. A man or a solution or a theory was either right or wrong, and he had little patience for partially right or partially wrong compromises. Although passionately devoted to politics, he was unwilling to make the accommodations and compromises that politics, even parental politics, demanded.

Victor was a ready compromiser in his politics, but he proved as strong willed as Fritz in the father-son negotiations, and by the end of the year his persistence had won out. It was agreed that Fritz would go to the university, as he insisted, but instead of studying the philosophy of history and political economy, he would prepare himself for a practical profession by studying chemistry.

When the time came to choose a university, Fritz faced still another problem. Although the *Realschule* had been much touted as an educational innovation in Vienna, the authorities at the University of Vienna did not recognize the new schools. To follow in his father's footsteps at that university, Fritz discovered, he would need a diploma from a classical gymnasium. With his credentials from a *Realschule,* almost the only German-language university he could attend was the University of Zurich, far from the excitement of Vienna and the politics of the Austrian Social Democratic party.

The University of Zurich made no stipulations for admission aside from certain academic criteria. The excellence of several of the faculties thus attracted many students who were excluded from the universities in their homelands for one reason or another. Students who lacked the usual prerequisites required by most universities, political exiles from Russia and Germany, Jewish students from Poland and Lithuania who were excluded by law from attending the universities—all mixed in the great faculties of the University of Zurich. Many of these students were highly talented and motivated, as they had to be to journey thousands of miles to a university in a foreign land, often to pursue advanced studies in a strange language. Many also came with interests far beyond the confines of their studies. Zionists, socialists, anarchists, and advocates of hundreds of other ideological and political movements—all scarcely tolerated at home—found a welcome atmosphere for quiet discussion and plotting in the placid community of Zurich. With their studies these students could mix regular association among the infamous exiles.

Fritz registered in the chemistry department of the university in October 1897. Within a month the other attractions of Zurich had reached him, and in November he spoke at a political meeting in a Zurich meeting hall. For Fritz, aged eighteen, the ensuing debate on Austrian politics marked a formal entrance into political life.

Fritz's opponent in the debate was an anarchist named Stefan Grossmann, a roving agitator who had come by his anarchism the hard way, after years of apprenticeship in the frustrating work of socialist organizing. Grossmann had worked with the Austrian Social Democratic party in Vienna, including a stint as a reporter for the *Arbeiter-Zeitung*. Convinced that he knew the Austrian party well from his firsthand experiences, Grossmann attacked the tactics of the party as procrastinatory, and leveled some sharp criticisms at the moderate leadership of Victor Adler.

Fritz, arguing from his extraordinary knowledge of Marxist theory and pointing up several recent achievements of the party, defended his father's tactics and leadership. In the end Grossmann was overwhelmed by Fritz's persistent arguments and the flood of documentation that Fritz could cite from memory. Grossmann finally conceded.

Grossmann had known Victor Adler in Vienna. With astonishment he noted after the debate how like his father Fritz had become. Fritz never learned to speak as well as his father, who had overcome a stammer to become one of the great orators of Austrian politics. But like his father, Fritz was slow and precise in his speech, using point after point to drill home his arguments. Already he looked like Victor, with the familiar full head of wavy hair, the drooping mustache (Victor had once consciously modeled his own appearance after Friedrich Nietzsche, a hero of his youth), and the small gold-rimmed glasses that framed his deep-set eyes. He even used many of the same gestures as his father. As he carefully wove his argument he would inscribe an imaginary circle with his finger; then, to emphasize or to accuse, he would thrust the outstretched finger through the center of the circle, as if to say, "There! There is your proof!" And like Victor, Fritz argued with cool precision. Even on the most volatile political questions, he presented his arguments with the deliberateness of a scientist presenting data.

One month after this first debate, which was followed by many more, Fritz participated in the founding of the League of the Austrian Social Democracy in Switzerland. The organization was formed to advance the cause of the Austrian party by propaganda and to solicit support for the party abroad. Some months later, in May 1898 when the Social Democratic daily newspaper *Volks-recht* was founded in Zurich, Fritz began contributing occasional articles as an associate correspondent.

But even these activities were not enough to fulfill the pledge Fritz had made to himself at the age of eight. He was no more satisfied with his studies than he had been in high school. He still wanted to devote his life to the labor movement. In the middle of his first semester at the university he wrote his father to express his dissatisfaction with the career compromise upon which they had agreed. What he really wanted to learn, Fritz wrote, was the life of a worker, and he wanted to learn it from firsthand experience. Hence he wanted to work for three months in a mine, and then work for nine more months in a factory, hopefully a machine factory. "If after a short time I see that it does not work out, which I do not believe will be the case, then I can always return and do something which you would consider 'wise.'"

Victor was terribly upset when he got Fritz's letter. From his own experience in labor politics, he knew well the consequences of not having an independent source of income. After spending his inheritance on *Gleichheit,* he had eaten further and further into what little money he and Emma had until in 1892 they had to sell the house they had received as a wedding present from Victor's father. (It was purchased by Victor's sometime friend, Sigmund Freud, who used the medical suite on the mezzanine for his own psychiatric practice.) After selling the house, Victor was forced to draw a small salary from the party to feed his family. The still small and semilegal party could scarcely afford any salary, and conscious of this fact, Victor went deeper into debt as he struggled to devote his energies to full-time party and newspaper work.

Moreover, Victor opposed Fritz's ideas as immature and overly romantic. What sense was there in trying to live the life of a proletarian unnecessarily? Of what use or service could that ever be to Fritz or to the party? And under all of his protests there lurked the fear he had harbored since Fritz was a weak and sickly child. Although the severe inflammations of myocarditis were not detected until many years later, to Victor the angina pains denoted a physical condition that could be propitious for what the nineteenth century carefully euphemized as melancholia. He never hinted the truth of his fears to Fritz, but using arguments of practicality and examples from his own experience, he did all he could to convince his son that politics would be an unwise career choice.

Fritz was undaunted by his father's arguments. He wrote back:

> It matters very little that as a worker I will not live as comfortably as I might live as a bourgeois. I know all too well that you have missed certain wants in your present situation. But would you today bring yourself to use your talents to become a comfortable private person, living in easy circumstances? How can you demand of me that I forbear taking the same steps out of my milieu that you once took?
>
> . . . I should work three years in order to have the security of being a member of bourgeois society? It is truly laughable of you!! I say to you that I would rather be editor of the tiniest party newspaper, and if I am too dumb for that, a worker in a factory, than do anything to prepare myself for a "bourgeois" profession.

In a later letter, Fritz struck out with the disrespect of a frustrated and heartbroken rebel: "You would have it that I keep the possibility of a bourgeois profession open for myself, and I say that I do not give a damn for it!"

In the spring Fritz came home for a holiday. He and his father, picking up where they had left off a year before, argued for most of three days about Fritz's future. Fritz had given up his plan of working in a mine and a factory, but he was determined to devote his life to the labor movement, and he wanted to study history, political economy, and philosophy in order to deal with problems of Marxist theory and practical politics. Victor was insistent that Fritz learn a practical profession, preferably one that would provide a relatively unstrenuous life.

After a sustained battle they again settled on a compromise: Fritz would switch from the chemistry department to the physics department. The change seems minor, but for Fritz it was important. He had concluded after less than a year of study that while chemistry might offer unlimited opportunities for successes in practical work, the theoretical bases of chemistry were too narrow to provide a foundation for the exploration of broad philosophical questions. Physics, however, was an altogether different discipline. One of Fritz's favorite books as a sixteen-year-old had been *Anti-Dühring,* Engels' brilliant polemical tract which attempts to relate Marx's idea of the dialectic to a broad framework of ideas. The principles of the dialectic, which Marx uses to structure human history, Engels develops as general principles of human knowledge by drawing analogies between the laws of nature and the laws of human society. Fritz was convinced that from a study of physics he could explore this connection further.

As he explained: "I was interested in physics as an enlightenment of mechanical materialism. The relationship between mechanical materialism and historical materialism was inscrutable to me, and it seemed to me urgent that I search out the theoretical basis of Marxism from this standpoint."

Never one to quibble over questions of theory, Victor judged that there were almost as many opportunities for practical work in physics as chemistry. He gave the new plan his approval.

Fritz, back in school, plunged into the study of physics with extraordinary zeal. Rather than lose a year of credit, he taught himself higher mathematics in the summer between his first and second years of school, and when he returned to the university in the fall he worked day and night at his studies and his experiments. He never drank, never smoked, never went out with the boys or with girls. His only friends were colleagues, with whom he stayed up night after night to argue theoretical questions.

Physics offered Fritz the uncompromisingly clear answers he had long demanded. In experimental physics, an hypothesis either fit the data or it did not; there was no need for rationalizations or hedging or compromise. And the opportunities for significant research in the still new field of physics were unlimited.

Early in 1899, in the middle of his second semester of physics, Fritz began work on the subject that was ultimately to become his doctoral dissertation: "The Dependence of the Specific Heat of Chromium on Temperature." The project required several semesters of rigorous laboratory work. Later that year, Fritz was appointed First Assistant in the Institute of Physics, a position he held until he was called up for military service in 1902. He was rejected for medical reasons.

In 1901, after three years of intense work, his dissertation was published. After he passed final examinations later in the year, he was awarded the Doctorate of Philosophy in physics. On the basis of previous examinations, he also received credentials as an intermediate school teacher of mathematics and physics.

The work in the Institute of Physics had been a full-time job, but Fritz also took time off from his experiments to continue his work with the newspaper *Volksrecht,* and to participate in 1901 in the merger of the League of the Austrian Social Democracy in Switzerland with the League of the German Socialists in Switzerland to form the League of International Labor Unions, a representative organization for the German-speaking workers of all nations. Fritz, then twenty-one years old, was named President of the new organization.

Victor did not share Fritz's excitement about the new appointment. His hope, that physics would lead to a quiet and sedentary career for his son, was completely trampled as Fritz spent longer and longer hours in the laboratories, at newspaper editorial meetings, and in political meetings. Over and over, Victor wrote to plead with Fritz not to try too much, not to work too hard.

"I have the impression," Victor wrote, "that you work too much; that is *un-Austrian*, don't do it."

On another occasion his plea went from humor to poignant concern:

> Your last letter has given me cause for the greatest concern. You seem to be demanding more of your nerves than they can bear. For the love of God, don't invite a nervous breakdown: Let the stupid exams go and rest for a few weeks. Whether you are finished half a year later or not is all the same. *But you must remain healthy! To me* you mean too much already—I could not bear to see you sick.

It was the closest Victor came to admitting the real cause of his concern.

In still another letter: "The central question is that you not exhaust yourself any more than you can physically bear. Time is not such an important matter; you are twenty-one years old and already you are in a great hurry."

Fritz was indeed in a hurry, so much so that he insisted on working even during the vacations. "You have richly fulfilled your duty," Victor wrote. "To sacrifice your already stingy vacations is suicide."

Only Fritz's reports that he was working on practical experiments in the laboratory seemed to appease Victor's concern. After Fritz had described an experiment he was working on, Victor wrote:

> That I want you to work in practice is not only that I want you to avoid material need—the bitterness of which I know as well as many of the poorest proletarians—but rather because I want to see you in the *flow* of life. In the flow of things, the flow of man—not outside where the real danger is. Whoever works only in theory, plays *va banque;* he must

set aside a whole hunk of life and has hundreds of chances that he will sacrifice his life on a false path which is set against him from the start.

Even this encouragement was qualified, though.

To avoid misunderstanding, [Victor continued] I mean party life last of all. If one does not have the best of luck, it can mean at best a monstrous waste of energy. I still cannot regret that I devoted my life to the party, because at the time there was no one else to do it, and it had to be done. But today, when I can find many replacements, I often want very much to return [to another life]. Yet I am too old to begin something new.

When Fritz passed his final examinations for the doctorate, Victor was overjoyed, assuming or hoping that Fritz would abandon his already strenuous studies and politics to settle down in a career. He wrote to his friend and socialist colleague Karl Kautsky: "To my joy, Fritz has now passed his final examination. *He* of course will think of it as relatively unimportant, and take offense at my joy. Oh, these kids!"

For three years Fritz had labored at physics, putting every moment into theoretical and laboratory work. But even with the doctorate, he was far from through, for the questions he had set out to explore remained unanswered, indeed unapproached, in the narrow discipline of his study for the doctorate. Rather than abandon his studies for a practical profession, as his father would have him do, he returned to the book which had first interested him in physics, the *Anti-Dühring* of Engels. After a careful rereading, he decided to devote the next few years to the study of metaphysics, hoping that he could begin to draw the important connections between Marxism and the sciences at which Engels had hinted.

When he wrote of the new plan to his father, Victor answered with a ten-page plea, urging, even begging his son not to continue with theoretical studies. He used argument after argument to try to dissuade Fritz from continuing with his strenuous life. And yet, even as he wrote his careful arguments, each of which he had written so many times before, Victor seemed to know that he could do little to persuade his strong-minded son.

What bothered Victor most of all was not that Fritz seemed bent on exhausting his mind and body, but that Fritz seemed almost inhuman in his unrelenting commitments to politics, to physics, and now to philosophy. Not once in all of their arguments and letters did Fritz admit his father into that innermost part of himself which might somehow explain these driving commitments. Always Fritz argued and explained as if he were presenting a scientific theorem or a political theory. Always his answers were cool, precise, and emotionless, without a hint of passion or desperation. And always, to his father, Fritz remained inscrutable.

Victor wrote at the end of the ten-page letter:

One thing I must say, something which has long lain on my heart: Why are you so bloody serious, so sad, so nervous, so gloomy? Why? A capable young man, capable of almost anything—why do you never laugh? Why never a spark of humor or youth in you? Why must everything be so portentous? Why are you so overdedicated, like the head of a family with six children all yapping for food? Why never just joyful? If you just once would commit some stupid silliness, I might be annoyed, but it would be comforting. That you are so phlegmatic, though, that gives me cause for great concern.

4

The Professor

During his second year at the university Fritz struck up a casual friendship with a Russian girl who was beginning her studies in chemistry just one year behind him. Katharina Jacoblevna Germanischkaja, called Kathia, was the only child of a well-to-do Orthodox Jewish family in Lida, a small town in the Vilna government of Lithuania. Her father was a manufacturer of mineral water, one uncle was an attorney and a Duma representative, another a physician. Kathia attended the gymnasium at Kovno, and was graduated with a distinguished record. But despite her achievements and the relative prominence of her family, as a Jewess she was not eligible for admission to the University in Lithuania. After long, heated discussions she convinced her father to allow her to attend the University of Zurich, and in the fall of 1898 she and her mother made the long trip to Switzerland. Kathia lived with her mother throughout her years at the university.

FRITZ

Fritz met Kathia at a lecture. Soon he brought her into his small circle of friends who spent their evenings in endless discussions of science, philosophy, and socialism. In turn Kathia led Fritz from the ruthlessly limited world of his studies to the literature and music that he had once allowed himself. After a few months he gave her a gift, the full score of *Das Rheingold* (his favorite opera) with the inscription: "To the enigmatic one who understands all." The enigmatic one soon discovered there was much she did not understand. Under Fritz's coaching she received an extensive introduction to Marxism and the labor movement. Within the year she transferred from the chemistry department to the physics department, and from apathy to involvement with the socialists in Zurich. The friendship developed rapidly, and at the end of 1901 Fritz wrote his father that he wanted to marry Kathia.

Victor, ever prudent with Fritz's life, wanted him to wait a few years before marrying. But Fritz was in his usual hurry. He invited Kathia to Vienna for a visit, and in a long letter to his father beforehand he described Kathia in such glowing terms that Victor was won over from the letter even before he met the girl.

"Kathia is so extraordinarily sympathetic to me," Victor wrote back, "and your imaginative sketch of her—I have no other —so loving, that I want nothing else than to spend a few days together with her and you in peace and quiet."

After the visit, Victor was in favor of the marriage. Then, when Fritz and Kathia began to discuss details, Kathia told Fritz that her parents wanted them to be married in an Orthodox Jewish ceremony. Kathia, who felt very close to her parents, wanted to have the ceremony as her parents wished. For Fritz, the religious question, like every other question, was not a matter for simple or genteel compromise.

The Adler family too was Jewish. Fritz's grandfather, Solomon Markus Adler, had been educated in a talmudic school in the tiny *shtetl* where his father lived and worked, and was sent to the Hebrew Institute in Prague to finish his studies. When he came to Vienna with his family in the 1850s, he and his wife continued to observe at least a modicum of Jewish rites in the home and at the synagogue for many years. Victor's birth was registered with the Jewish community, and throughout school, when the class spent the required hours on religion (which in Austria meant Roman Catholicism), Victor was given special classes in Hebrew and Bible literature.

The 1860s and 1870s, when Victor was a schoolboy, were the heydays of the Jews in Vienna, an era of prosperity and toleration when the Jews came to dominate much of the cultural and financial life of the city. It was also a period when many Jews dropped their religious and cultural affiliations with Judaism to become assimilated with Gentile society. Although there were almost no legal blocks in the way of the Jews of Vienna, the self-consciousness bred by generations of life in the ghettos of Eastern Europe made many Jews hesitant about the apparently open doors of toleration. Despite the fortunes they had earned and the commanding roles they played in the culture of the city, many Viennese Jews felt nervous when they sat next to a Prince Schwarzenberg or a Lobkowitz in the Café Sachar. The answer was conversion.

Solomon Markus Adler, whose real religion was liberalism anyway, followed the wave of conversions. In the late 1870s he went to Rome one Easter and came home a Catholic; his wife brought back a rosary the Pope had given to her. Although he never attended Mass, Solomon Markus Adler was quick to proclaim the advantages of conversion, and he soon convinced every other member of the family to follow his course, except Victor.

With the birth of Fritz, Victor was forced to decide whether the boy should be brought up as a Jew or not. For what he called "cultural reasons" he finally decided on conversion, but to defy his father, who had counseled conversion to Roman Catholicism, and at the same time to avoid the bureaucratic difficulties of a declaration of atheism in Austria, he had himself and Fritz baptized as Protestants.

Fritz legally remained a Protestant until the age of eighteen. Like his father he never attended any church; in fact, his Protestantism was no more than a word written on the dozens of documents forever demanded of citizens by the Austrian bureaucracy. The bureaucrats understood only three answers to the question "Religion?" Any answer except "Catholic," "Protestant," or "Jew" meant an interminable wrangle. Yet even as a child Fritz was distressed by the hypocrisy of the word "Protestant" on his documents, since he was an adamant atheist. Never willing to compromise on other questions, he saw no reason to allow convenience to change absolute truth. When he reached the legal age of majority, eighteen, he reregistered as an atheist, and militantly proclaimed his atheism whenever a situation demanding religious views arose.

When Kathia and her parents requested the Orthodox Jewish ceremony, Fritz did not know what to do. To go through with the ceremony was to compromise principles; to refuse was to force Kathia to break with her parents, and possibly to jeopardize their relationship. Fritz wrote his father for advice.

"That she has a special respect for her parents," Victor wrote back, "I would be the last to take amiss. She obviously has strong and deep bonds with her parents. . . . This circumstance itself will give you plenty of cause for concern, but one warning I can give you: A Jewish heart is still only a heart, and to have it is still more important than our cultural and aesthetic whims."

This time Fritz followed his father's advice. In January 1903 he took the long trip to Russia and suffered the ritual formalities of the Orthodox wedding at the home of Kathia's uncle. Afterward they were married again in a civil ceremony in Zurich.

It was not a happy marriage. Fritz had hoped that marriage would draw Kathia away from her dependence on her mother, but shortly after the wedding Kathia's mother moved in with the newlyweds. When a child—Johanna Alice—was born in December 1903, Kathia began to substitute an extreme dependency upon the child for the old relationship with her mother. Gradually she lost all interest in Fritz's activities as she became absorbed in a symbiotic relationship with the child. The birth of a second daughter—Emma Frida—in June 1905 only aggravated the situation. As Fritz grew estranged from the uncomfortable home life, he turned toward his work with increasing vigor.

After the marriage Fritz gave up his position as First Assistant in the laboratory of the Institute of Physics to devote himself to full-time independent study. From his father, his uncle Sigmund (Victor's brother), and from Kathia's family, the couple received enough money to support them for several years. The first year Fritz developed two laboratory instruments—a control instrument for thermal elements and a disjunctor for high voltages. In the summer of 1903, Fritz was reappointed to a position at the Institute of Physics, giving him access to laboratories where he could build and test the instruments. He later wrote two articles describing his researches for a scientific journal.

Despite the success of Fritz's work in experimental physics, the question that had first drawn him to the study of physics—the relationship between mechanical materialism and the historical materialism of Marx and Engels—remained unanswered. Then, during the summer of 1903, Fritz began reading extensively in the works of Ernst Mach and his followers.

Mach was the first philosopher to extend positivism and skepticism from metaphysics to science. The scientist, argued Mach, was as great a sinner as the philosopher when he laid claim to knowledge that transcended phenomenal experience. Several of Mach's followers, such as Richard Avenarius and Wilhelm Ostwald, extended Mach's argument to the point of denying the possibility of scientific knowledge beyond observable or measurable phenomena, with the result that a great variety of scientific "systems" became in their view both conceivable and workable. Some members of the school, such as Ostwald, even proposed new hypothetical frameworks for the organization of scientific phenomena. Ostwald's system, called *energetism,* defined matter as a manifestation of energy, and reduced spiritual phenomena to a category of "psychic energy."

When Fritz first reread Mach's *The Science of Mechanics,* he disagreed with much of Mach's argument, and thought of writing a critique of Mach's treatment of Newton. But after laboring the question for two years, reading and rereading the literature in the field with his compulsive, almost talmudic thoroughness, he had swung away from his previous staunch adherence to philosophical materialism to become an advocate of Mach's empirocriticism. Like Mach, he began to view scientific "laws" as useful but relative principles, each absolute only within the framework of the system in which it had been conceived.

The essay that emerged from these studies was completed in 1905 and given the title, "The Metaphysics of the Ostwald Energetic." Ostensibly an analysis of the epistemological consequences of Ostwald's philosophy, the article is actually an account of Fritz's own philosophical development from mechanical materialism to empirocriticism. The introduction of the essay is written in the first person singular (unheard of in a serious German scientific article), making Fritz's simple and direct argument very credible.

Before the article was published in the Leipzig *Quarterly for Scientific Philosophy and Sociology* (1905), Fritz sent a copy of the manuscript to Prague for the perusal of Ernst Mach, then a professor at the University of Prague. Mach wrote back:

Illness in my family and my own indisposition have reduced my receptivity, but I believe that I can state that your work includes enough new and important expositions to be significant. You should not expect a raving success among the physicists, though. They, with few exceptions, have a real aversion to serious reflection, since it might drag them out of their own narrow professional circle. But just once, someone has to make the break. Please do not hesitate to publish the manuscript. I think Ostwald will be most pleased with what you have written. I am certain that *I* will learn the most from it. This kind of question has not been thought out for too long.

The unqualified praise of a man with the stature of Ernst Mach was exactly the encouragement Fritz needed to settle the restlessness of his intellectual labors. To achieve this kind of success on a first attempt in a field as exacting as epistemology was an extraordinary achievement. When Fritz sent the manuscript and the letter from Mach to his father, it was obvious that Victor felt many of his qualms about Fritz's career settled by the success.

Mach's letter [Victor wrote] has pleased me enormously, and has reassured me to some extent that you have not lost yourself in transcendental clouds. You perhaps have never understood the anxious feelings of someone who to his own misery understands nothing of the things you are doing and who naturally fears that you will lose yourself in self-deception or horrible speculation.

Victor concluded his letter on a somewhat different note: "On the question of material matters, I shall say nothing. I sense how much it bothers you, and I hesitate to depress your high spirits."

The "material matters" to which Victor referred were only indirectly related to the philosophical materialism that Fritz was studying. Despite his own poverty, for several years Victor had been sending small sums to Fritz periodically to allow him free time for his philosophical and scientific pursuits. Although Victor was reluctant to raise the question of finances, by 1905 Fritz was the father of two children. Victor finally wrote to encourage him to find a position that would at least enable him to feed his family. "The great thinkers, from Nietzsche to Helmholtz," Victor assured, "have all had to support themselves through school teaching or some such profession."

Fritz agreed. He first tried unsuccessfully to have his mother's brother, Heinrich Braun, secure him a position with an industrial concern in Berlin. Then, after writing a number of letters of his own, he found a position as a Scientific Associate of the newly founded Museum for Masterworks of Science and Technology in Munich.

In late June 1905 Fritz moved with his family to Munich to take up his duties organizing the physical science section of the museum. The work was mainly administrative, and exhausting enough to assure that Fritz had no time for his philosophical studies. Indeed, only the absolute need of money had prompted him to take the job in the first place, and only the continued encouragement of his father prompted him to stay as long as he did, fifteen months.

In Vienna, far from the quiet museum in Munich, Victor Adler was elected to the Austrian parliament in 1905. In his new role as the leader of the small Social Democratic delegation in the parliament, he was leading the Austrian labor movement in the greatest of its struggles with the government, the campaign for direct and equal suffrage that culminated in a mass strike on November 28, 1905. Only the news of the revolution of 1905 in Russia and the bloody reprisals which came in the wake of that revolution were more exciting to Fritz. In letters to his father he made it quite clear that he had not forgotten his interest in the labor movement.

Again, in the very letters he used to describe his own activities, Victor renewed his efforts to dissuade Fritz from any interest, except that of a spectator, in party affairs.

That you have kept your political aspirations, [Victor wrote] I understand full well, but I hope and I really know that you are completely busy with the train of your scientific thought —quite apart from your professional work. Should it really be me that is keeping you away from politics—a rather childish explanation of the history—it would give me no cause for self-reproach, rather for merit. It also does not hinder me that we are now by chance in the midst of some very interesting political episodes, which take up a great deal of my energies. I mean, that in spite of everything, the possibility of scientific work, in general and especially for you, is much more worthwhile.

Fritz was unconvinced. Less than two weeks after he received this letter from his father, he wrote to Karl Kautsky, the editor of *Neue Zeit* and the heir of Engels as the keeper of Marxist orthodoxy, to seek a position on the staff of the journal. Fritz had written several articles for *Neue Zeit*, including a long analytic article on "Engels and Natural Science," which incorporated many of his views on epistemology and metaphysics. The reason he wanted an appointment to the staff of the journal, Fritz wrote, was so that he could support himself through work in socialist theory, work which would be useful to the labor movement.

I have had this wish as long as I can remember, [he continued] but only after numerous detours have I gotten to a position where it is possible to realize my wish. One hindrance has been my father, who has sought to pull me in another direction which did not accord with my plans; the other hindrance has been my desire, above all, to learn the exacting sciences well, as a foundation for an overview of the vast realm of knowledge today. As a compromise between the technical career which my father sought for me and the rejection of any bourgeois profession on my part, I temporarily became a physicist.

FRITZ

Now my father wants me to stay on this track, either as a professor or as a scientific adviser to a factory. I have no wish whatever for the great material success this path might lead me to, since my true interests are what they have always been.

Kautsky could not offer a position, and with the dream of working full-time as a socialist theorist apparently stifled, Fritz settled on what was admittedly a second choice: he would work as a scientist at a university, keeping his studies as close as possible to the theme he had been following when he worked on the Ostwald article. With a good appointment he would have free time to pursue his studies, and at the same time he might have enough time to dabble in politics.

The obvious place to apply was Zurich, which he knew well. But Vienna offered the great attraction of Ernst Mach, who had moved there from Prague. Vienna also offered the alluring possibility of working with the Austrian Social Democratic party.

Victor, of course, objected, knowing that if Fritz were to return to Vienna he would plunge headlong into party activities. "In Vienna you would be torn into a hundred pieces in four weeks," he warned in a letter. The warning probably had little effect, but there was no position open at the University of Vienna so Fritz once again returned to Zurich, in the spring of 1907, this time to take up a position as a *Privatdozent* at the university.

At Zurich, as at most German universities, regulations provided that no one could become a professor until he had served as a *Privatdozent,* or unpaid lecturer. The position has no analogue in the universities of America or Western Europe. Essentially it provides a talented young man with the opportunity to offer lectures and thus to show his teaching ability; since a great number of young men accept these posts, it provides the university authorities with a large number of candidates from which to choose the limited number of professors. The disadvantage of the system is that the *Privatdozent* receives no pay except the small fees paid by students, and must therefore have private means or another source of income to support him while he waits for an appointment as a professor.

Concurrently with his appointment as *Privatdozent,* Fritz returned to his old position in the Institute of Physics, took a part-time position teaching physics in a local high school, and began tutoring doctoral candidates and other students. Yet all of these small salaries were not enough to support the family. Fritz tried to avoid writing his father, knowing that Victor could scarcely afford any sum. But Victor understood the situation too well.

"It is remarkable that you do not need money," wrote Victor on one occasion. "Are you so rich? Or do you mean that I am too poor? Both strike me as not quite right. Rather, you are over-concerned about me and apparently torment yourself. Write me how you stand, and I will send you what I can."

Even when Victor indicated a willingness to help out, Fritz was reluctant, perhaps ashamed, to ask. Often he would write in the embarrassed tone of a student: "Mathematics makes for horrible hunger and I eat more than before." On Fritz's birthdays Victor often sent gifts of money. After one such gift Fritz wrote back: "The hundred fifty francs came at exactly the right time. The family fortune had sunk to fifty centimes."

At the university Fritz continued his researches in philosophy and the epistemological bases of physics. In a series of articles he wrote for *Neue Zeit* and *Kampf* (the theoretical journal of the Austrian Social Democracy), he expanded upon his earlier work with Mach to develop some ideas on the relationship between Mach's empirocriticism and the historical materialism of Marx. Mach himself had paid little attention to the ideas of Marx and Engels, but for Fritz there was a clear parallel between Mach's writings on individual and social organization of experience and

Marx's writings on the philosophy of history. Mach showed the relativity of descriptive systems, and by extension his viewpoint could show the "validity" of systems which "fit" the observable phenomena, whether of physics or history. Fritz even went on to argue that study of the philosophy of Mach could give important stimulus to Marxist research.

Fritz was the only German Marxist to take up the cause of Mach in the theoretical journals. But elsewhere Machism was a volatile question, and Fritz's articles soon brought him into the midst of one of the great theoretical melees that accompanied the growth of the socialist movements in Europe.

In Russia Mach had built up a legion of followers, including Bogdanov, Lunatscharski, Basarov, and Maxim Gorki. After the collapse of the revolution of 1905, the various factions of the Russian Social Democratic party began to polarize around different responses to the theoretical issues of Machism, with Plekanhov, Deborin, and especially Lenin characterizing the followers or supporters of Machism as "reactionaries." The theoretical struggle had direct political overtones, for in Lenin's view whoever refused to surrender their adherence to Machism had to be drummed out of the party. The battle waged on in journals and clandestine papers until Lenin introduced the ultimate weapon, a four-hundred-page *summa* on Marxist orthodoxy entitled *Materialism and Empirocriticism*.

Lenin was no philosopher. His book is argued like a theological treatise, "proving" all sorts of statements with ever-available verses from the Gospel According to Marx and Engels.

One chapter of Lenin's book singled out Friedrich Adler as "the only German author who is anxious to supplement Marx with Mach." "We must give the naïve instructor his due," Lenin wrote, "and admit that he rendered a service to Machism that did more harm than good."

Because Lenin's arguments were directed more toward Russian political struggles than to the philosophical issues involved, Fritz was scarcely affected or even responsive to Lenin's criticism. To his father he wrote:

> Lenin has written a large book of four hundred and fifty pages against Machism, in which he carefully attacks me, but without really disturbing me at all. He is capable only of petty arguments, since he does not really understand the question. Still, the book is a remarkable achievement. In about one year he has gone through the entire literature, of which he previously had no idea, and then has been able to make criticisms.

In another explanation, Fritz wrote to Kautsky to explain his views vis-à-vis the Russian polemics. Like the other Russians, he wrote, Lenin makes the mistake of identifying Marxism with the Social Democratic party. "To me," he continued, "Marxism is a *Weltanschauung*—a world view." The party is only a means of organizing men who share this world view into an effective force. His own life interest, the letter explained, was not the party and the petty squabbles of party politics, but the idea of Marxism—the vision and theory that would someday change the world.

By 1908 Fritz was nearly thirty years old, with a growing family to support, and it had become increasingly difficult to maintain an existence as a scientific and philosophical prodigy. His total income from various tutoring jobs and the miniscule royalties he received from his writings could scarcely supply bread for the table, and unless he could secure some permanent position the future looked bleak indeed. In industry, or even in teaching, Fritz could easily find a position. The problem was to find a source of income which would not compromise his absolute revulsion of "bourgeois" work.

The only real possibility of continuing his theoretical work undisturbed and at the same time earning a reasonable income was an appointment to the professorship of physics at the university. To his extraordinary good fortune the professorship had fallen vacant in 1908, and he was the leading candidate for the post. His scientific and academic credentials were impeccable, his publication record was excellent, although it was somewhat unusual to be published in socialist rather than academic journals, and his lectures at the university were well-subscribed. Most important of all, the Board of Education of the Canton of Zurich, which had to approve the appointment, was strongly sympathetic to the Social Democratic party, and leaned favorably toward Friedrich Adler for his own political views and because of his father's prestige in Social Democratic politics.

There were other candidates, however, including a sometime friend of Fritz's student years. This other candidate, Fritz wrote home to his father,

. . . is a man named Einstein, who studied at the same time as I did. We even heard a few lectures together. Our development is seemingly parallel: He married a student at about the same [time] as I, and has children. But no one supported him, and for a time he half starved. As a student he was treated contemptuously by the professors, the library was often closed to him, etc. He had no understanding of how to get on with the important people. . . .

Finally he found a position in the patent office in Bern and throughout the period he has been continuing his theoretical work in spite of all distractions. Today he is in the school of Bolzmann, and one of the most distinguished and recognized. And this school, not that of Mach, is the mode today.

Shortly after he wrote this letter, Fritz addressed the Board of Education as they were deliberating the final choice for the new appointment:

If it is possible to obtain a man like Einstein for our university, it would be absurd to appoint me. I must quite frankly

---

say that my ability as a research physicist does not bear even the slightest comparison to Einstein's. Such an opportunity to obtain a man who can benefit us so much by raising the general level of the university should not be lost because of political sympathies.

Einstein was appointed. When Professor Alfred Kleiner, Director of the Institute of Physics, informed him of the new appointment, Fritz "had the feeling of an immense liberation." Although it might have been possible to obtain a professorship somewhere else, the chances were slim. Fritz, in fact, had already decided about his future. Again, he wrote his father to raise the taboo:

I believe that I must abandon theory to search for some practical activity. And that can *only be a party activity*. . . . That is the only thing other than epistemology which is important to me. To renounce science *and* party, to become the father of a family *pur et simple,* that I could never do.

Once again, Victor tried to dissuade Fritz from party activity. But Fritz was thirty years old now. He had outgrown the familiar arguments. He answered his father's pleas with a firmness which put an end to the discussion:

I did not become an engineer, as you wished, because it absolutely did not accord with my natural predisposition. I have not . . . sought a position at the university, as you wished. I have taken every step toward what I have become against your advice. Today it appears to you that for me to busy myself with theory, which you previously opposed, is the most desirable goal. This is in no way a reproach, but only the simple fact that I cannot any longer acquiesce to your prudence.

5

The Worker

Like most of the other socialist parties in Europe, the Swiss Social Democratic party was beset with factionalism. The founders of the party had been moderates who maintained a program of limited action to prepare the working classes for the day when the inexorable processes of history would bring the collapse of the bourgeoisie and the triumph of the proletariat. They were continually challenged by the anarcho-syndicalist wing of the party, under the leadership of the physician Fritz Brupbacher. Brupbacher's faction had little patience with the deliberate tactics of the orthodox wing of the party. If the party was to be truly revolutionary, they argued, it should work actively for revolution. To that end they advocated the immediate organization of revolutionary strikes and other provocative activities. By 1910 the appeal of the anarcho-syndicalists had grown so large in several cantons, especially among the traditionally anarchistic watchmakers of the Jura, that the Brupbacher faction had taken over both the leadership of the party and the editorship of the party newspaper, *Volksrecht*.

The moderates were alarmed enough by the anarcho-syndicalist takeover to rally their own strength, and in April 1910 to secure the resignation of Max Tobler, the anarcho-syndicalist editor of *Volksrecht*. In the hope of reuniting the party, they decided to offer the editorship of the newspaper to Friedrich Adler who, as an outsider to the intraparty struggles, might be acceptable to both factions.

Fritz had followed the activities of the Swiss Social Democratic party since his arrival in Switzerland in 1897. Although his studies had allowed him little time for party activities, he had been an occasional contributor to *Volksrecht,* and he had regularly attended party meetings when he was in Zurich. The offer of the editorship came as a total surprise. Like the opening of a professorship in the physics department at the university, it was timely. This time, Fritz accepted. His hope was that of the men who offered him the position—that he could somehow reunite the Swiss party in the same way his father had once united the divided factions of the Austrian labor movement.

The work with the newspaper proved to be everything Fritz expected. Although it was a full-time job, he insisted on holding his position as a *Privatdozent* at the university as well, using his occasional brief holidays from the newspaper as opportunities for lecturing at the university.

Just one week after he started as editor, he wrote to his father: "I work like a horse, never go to sleep, and I feel as though I were reborn, exactly as though I were on an alpine hike . . . . I have been at it with fire and flame, and the men here are rather flabbergasted, as this tempo is not their style."

Within a few weeks Fritz had completely reorganized the editorial procedures of the newspaper. He personally supervised the organization of news items and wrote lead articles and editorials himself. "I am agreeably disappointed with myself," he wrote after he had gotten the newspaper into what he considered a decent working order. "I feared quietly that, in the beginning especially, I would have far more inhibitions about writing and also in the entire work. To my utter surprise it has turned out that, among other things, I was also born to be a chief editor!"

At last, Fritz was doing what he had dreamed of doing since childhood—working body and soul for the labor movement, in the midst of the day-to-day campaigns for rights, for suffrage, for decent wages, for the myriad of causes that would somehow wipe out inequality and injustice. But compared to the dramatic and sometimes bloody struggles of the Austrian Social Democratic party, the activities of the Swiss Social Democrats were quiet and placid. Although industry and the working class were both highly developed in Switzerland, only rarely had the Swiss Social Democratic party been forced to fight for rights, which the government and the industrialists had willingly conceded to maintain the public order so sacred to the Swiss. The great causes that had united the international socialist movement, such as May Day demonstrations, were readily tolerated in Switzerland, where May Day was already something of a national holiday. If the workers of Zurich or other industrialized cantons wanted to celebrate with a parade each year the government would hardly object. Even the rising militarism which socialist parties in Austria and Germany and France fought with alarm was scarcely a subject for discussion in perennially neutral Switzerland.

It was only a few months after he had accepted the position as chief editor of *Volksrecht* that Fritz began to have doubts about the decision he had made. He was certainly not sorry that he had turned down the security of academia for the perils of the labor movement. Rather he was concerned about how long he could maintain his interest in the comparatively placid activities of the Swiss labor movement. "On the whole," he wrote to his father, "I am now satisfied that I made the break; that does not mean that I would not like to make still other breaks." Growing up in

Vienna, hearing about the activities of the Austrian party from his father every day at lunch and dinner, following the growth and daily activities of the party and the leader of the party—his own father—year after year, Fritz could hardly think of his activities in Switzerland as anything but an apprenticeship for work with the Austrian Social Democratic party.

Somehow finding time in the midst of his duties as editor and his duties at the university, Fritz wrote an article on "The Tactics of the Austrian Social Democracy" for publication in *Kampf*. His views are those he had held in his first political debate —exact agreement with his father's moderate, nonprovocative policies. The article is scholarly, but almost adulatory, using theoretical arguments to prove the correctness of Victor Adler's leadership of the party. Ten years of exile in physics and ten years of intermittent fighting with his father had not changed Fritz's politics at all.

Exactly one year after he had accepted the editorship of *Volksrecht,* Fritz received a letter for which he had waited and hoped. Karl Seitz, Vice Chairman of the Austrian Social Democratic party, wrote Fritz in April 1911 to offer him a position as a Secretary of the party, adding that because of the imminence of the new parliamentary elections, Fritz should come to Vienna immediately to take up his new duties.

It is impossible to determine whence the initiative for the invitation came. Certainly, as Chairman of the party, Victor knew about it. Indeed, the invitation may have been Victor's admission that he had lost the long struggle over Fritz's profession and career.

Fritz accepted. Before he quit his posts at the university and at *Volksrecht,* he wrote his father again—for the last time— to ask for five hundred francs to pay some "running accounts" in Zurich. Within a month he was in Vienna and had taken up his new post, and only two months later Victor had come around enough to write to August Bebel, Chairman of the German Social Democratic party and a close personal friend: "That Fritz is here is for me a true blessing, as I am sure you can imagine."

Kathia did not share Fritz's enthusiasm for the move to Vienna. She resented her husband's choice of politics over a more lucrative profession, and the birth of their third child, Felix, in January 1911 provided the excuse for her resistance to the move. The milk in Vienna would not be good for the children, she argued, and while she finally consented to the move, at her insistence they lived in Brunn am Gebirge, a distant suburb on the edge of the Vienna woods. The long commute meant that Fritz saw less and less of his family, and as the pace of politics in Vienna accelerated, he began to spend many nights in the city. When the children were old enough to ask why their father was home so seldom, Kathia would answer that he was too busy for them, a statement that reflected the truth of consequences more than motivations.

Before Fritz came to Vienna, three secretaries—Ferdinand Skaret, Leopold Winarsky, and Julius Deutsch—divided the normal day-to-day administration of the Austrian Social Democratic party. Fritz's position was a new Secretariat, created specifically to take up the separate problem of election propaganda and campaign coordination for the forthcoming national election.

His new colleagues readily accepted Fritz into the party organization. Although he did not have the remarkable flexibility or sense of humor of his father, who seemed to know instinctively when to be precise and when to muddle through in Viennese dialect, Fritz was quiet, diligent, and soft-spoken, even taciturn, in his relations with other party officials and with the rank and file. Never did he use his position as Victor Adler's son, his past record of scholarship, or the editorship of *Volksrecht* to pull rank. A few of the party workers jokingly called him "The Professor," but more as a reflection of his donnish attitude than as a recognition of his academic achievements. To most of his colleagues, and to the rank and file of the party, he was simply another worker for the cause, willing to do whatever the party demanded.

Indeed, even as he came to the complex politics of Vienna, Fritz never forgot the chiliastic notions of Social Democracy that had driven him since he first pledged himself to the movement at the age of eight. He still fervently believed in the inevitability of the Revolution. There might be battles lost in the great war between liberty and tyranny, between freedom and oppression, but ultimately the great victory would come. And when the day of revolution finally dawned, it would mean the collapse of immemorial despotism and the end of distinctions between classes and nations and religions. Then would come the great age of freedom, when mankind would forever be cleansed of oppression, hatred, and envy, of the meanness and foulness that led to wars and to every other violent disfiguration of mankind.

Fritz's initial duties in Vienna were rather menial. He clipped newspapers and collected documents to illustrate the positions of other parties and candidates. He prepared speeches for the election campaigners and assigned speakers to the various rallies. He wrote election leaflets and prepared the agendas for election meetings of the Executive Committee of the party. These tasks all imply a certain behind-the-scenes power, but they seem a rather dreary list of duties after years of high-level physics and metaphysics, or even after the responsibilities of the editorship of a daily newspaper. Yet to Fritz they were "the fulfillment of a wish long held, to be able to work for the Austrian party."

In addition to his regular party duties, Fritz took over the editorship of a small, popular biweekly journal, *Das Volk*. He also began contributing articles and time to *Kampf,* the theoretical journal for which he had written so many articles. Two years later he became an associate editor of *Kampf*. Finally, Fritz (always the teacher!) offered lectures on Elements of National Economy at the Workers School in Vienna.

As the campaign preceding the parliamentary elections reached a peak in early June, Fritz began to work a day-and-night schedule. In addition to his other duties he led numerous political rallies and gave dozens of speeches in support of Social Democratic candidates in Vienna and the provinces.

For the June issue of *Kampf* Fritz wrote a short article on "The Value of Parliamentary Institutions," which argued the importance of elections and of the campaign to secure parliamentary representation for the working classes. For many years there had been a small but vocal dissident group within the Austrian Social Democratic party which argued that election campaigns were senseless. Instead, the dissidents argued, the party should concentrate its strength on direct action—strikes, a general strike, even violent protests—to achieve the goals of the party. In his article Fritz disputed the advocates of direct action, whom he termed "naïve." Drawing an analogy with the way in which a turbine, a dynamo, and a transformer can harness and transform the energy of a waterfall into useful electricity, he asserted: "Parliamentary institutions are only the transformer of the energy of the working classes." Thus it was imperative for the party to build a massive electorate on June 13, so that a large Social Democratic parliamentary delegation could transform the might and energy of the proletariat into action.

The article was more interesting for the fact that Fritz still agreed completely with his father's political views and still found it easiest to explain his ideas in scientific analogies than for the impact it had on the electorate. Indeed, the article probably had little influence on the rank and file of the party, most of whom would certainly never read a journal as erudite as *Kampf*.

In the first election under universal suffrage, in 1907, the Social Democrats had surprised everyone in the empire by receiving 1,040,100 votes out of the 4,676,636 cast, making them the largest party in Austria. When the election returns from the 1911 election were tabulated, the Social Democrats received more votes then any other party. Their vote total had gone over the figure of 1907. But since 1907 the total number of voters in Austria had increased substantially, and the disputes between the Czechs and the Germans within the Social Democratic party had done little to increase their support in the crucial areas of Bohemia and Moravia. The party dropped from eighty-nine representatives in parliament to eighty-two.

With the conclusion of the election campaign, Fritz was assigned new duties, this time far closer to the role in the party that he had long dreamed of playing. His Secretariat was made into the coordinating center for the international activities of the party, which gave him the responsibility for the general correspondence of the party with other socialist parties, and the special correspondence with the Bureau of the Socialist International. For Fritz the new appointment meant that he would be in regular communication with the great leaders of the international socialist movement, the men whom he had once called "Uncle."

Fritz took no time off after the strenuous election campaign and after months of exhausting labor, which often had him working up to eighteen hours a day, the prediction his father had made about his physical frailty proved true. One evening after Fritz had eaten a large fish dinner, he was struck with acute chest pains, which he dismissed as heartburn from a bad case of "fish poisoning." When he felt better a few days later, he decided that a short rest would do him good, but instead of the few days in a spa or at a resort which his father recommended, Fritz decided to take an extended hike with Kathia in the mountains.

On the first day of their hike Fritz was stricken with pains far more severe than the original "heartburn" from the fish dinner. He saw a physician, was informed that he had a rather bad case of myocarditis, and was told to spend at least three months in bed and away from politics. The findings of one X-ray examination were so discouraging that Fritz seriously contemplated dropping his political career to go back to physics.

The physician's orders were like a prison sentence to Fritz. Although he could still read the newspapers and party materials which his father and other colleagues brought him, he was unable to participate in any party meetings, rallies, or other activities. The months he spent in bed, from August through November, were exciting days for the Austrian Social Democratic party.

The summer of 1911 was marked by a substantial increase in the cost of living in Vienna. Bread and meat prices, especially, rose dramatically. When wages did not follow the price rises, many working-class families found themselves dropping from the regimen of meat dinners two or three days each week to one day, and sometimes, to none. The Social Democrats blamed the agrarian sympathies of the government and the harsh trade agreements with Hungary for the price rises. When groups of workers held spontaneous demonstrations in Vienna to protest prices, Prime Minister Baron Paul von Gautsch accused the Social Democratic party leadership of "arranging" the protests. Should there be any further pressure from the streets, he warned, the government would maintain law and order with force. He kept his word.

One month after his warning, Viennese workers gathered anew before the Rathaus to protest the still high prices. When police were unable to disperse the crowd, infantry and cavalry were dispatched to the scene. In the melee that followed, several workers were killed, many more were wounded, and hundreds were beaten and jailed. In the following weeks stiff prison sentences were dealt out to eighty-two persons. Hundreds of others received shorter sentences.

The situation was tailor-made for the righteous declamations of the party against the cruel tyrannies of the class society.

FRITZ

Just before the new parliament convened, Victor Adler told a sympathetic audience of workers in the Favoriten district that while it was naïve to expect a capitalistic state to give food to every family, there was no reason to excuse the state when it deprived its citizens of available meat just to please agrarian lobbies. He was careful to dissociate himself from any advocacy of radical action, but he finished his speech by asserting unequivocally that there could be no justice or equality of treatment in the courts until the class struggle was over.

The man who received the brunt of the public blame for the brutal repression of the September protests was not the Prime Minister, but the Minister of Justice, Dr. Viktor von Hochenburger. It was he who had called out the troops, and in a new series of spontaneous demonstrations it was he who was blamed for the deaths of the martyrs of September and for the harsh prison sentences.

The new parliament, of course, was reluctant to discuss the price rise which had led to the first disturbances. But on October 5, 1911, the delegates did consent to discuss the disturbances themselves. In the middle of Victor Adler's long speech criticizing the violent measures the government had taken to put down the disturbances, five shots rang out from the gallery of the chamber. The shots had been aimed at the Minister of Justice. Hochenburger was wounded only slightly, but when the commotion finally died down in the chamber the Prime Minister stood up to accuse the Social Democrats of inspiring the would-be assassin with their "hate speeches."

The assailant was later identified as Nikolaus Njeguach, a cabinetmaker's assistant from Šibenik. At his trial some weeks after the attempted crime, Njeguach declared that he had been driven to shoot at Hochenburger when he noticed him laughing and joking during Victor Adler's recital of the woes of the common people.

Njeguach, sentenced to a term of seven years, died in

prison. No real connection between his act and the Austrian Social Democratic party was ever proved in the trial or in the hundreds of allegations made in newspaper editorials. But for the government and for a large segment of the Viennese public, there was now evidence aplenty of the danger of the "Reds" in their midst.

It was in this atmosphere of a "Red scare" that Count Karl Stürgkh was named Prime Minister of Austria.

6

Count Stürgkh

Count Stürgkh was the scion of an impoverished noble family from provincial Styria. Following the only path upward that remained open to a destitute aristocrat with scruples about "bourgeois" money, he decided at an early age to devote his life to the imperial bureaucracy, where his ambition and diligence were rewarded in a sterling career. For almost three decades he served in various ministries and as a deputy of the landed gentry electoral college in the parliament, building a reputation as an expert on secondary education and as an unyielding conservative, not to say reactionary, on almost all political questions.

Count Stürgkh never married, never seemed to play; indeed, nothing detracted from his single-minded devotion to duty. Unfriendly cartoonists caricatured him in a clerical surplice, lampooning both his ultramontane politics and his celibate zeal for service. But Count Stürgkh, oblivious to their jibes, continued his distinguished career. In 1907 he was appointed to the House of Lords. In 1909, his reputation as an expert on secondary education and the patient intervention of a well-placed friend, the financier and newspaper magnate Rudolf Sieghart, earned Count Stürgkh an appointment as Minister of Education. He spoke ineffectively and wrote even worse, but in the bizarre politics of Austria he acquired a reputation for clear, methodical thinking, and after the calculated blundering of Baron Gautsch had brought the government to a crisis in November 1911, Emperor Franz Josef asked Count Stürgkh to form a new government. Pundits noted that his first speech as Prime Minister was remarkably lacking in political insight, but that was probably just as well, for in the labyrinthine politics of Austria-Hungary, a firm statement on any issue was sure to irrevocably alienate some nationality or interest group.

The Habsburg empire was probably the most peculiar state in Europe. For centuries the Habsburg dynasty had ruled; whom and where they ruled remained forever a moot question, decided usually by circumstances far beyond their own control. What the dynasty acquired through the dowry diplomacy of a series of brilliant marriages, it lost through reckless and disastrous military campaigns, until Emperor Franz Josef could justly boast that he had lost more possessions than most kings would ever hold. The final form of the Habsburg domains was decided in 1866, when the armies of Prussia soundly defeated the Habsburg forces on a Bohemian battlefield near the town of Sadowa. His hegemony in Germany usurped by the upstart Prussians, Franz Josef turned to the peoples of Eastern Europe to build anew a great empire.

What emerged was Austria-Hungary, a Siamese twin of two states, Austria and Hungary, connected only in the person of the monarch, who was Emperor of Austria and Apostolic King of Hungary. To the outside world it was a single great empire, represented everywhere by distinguished ambassadors and consuls, often bewhiskered in the fashion of the Emperor; but the actual institutions of the empire as a whole were confined to the Emperor and his court, the Ministry for Foreign Affairs, and the Ministry of War. There was no common prime minister, no common cabinet, and no common legislature. Every ten years the *Ausgleich* between Austria and Hungary had to be renewed, and the revival of such sensitive issues as tariffs, duties, customs, and quotas provided an open stage for the raucous interplay of centrifugal nationalistic forces.

In return for their support of a single great empire for foreign affairs and war, the Magyar gentry of Hungary demanded and received virtual rule of the lands of the Crown of Saint Stephen, an enormous area which encompassed what is today Hungary, Slovakia, and huge areas of Romania, Yugoslavia, and the Soviet Union. Left to their own devices, the Magyar minority made precise laws to guarantee the rights of the other nationalities —Slovaks, Croats, Romanians, Serbs, Ruthenians, Gypsies— admirable laws which were not operated in a single instance. Exercising a tyrannical rule over the other nationalities, the Magyars perpetuated the feudal government that suited their purposes. As long as they paid their share of the joint taxes and supplied their share of the joint fighting forces, the Emperor voiced no objections.

The western half of the empire was not even united in name. Germans called it Austria, a name which it had renounced by solemn oath. But for lack of a comprehensive and still inoffensive name, the lands which today form not only the Austrian Republic but also the western half of Czechoslovakia and substantial areas of Poland, Italy, Yugoslavia, and the Soviet Union were officially called The Kingdoms and Provinces Represented in the Parliament. The keepers of regalia never succeeded in fitting that tongue-twister to a suitable coat of arms.

As another price of defeat in 1866, Franz Josef had to surrender to the demands of the German liberals by granting a constitution for Austria. The liberals thought it their duty to protect the rights of the individual from the state. They could scarcely imagine a state under popular control, least of all their own. As in Germany, the liberals of Austria regarded the state as a remote authority which relieved them from the problems of government and allowed them to devote their full energies to the pursuit of enlightenment and *Gemütlichkeit*—a calling far more noble than the trivia of government. As long as they demanded only a few concessions of civil rights and nothing approaching popular control, Franz Josef was all too glad to acquiesce to their demands by reviving a constitution that he had offered once before, after the defeat of 1859, the so-called February Patent. Making a few minor changes to placate more recent demands, Franz Josef promulgated the new constitution in a spirit that recalled the words in which he had addressed his ministers after announcing the earlier version:

> His Majesty demands from all his Ministers the solemn promise that they will protect the Throne with full energy and single application against the extortion of further concessions, whether by pressure from the Parliament or the Diets, or by revolutionary attempts on the part of the masses. In particular, His Majesty deigns to insist that the competencies of Parliament, as described, be strictly regarded, and that any attempt on the part of that body to interfere in the conduct of foreign affairs, in military affairs, and in the matter of the command of the army, meet with the most determined refusal . . .

The orders were strictly heeded. Indeed, whenever parliament made too vigorous use of the liberties granted to it, it would be prorogued in the interest of governmental efficiency, and the ministries would rule Austria under Article Fourteen of the constitution, which provided that "in cases of urgent necessity, where the consent of parliament could not be obtained," the ministries could pass any measure they deemed necessary on their own joint responsibility. The procedure was used seventy-six times in the course of one eight-year period, and thirteen different budget estimates were forced through recalcitrant parliaments under the threat of Article Fourteen. Yet whenever government and citizens alike began to rejoice in the smooth efficiency of absolutism, as ministries would temporarily take over legislative powers, the Emperor was likely to decree, for reasons of state (that is, to placate the liberals), that there must again be a return to parliamentary government.

The real power in Austria rested not with parliament or the provincial diets, but with the army and the ubiquitous imperial bureaucracy. From ministers to elementary-school teachers, railway employees, and foresters, officials of the state were appointed by the Emperor and were ultimately accountable to him. Professors in the universities, even members of the great theaters in Vienna and Budapest, were appointed by the Emperor; academic or dramatic abilities, in the usual sense of the terms, were not always the key criteria for these appointments. One of two abbreviations, *K.-K., Kaiserlich-Königlich* (Imperial-Royal) or *K.u.K., Kaiserlich und Königlich* (Imperial and Royal), was applied to every state institution, and while only the most abstruse and esoteric lore could distinguish which institutions were to be accorded which abbreviation, the pervasive presence of the imperial bureaucracy was obvious to any citizen of the empire a dozen times each day.

As a rule, members of the bureaucracy at any level were diligent, serious, and polite, as long as their authority remained unquestioned. The multiplication of offices and the extreme ranking of the hierarchy often deadened initiative, but what the system lacked in efficiency it made up for with an extraordinarily obscure jargon, which made it seem as though matters were constantly being processed. The favorite term was *Asserviert*, usually applied to a document in the abbreviated form, *Ass.* The term meant "awaiting further consideration," an example of that circumspect attention which does not lose sight of matters but equally does not rush them. It implied attention to a minor request and spared officials the opprobrium of rejecting requests from important personages. Although the proverbial Austrian *Schlamperei* often kept matters "awaiting further consideration" for twenty or more years, things did somehow get done, if only through the magic procedure which Austrians call *fortwursteln*. The dictionary defines the process as "to muddle through"; Austrian bureaucrats would more probably define it as a variety of Providence.

The zenith of this great bureaucracy was the Emperor himself, whose titles form the longest listing in the Almanach de Gotha, and even there must end with an "etc." The Old Gentleman, as the Viennese called him, accepted as unchallengeable dogma the archaic conception of the divine right of kings to rule. He considered himself a father, responsible for the well-being of a large, unruly family, and as supreme head of a household he was willing to undertake the incredible minutiae of routine business which his office demanded. Though a stern father to his peoples, he was regarded with the love and sentiment not of a father but of a grandfather, a man of consummate dignity in the face of insuperable odds. Many a rabid nationalist in the empire, losing no love over other nationalities or the German bureaucrats, nonetheless remained *Kaisertreu* throughout the long reign of the Old Gentleman.

When Franz Josef became Emperor, in the aftermath of the Revolution of 1848, his first Prime Minister, Prince Felix Schwarzenberg, told him: "Your Majesty, you're young and I'm old, and I've a great deal of experience. I beg you to promise that in the future you will never speak to any minister or general, and so on, about other affairs than those within his competence. This is the only way to protect yourself against intrigues." The young monarch gave his solemn word, "as man and as Emperor," and kept it meticulously throughout his long reign. As the exigencies of politics demanded, Franz Josef would summon and sack whole ministries, like so many lackeys. Always he hoped that somehow he might come up with the magic formula for stability, although he probably knew all along that only political alchemy could produce such a formula in Austria-Hungary. For Franz Josef, as for the lowliest bureaucrat, the only solution, often, was *fortwursteln*.

In public appearances Franz Josef's indefatigable spirit never waned. Every appearance ended with the same noncommittal phrases: "It was very nice, it has pleased me very much." But when Count Stürgkh was appointed Prime Minister, Franz Josef was eighty-two years of age, in the sixty-second year of the longest and surely the most tragedy-ridden reign in modern history. His brother, his son, and his wife had all died violent and unexpected deaths, and his empire had suffered the ravages of war and the threat of war with uncanny regularity throughout his reign. Finally, Franz Josef's strength did begin to wane, and as his powers of concentration began to give out, the bureaucratic matters which had once received his personal attention began to fall more and more to the supervision and authority of his ministers. He still rose from his fabled camp bed every morning at four, still put in twelve- and fourteen-hour days with the conscientiousness of a troubled father, but try as he might, the Emperor could no longer personally oversee the myriad of administrative details. He gradually lost the power to supervise effectively the great bureaucracy and the army, and was powerless to keep his ministers and generals from usurping those powers.

The crisis that brought Count Stürgkh to the Prime Ministry of Austria was another episode in the continuing struggle of the nationalities of the Habsburg empire. To the uncomprehending amazement of most of Europe, these recurrent crises were violent enough to bring the machinery of government in Austria to a grinding halt several times each year. Yet in the breathing spaces between governments everyone seemed to get on famously with everyone else and behave as though nothing at all had been the matter. In their bizarre details the conflicts of the nationalities were an incredible labyrinth. In basic outline they were a direct consequence of the continuous will to rule of the Habsburg dynasty.

Until the defeat of 1866, the Habsburg domination in Germany was matched by the ascendancy of the Germans of Vienna and the Austrian lands. Identifying with the Habsburg dynasty, the Germans of Austria saw themselves as an imperial race, boasting of a political and cultural tradition that no other people of the empire could rival. But by the end of the nineteenth century, the Habsburgs ruled over a vast Central European empire of essentially non-German peoples, and the Germans of the empire found themselves a minority, forced to struggle to maintain their hegemony over superior numbers of Slavs, Magyars, and Italians.

The preeminence of the Germans was first challenged by the Italians, who secured their independence in the 1860s. When the Magyars of Hungary secured equality with the Germans of Austria in the *Ausgleich*, or compromise of 1867, the Slavs of the empire—especially the Czechs of Bohemia and Moravia but also the Poles of Galicia and the Slovenes, Croats, and Serbs of Illyria, Croatia, and Dalmatia—began to advance their own demands. The revival of long-dormant literatures and the rebuilding of long-stagnant economies added impetus to these claims, until by the end of the nineteenth century economic, political, and cultural objectives were fused into a solid program of national rights.

The Germans of the empire bitterly resented and fiercely resisted the Slav demands, and until 1907 the peculiar electoral geometry of the constitution guaranteed that the minority of Germans, by qualifying for extra voting strength through their wealth and education, could control a majority of the seats in parliament. After universal and equal suffrage was ceded by the Emperor in 1907, in an unsuccessful attempt to play the working-class and

Slav votes against one another, the Slavs began to assume parliamentary representation commensurate with their majority of the population in the empire. What had been threatening demands then became paralyzing politics.

The real dispute of the nationalities was over the political aspirations of the Slavs. But to the astonishment of onlookers, this dispute was fought almost exclusively in the symbolic terms of linguistic battles, the more important and bitter of which concerned the Czechs and Germans of Bohemia and Moravia. A Czech in Vienna would demand a railway ticket printed *Praha* instead of the German *Prag*. A German in Bohemia would refuse a postcard which had the word "postcard" printed in both Czech and German instead of German alone. In the provincial diets and in the parliament, the very foundations of the empire would rock with debates over the name of a tiny railroad station in provincial Moravia.

Neither the Slav nor the German blocs in the parliament could muster a majority, especially since the Social Democrats, the largest party, took no side in the nationality disputes. Yet the Slav and German blocs were each large enough to obstruct thoroughly the proceedings with which they took issue, and incidentally to convert the decorum of the polyglot sessions in the celebrated neoclassical House of Parliament into what some wags called a menagerie. A Czech deputy once spoke in German for thirteen hours and thirty minutes without resting, a record which pales alongside the filibuster of a German deputy named Lechner, who with the relative advantage of speaking in his native tongue, managed an address of thirty-six consecutive hours—a truly remarkable effort since he is said to have been to the point throughout. When filibusters were insufficient to prevent the passage of legislature, both Slav and German deputies were willing to apply more colorful and ingenious obstruction techniques. One deputy, a former Master of the Watch, regularly brought his cavalry bugle into the hall and blew it sonorously to disrupt various proceedings. Others tooted horns, shrieked whistles, banged on desks, or threw inkpots through the air.

Since 1902 a great fountain, topped by an enormous statue of Pallas Athene, has stood in front of the House of Parliament in Vienna. As soon as it was built, the statue gave rise to more than a few cruel jokes.

"Why of all things did they put Pallas Athene there?" a jokester would ask.

"Because she is the goddess of wisdom," would come the answer.

"So?"

"Well, they must put her outside, since she is unwelcome inside."

It would have been funny if it had not been true.

As a parliamentary deputy, Count Stürgkh had been a vigorous opponent of universal suffrage. Indeed, from the beginning of his political career he felt only a profound distrust for the masses. In the complexities of Austria, he would argue again and again, only the Emperor and his ministers could be expected to have the wisdom and knowledge necessary to make sense out of chaos. Yet there was no trace of aristocratic hubris in Count Stürgkh's political views. The world was simply a given; it could not easily be changed. Austria too was a given. It could not be expected to survive the drastic changes which would-be reformers, filled with irrelevant Western European ideas, would introduce.

Quite correctly, Count Stürgkh had predicted that the introduction of universal suffrage would release a wave of irredentist opposition to Habsburg rule. Seeing the correctness of his own predictions, he became increasingly determined to see that the petty struggles of the nationalities should not bring his own government into the quagmire of bickering. As he assumed the office of Prime Minister, he made optimistic speeches, including a memorable declaration that the Czechs and Germans were separated by a wall "the thickness only of a piece of paper." But he knew well that the paper was of impenetrable thickness, that it was the conflict of two historical claims which could never be reconciled by schemes of compromise. Indeed, even before he was sworn into office it was widely known that he intended to rule with the aid of the notorious Article Fourteen. Although the article had been used quite frequently to slip various bills, usually military budgets, past the recalcitrant parliament, no one had ever succeeded in ruling for a sustained period without the parliament.

With what appeared to be a flagrant disregard of political sensitivities and realities, Count Stürgkh appointed a cabinet made up almost wholly of German conservatives, including, for the first time since 1867, a cleric as Minister of Education. The latter appointment, in particular, was sure to antagonize the Social Democrats, the anticlerical German radicals, and the large Jewish interests in the empire. Yet, despite what looked like very bad auguries for the future, the first months of Count Stürgkh's ministry were marked with some rather spectacular victories in getting important military bills through a potentially intransigent parliament.

For several years the political situation in the Balkans, traditionally regarded as an Austrian sphere of influence, had been in turmoil. In 1908, under the advice of his Foreign Minister, Count Alois Aeherenthal, Franz Josef had formally annexed the two principalities of Bosnia and Hercegovina, former Turkish territories that had been occupied by Austrian authorities as protectorates since 1879. The annexation was little more than a formality, but the move set off repercussions in Turkey, Russia, Italy, and every other great power with interests, real or imagined, in the Balkans. The Russians, weakened by the 1904 war with Japan and the Revolution of 1905, were forced to acquiesce to the Austrian annexation by an ultimatum from Kaiser Wilhelm II of Germany, and as Tsar Nicholas put it, by the appearance of the Kaiser "in shining armor" alongside his ally, Austria.

Instead of its original purpose of clearly demonstrating the Austrian sphere of influence in the Balkans, the annexation made the Balkan states ever more distrustful of Austrian ambitions, and left the Russians determined to revenge the humiliation they had suffered at the hands of Austria. By March 1912 Serbia and Bulgaria had formed an alliance—to take Balkan politics into their own hands—and by October of the same year, Serbia, Bulgaria, and Greece were at war against Turkey in the first of the Balkan wars.

In Austria the renewed turmoil in the Balkans was viewed as a dangerous disturbance of the status quo. The collapse of the Turkish empire could lead to dreaded Russian intervention in the Balkans, and even if the Turkish empire somehow held together, the Russians could be counted on to support Orthodox Serbia and Bulgaria in claims that might interfere with Austrian designs.

Moreover, the military threat at the "back door" of the Austrian empire led to serious questions about the preparedness of the Austrian military forces. If, as seemed highly possible, these Balkan wars led to a general European war, would Austria be ready to fight on several fronts? In the middle of the nineteenth century, old Austria had carried an armaments bill the same size as that of France or Russia. By the time of Count Stürgkh's ministry, although ranking only after Russia and Germany in population, Austria-Hungary spent less on armaments than any other great power—a quarter of Russian or German expenditures, a third of British or French—less even than Italy. With war threatening along the Balkan frontiers, the very frontiers that had once witnessed the invasions of the Turks to the walls of Vienna itself, the Austrian forces looked woefully inadequate.

By the summer of 1912 Count Stürgkh had capitalized on the war panic to coax parliament into passing a new Army Law.

The bill reduced the term of training for recruits, and increased the annual contingent of recruits and the size of the *Landwehr* or National Guard so that the war footing of the empire would reach an initial mobilization of 1.5 million men instead of the previous 900,000. The same bill also softened the military penal code, which had not been altered in more than a century.

A few months later Count Stürgkh cleverly overcame obstreperous Social Democratic opposition in parliament to secure the passage of a War Service Act. This bill provided that, in case of war, civilians could be compelled to supply manufactures and agricultural products for army needs or could be drafted for labor in industry. The ministries, under the new law, could commandeer the entire equipment and military resources of the country for natural defense. In other words, the bill provided for a total mobilization of the country in case of war, and granted the ministries the dictatorial powers necessary to conduct that mobilization.

Count Stürgkh's successes in securing the passage of the two military bills consolidated his position as Prime Minister, and assuaged the doubts of those influential voices that had predicted the early collapse of the ministry. By May 1913 Count Stürgkh was fairly floating through the incredible difficulties of his office, until a military scandal rocked Vienna and Austria, shaking irreparably whatever scant confidence the public may have felt in the bureaucracy and the military, and making many parliamentary deputies regret the powers they had granted the new Prime Minister in the two recent military bills.

The scandal began in the midst of the Balkan crisis of 1912, when the Russian and Austrian armies were threatening mobilization against one another. It leaked out in official circles in Vienna that the most important secret document of the Austrian Army, the plan of march, had been sold to the Russians. This meant unparalleled catastrophe if war had threatened, as the Russians would have been ready for every Austrian tactical move. The Austrian General Staff reacted quickly to the news of the treason by assigning to Colonel Redl, the head of the Counter-Espionage Department of the General Staff, the task of uncovering the traitor.

Meanwhile, the Foreign Ministry, as usual distrustful of the General Staff, gave orders for an investigation of its own, without informing the General Staff. The two investigations proceeded quite independently, with the bumbling buffoonery of an operetta, until the curtain fell on a surprise ending. Detectives of the Foreign Ministry discovered that the traitor was none other than the trusted Colonel Redl. In the wild round of telephoning that ensued, the news went to Field Marshal Conrad von Hötzendorf, Chief of the General Staff, who is said to have turned white as a sheet, and finally to the Imperial Palace. After hectic conferences it was decided that at all costs the affair, with its scandalous implications, was to be terminated as quickly as possible. "To save the army from worse dishonor," as Hötzendorf put it, drastic though traditional measures were taken. Two fellow officers escorted Colonel Redl to his room in the Hotel Klomser, left him there with a revolver on the table, and paced the hall outside the room until two o'clock in the morning, when they heard a pistol shot from within.

The next day, the papers carried only a short obituary of the capable officer, Colonel Redl, who had died "unexpectedly." But too many people were implicated in the affair for the details to remain a secret, and bit by bit the scandal became a sensation in the Viennese press. Unknown to most of his colleagues and his superiors, Redl had been a homosexual, at the mercy of blackmailers who drove him to his desperate act of treason to raise money. When these lurid details exploded in the press, the prestige of the army was permanently tainted in the eyes of the public and the parliament. Count Stürgkh was careful to dissociate himself from the whole scandal, but it became increasingly difficult for him to railroad any legislation through the now implacably hostile parliament.

Only a few months after the peak of the Redl Affair, Count Stürgkh's honeymoon in the Prime Ministry ended, as the parliament and the Bohemian Diet returned precipitously to their old disruptive tactics. In the Bohemian Diet, the Czechs were a majority but the Germans had sufficient numbers to obstruct business thoroughly with a few well-timed filibusters. Local finances were in chaos, and the industrial production of the entire province, the heart of the industrial might of the Habsburg empire, seemed precariously threatened by the paralysis of the diet. After a few half-hearted pleas to the parliamentarians and a scarcely serious attempt at mediation, Count Stürgkh, convinced that further efforts at compromise were useless, acted with a decisiveness rare in Austrian politics. In one fell swoop, he decreed—over the signature of the Emperor—that the Bohemian Constitution was suspended. The doors of the diet were locked and the delegates sent home. With the Emperor's consent, Count Stürgkh appointed an Imperial Committee, with representatives of both nationalities, and announced that the committee would look after affairs until conditions were propitious for a new election.

Czech and German spokesmen alike berated the Prime Minister for his arbitrary actions, but the fact that direct rule under the ministries was able to restore order to the chaotic finances of Bohemia and to improve drastically the industrial conditions took much of the wind out of their complaints. Indeed, to Count Stürgkh, the success of the move in Bohemia seemed to suggest a solution to the wretched condition into which the legislative bodies of Austria had slipped since the granting of universal suffrage. As long as the diets and the parliament were unable to overcome their own internal antipathies long enough to pass much-needed legislation, they served no purpose in the Habsburg empire except to heat still further the already boiling pot of the nationalities.

When parliament reconvened in March 1914 after a winter recess, the Czech deputies opened a blistering attack on the

Prime Minister for failing to call new elections in Bohemia. Count Stürgkh remained oblivious. As one of his colleagues put it: "I believe that Stürgkh actually wants an obstruction, so that he can enact the Fourteenth!" Within a few days the attacks escalated into the familiar cacophony of obstruction, rallied around the battle cry, *"Ohne Landtag, kein Reichsrat!"* ("Without the Diet, no Parliament"). Again, Count Stürgkh acted without delay. After the obstructions had gone on for a few days, he sent a note to the House of Parliament ordering that the parliament be prorogued. The ministries, declared the note, would rule Austria as they ruled the provincial affairs of Bohemia, by direct order and without legislative interference. Article Fourteen of the constitution granted the necessary powers to the Prime Minister, and Count Stürgkh was determined to ignore the vociferous complaints from all sides in parliament. Austria was to be ruled with quiet efficiency.

A wail of protest arose from parliamentarians of every faction, but to many Viennese, including the once skeptical Emperor, the advantages of what was quickly known as the Stürgkh System were readily obvious. By the summer of 1914 Count Stürgkh had reduced the cantankerous parliamentarians to a docility that enabled the ministries to function freely as both executive and legislative authorities. The military was already prepared for effective and efficient mobilization in case of war, and the main outlets of Slav opposition to war against Mother Russia had been carefully bottled up. Finally, Count Stürgkh, for the first time in anyone's memory, had managed to combine the authorities necessary to act in both provincial and Austrian affairs in a single office, enabling the Prime Ministry to function with a decisiveness undreamed of in Austrian politics. As tensions in the Balkans rose toward their familiar summer high, Austrians could be comforted to know that in any kind of emergency their government could act with the swiftness of concentrated authority. No obstructions of parliament or the diets could stop the important machinery of government which might be needed in case of mobilization. To those who cited the constitution or screamed of the perils of tyranny, Count Stürgkh had a simple explanation: Provisional absolutism was the only alternative to parliamentary paralysis.

Early in the hot and sultry summer of 1914, on June 28, a Serbian nationalist named Gavrilo Princip fired two shots that ultimately put the Stürgkh System to its greatest test. The Archduke Franz Ferdinand, nephew of the Emperor and heir-presumptive to the throne, had been on a state visit with his morganatic wife, Countess Sophie Chotek, to the Bosnian capital of Sarajevo when the bullets of the assassin killed them instantly. As their bodies were born through the Adriatic toward Trieste on the dreadnought *Viribus Unitis*, at the Ballplatz (short for Ballhausplatz, the great baroque home of the Austrian Foreign Ministry) a select group of men, including Count Stürgkh, met to draft a response to the assassination. The Hungarian Premier, Count Tisza, urged diplomatic action to avoid larger European complications. He was overruled as the men of the Ballplatz decided to capitalize on the situation for a final solution to the "Balkan Question." On July 23 they sent an ultimatum to the Serbian government, demanding assurances that would mean an effective end of sovereignty for Serbia. The Serbian government acquiesced to most of the conditions of the ultimatum, leaving the door open for further diplomatic negotiations on the other conditions. The men of the Ballplatz slammed the door: On July 28, 1914, Austria-Hungary declared war on Serbia.

7

The Peacemongers . . .

By 1912 Victor Adler was a very ill man. He was sixty years old, and for more than twenty-six of those years, since he began his full-time involvement with the labor movement, he had pushed himself too hard. Often he had worked fifteen-hour days, seven days a week, and without vacations. The work had taken its toll. For more than ten years he had suffered from emphysema and a bronchial catarrh which left him racked each morning in an hour-long seizure of coughing to clear the mucus from his lungs and throat. In 1908, just before he finally took a much needed cure at a spa, he wrote to August Bebel: ". . . [I] can scarcely breathe and cannot walk one hundred steps." By 1912 he was so exhausted that he needed to return to the spa every few months just to regain enough strength for another short bout with the authorities or with the dissidents within the party.

In February 1913 Victor wrote his will. He left his few personal possessions, his furniture and his library, to his family. In his instructions for the funeral he cleared up an old question by requesting that he be buried with no religious ceremony of any kind. He ended with a testament: "From the party and from my work I take the most difficult farewell. To it [the party] I leave my best: my son Fritz."

The will was premature. Victor never recovered completely, and in the next few years he saw his condition gradually worsened by the added complications of heart disease, but through sheer willpower he somehow managed to continue limited work for the party. Because he was so weak that he could not cross a street unaided or get into a streetcar, the party supplied him with a small carriage for his transportation. He used it only reluctantly, calling it an unnecessary luxury and begrudging the pampering. Victor was not easily put out to pasture. "I am increasingly able to reconcile myself to my situation as a pensioner," he wrote Fritz from a spa in March 1914. "But it is still hard to accept fully. . . . My one consolation is that you young people can work so wonderfully, and that my condition is a burden only subjectively for me, and not objectively for the party—although it remains for me a very tender subject."

As Victor's strength waned, Fritz began more and more to take over the exhausting administrative chores that his father had once handled personally. Fritz answered the volumes of correspondence from various other socialist parties and from the Bureau of the Socialist International, and as the government began to mount an increasingly active foreign policy, he began to fill in for his father in the writing of antiwar speeches and the organization of antiwar rallies. It was not nepotism that assigned these tasks to Fritz, and his increasing responsibilities met with few objections from other party officials. He was accepted as the most qualified for the tasks because he knew the necessary languages (he knew French and English and Kathia could help him with Russian) and because as the son of Victor Adler he was well known to most of the major leaders of international socialism.

Yet, although he could fill in for his father in many administrative duties, Fritz could not step into his father's shoes as Chairman of the party. Unlike his father, who knew well how to cajole and charm officials and to thread the narrow line between the demands of the censors, Fritz remained adamant and uncompromising in his politics. He still treated the complicated situations of Austria as if they were physics problems for which there was but one sure solution. Even when he knew articles he had written for his little magazine, *Das Volk,* or for *Kampf* were sure to be confiscated by the censors, he would go ahead, defying the agents to stop him. Twice they did, in 1912 and 1913, and in both instances he was convicted of publishing inflammatory articles. The penalties were small fines, not enough to deter Fritz.

Moreover, despite his ill health and the substitution of his son's signature on many letters, Victor Adler was still the official Chairman of the Austrian Social Democratic party. It was to him that the government turned when the Social Democrats were blamed for inciting demonstrations and riots. It was to him that the bank creditors looked in January 1914 when the party's bread factory, the Hammerbrotwerke, ran into severe financial difficulties. And most important, although Fritz could carry on the international correspondence of the party, it was Victor Adler who had to represent the Austrian Social Democratic party at the great congresses of the Second International.

The Second International was founded in Paris in July 1889, on the one-hundredth anniversary of the storming of the Bastille. In the beginning it was a rather motley collection of revolutionaries and reformers: mystics, forever predicting the date and hour of the coming world revolution from clues in the Biblical and Marxist Scripture; anarchists, eager to be done with talk and tergiversation to get on with the business of revolution and resurrection; humane and liberal reformers, blithely ignorant of Marxism and almost any other doctrines but eager to work body and

79

soul on behalf of the laboring poor of the world; and the majority of Marxist Social Democrats, confident of their future role in the ineluctable progression of history. In the world of nationalism and imperialism, robber barons and cartels, the twelve-hour day and the seven-day week, this motley crew, armed only with the vision of a new world and the precedent of Marx's own ill-fated International Working Men's Association, set out to build an international organization of the workers of the world.

In the era before the League of Nations or the United Nations, the Socialist International was perhaps the only truly international organization in the world, the only forum where men from dozens of countries, speaking many languages, could come together to discuss and plan peacefully for common ends. Their official name, The Second Workingman's International, was international; their anthem was the *Internationale;* their flag was solid red, representing the blood of Everyman. At the first congress, Vaillant and Liebknecht, the leaders of the French and German Socialist parties, were named Co-Chairmen of the meeting, at a time when colonial crises and revanchist fears kept France and Germany near the verge of war. At the 1904 congress, in Amsterdam, in the midst of the Russo-Japanese War, the delegates from Russia and Japan, Plekhanov and Katayama, sat next to one another. When they clasped hands all 450 delegates to the congress rose to their feet in a tribute of thunderous applause. Each made a speech declaring that the war had been forced upon their countries by capitalist interests and was not a matter of the Russian people fighting the Japanese people. The audience listened in an almost religious silence, then burst into applause again.

Although he did not attend any of the biennial congresses until 1910, when the International met in Copenhagen, Fritz had followed the activities of the International since the founding, when he was not quite ten years old. He was vacationing with his mother, brother, and sister in the Salzkammergut, when his father and another delegate stopped there on their way to the Paris meeting in 1889. Family discussion for the next few days was nothing except the potential for the growth and influence of the International. In the Adler home, the topic was never dropped.

Victor Adler, of course, attended every congress as the representative of the Austrian Social Democratic party. In the very letters in which he tried to dissuade Fritz from participating in the labor movement, Victor provided a running chronicle of the International. These letters and the published transactions of the congresses, which he read carefully, kept Fritz well apprized of the activities of the International, even in the years when his interest in the labor movement had seemingly taken a back seat to his interest in physics and philosophy.

Especially after the death of Friedrich Engels in 1895, the leadership of the International was rather fragmented among the epigoni—those leaders of different national socialist parties who could only with difficulty surrender their national interests to the interests of the whole International. Although the Austrian party was rarely in the vanguard of leadership of the International, lacking both the prodigious strength of the German Social Democratic party and the equally influential revolutionary heritage of the French party, Victor Adler was from its founding one of the leaders of the Second International. At an early congress Victor told the delegates: "We in Austria have a little International ourselves, we are the ones who know best the difficulties which have to be overcome." The speech characterized his role in the International: He was the compromiser. His status as one of the Grand Old Men of the International, the prestige of his close friendship with Friedrich Engels, and his experience in the nationality problems of Austria-Hungary enabled him to reconcile the often violent disputes of tactics and strategy into which the different parties embroiled themselves. To many, both inside and outside the socialist movement—and especially to Fritz—Victor Adler was the one man who symbolized the spirit of the International.

Each of the congresses dealt with the wide range of problems of the labor movement, and each concluded with what the participants proclaimed as epochal resolutions. At Paris in 1889 the resolution called for socialists everywhere, if possible, to celebrate May Day as an international workingman's holiday. At Brussels in 1891, Zurich in 1893, and finally at London in 1896, the anarchists were officially purged from the International in favor of a "pure" Marxist line. In Amsterdam in 1904 the doctrine of revisionism, which among other proposals called for limited tactical cooperation with bourgeois parties, was officially rejected. At Stuttgart in 1907 a universal program of antiwar action was voted unanimously. At Copenhagen in 1910 the "bourgeois nationalism" of such groups as the Czech separatists within the Austrian party was officially declared heresy. In every case Victor Adler had been a central figure in the executive committees that had drafted the final resolutions. In every case he had helped to reconcile the warring factions and had ironed out the important compromises that kept the International functioning in an atmosphere of untempered faith.

To some observers the resolutions and accomplishments of the International did not warrant this faith. Most of the firm decisions, such as the condemnations of revisionism and "bourgeois nationalism," had been taken to serve the dictates of Marxist dogma and the internal identity crises of the stronger parties. The largest of the parties, the German Social Democratic party, was four million strong, but so racked with bureaucratic inertia and fear of the Prussian and Reich governments that it was paralyzed politically. Using the leverage of their election strength and their incomparable party discipline, the Germans willy-nilly condemned other parties of the International to follow their policy of standing by and awaiting the inevitable collapse of bourgeois society. When socialist parties in some of the democratic states offered the idea that their own political situation made it possible to secure ministerial posts and perhaps to give the "tottering" bourgeois society a push from within, the Germans condemned the idea as "revision-ist." By browbeating, the Germans could coerce enough other parties to support their views to assure the defeat of revisionist measures or resolutions.

On the issues that lent themselves to specific solutions, such as the question of May Day demonstrations or the idea of a general strike to forestall preparations for war, the Germans, para-lyzed by their own fears, condemned the International to tergiver-sation. Congresses were forced to settle for compromise resolu-tions, substituting rhetoric and faith in the magic efficacy of the International for specific programs. Despite the sharp differences in tactics and strategy, the parties were united by an unyielding faith that in a moment of real crisis the working class would be capable of some united action expressing its strength. What, asked the optimists, could governments do in the face of the concerted opposition of millions of workers, organized nationally and even internationally into a powerful and disciplined force? What alli-ances or pacts of autocrats could stand up to the irresistible force of the workers of the world?

The dispassionate observer, weighing the evidence, might find faults. But Fritz was no dispassionate observer, and his opin-ions on these questions were neither judicious nor judicial. Raised in a home where the dinner-table conversations had always been Rights, Peace, and the Ultimately Victorious Struggle Against the Ruling Classes, Fritz was eager to believe in the Second Interna-tional with a religious fervor. To Fritz, who had never witnessed the acrimonious debates and endless politicking that preceded the votes at the congresses of the International, the final unanimous acceptance of the resolutions (rather like the final unanimous ac-ceptance of nominees at the conventions of American political parties) was itself the symbol of the power of the International. "The significance of the International," he once wrote, "cannot be measured by what it has done, but by what it is." If hundreds of delegates, representing millions of workers all over the world, could unanimously agree on resolutions opposing oppression and war, what could ever stop the International? That the governments of Europe might continue in their scrupulous disregard of the resolutions of the International, or that the parties of the International might themselves ignore those resolutions, were two skepticisms which Fritz did not allow himself. The triumph of the International was as sure as the imminent collapse of capitalist society, a simple matter of time, discipline, and steady hard work.

In 1912, when Fritz began to handle the correspondence of the Austrian party with the Bureau of the Socialist International in Brussels, the chief problem confronting the socialists of the world was war. From Marxist theory the socialists could argue that wars between nations were capitalist wars, waged only to profit the munitions and armaments makers and to appease the avarice of the capitalist ruling classes. The chief culprits—imperialists and militarists—were easily identified, and the "hurrah" chauvinism of the late nineteenth and early twentieth centuries was easily dismissed as another false illusion, perpetrated by the ruling classes to seduce innocent workers and peasants away from their true interest in the class struggle. What did the workers of the world have to gain by fighting one another? Surely a worker in Austria had more in common with a worker in Russia than either of them had in common with their respective ruling classes. And, socialists noted with an eye to the future, the blood of proletarian soldiers should not be squandered in wars to profit the capitalists. If workers' blood was to be shed, it should be shed in the only war worth fighting; the class war that would ultimately eliminate classes, and with classes, the class rule that was the root cause of the senseless wars between nations.

Yet, despite the coherence of their arguments, the socialists were powerless to stop wars. Even in the few countries where socialists had been able to muster strong parliamentary representation, they could exercise little real influence on their governments. They might make regular motions of disapproval—of the Moroccan policies of Germany and France, of Italian aggression in the Mediterranean and in Africa, of the Austrian annexation of Bosnia-Hercegovina, of the Balkan wars—but the motions were expressions of feeling, not instruments of action. Nowhere were the socialists a majority in a parliament. Even if they had been a majority, in states like Austria, Germany, and Russia, where the threat of war was most expected, constitutional restrictions reduced the power of parliaments to advice and consent, with scant provision for dissent. Hence, despite their resolutions and their rallies, the socialists could do nothing to stop the governments of Europe from embroiling themselves in an endless series of petty wars and detentes. If it was not the colonial squabbles, it was the power struggles in the Mediterranean or the Balkans, or the ever-escalating arms race, then entering a new phase as the British and German navies competed to build bigger and more destructive warships, until they culminated their race with the "invincible" dreadnoughts.

Because they were powerless to influence their governments at home, the socialists of the world turned to the International in the hope of stopping wars. From the very first congress, wars and imperialism had been on the agendas of the great meetings. In Stuttgart in 1907 a coordinated antiwar policy was the chief item of the Congress. The resolution at Stuttgart was adopted only after long and acrimonious debates, and it was only after much haggling in committees and subcommittees, together with the careful mediation of Victor Adler, that any resolution could be forged out of the mutually conflicting demands of many parties. What emerged was a hodgepodge, calculated more to assuage the internal qualms of the various parties than to meet the threat of war.

From the reluctant Germans came the usual Marxist platitude that war was inherent in the capitalist system and would not disappear until the destruction of capitalism. The Germans also proffered the vague instruction that in the meantime the socialists everywhere should press for the abolition of standing armies and the reduction of armaments. From Jean Jaurès, the eloquent and popular French socialist leader and the chief advocate of direct action to meet the threat of war, came an optimistic list of examples of international socialist cooperation (an impressive but meaningless list, since the socialists had actually influenced government policies in none of the instances cited), and the statement that in case of a threat of war:

> . . . it is the duty of the working classes and their parliamentary representatives in the countries taking part, fortified by the unifying activity of the International Bureau, to do everything to prevent the outbreak of war by whatever means seem to them most effective, which naturally differ with the intensification of the class war and the general political situation.

The last sentence of the resolution was the contribution of Rosa Luxemburg and Lenin, both of whom had participated in the Revolution of 1905 in Russia, where they had seen the truth of what Engels had once predicted, that war could so weaken the machinery of capitalist governments as to make revolution possible. Their contribution (probably accepted because no one else believed it) gave the Stuttgart Resolution something of a revolutionary twist:

> Should war break out in spite of all this, it is their duty to intercede for its speedy end, and to strive with all their power to make use of the violent economic and political crises brought about by the war to rouse the people and thereby to hasten the abolition of class rule.

Such was the antiwar policy of the Second International. Like most of the other resolutions of the International, it was long on optimism and short on specifics. There was not a line in it that listed a specific action socialists would use to meet the threat of war from potentially belligerent governments.

8

. . . Prepare for War

Fritz's first major duty when he was assigned the international affairs of the Austrian Social Democratic party was to make the preliminary arrangements for the next congress of the Socialist International, scheduled for the summer of 1913 in Vienna. It was to be the first time that the socialists of the world would meet in Austria. The party in Vienna was excited in expectation.

Fritz had scarcely begun to formulate the needed plans and arrangements when, in the early summer of 1912, war threatened in the Balkans. Since Austria was a potential party to the hostilities, the International congress scheduled for the following summer was in jeopardy. When the Stuttgart resolution was passed, five years before, the socialists had expected war to start over a colonial question, such as the crises at Morocco or Fashoda. Now war threatened on the very edge of Europe. Joined by Jean Jaurès, who called for "immediate, passionate, effective international action" to contain the situation in the Balkans, Victor

Adler pressed for the immediate summoning of an extraordinary International congress to answer the growing threats of war everywhere. Other socialist leaders seconded the idea, and in short order the congress was arranged for the end of November 1912, at Basel.

Five hundred fifty-five representatives from twenty-three different socialist parties assembled in the great cathedral of Basel, graciously loaned for the occasion by church authorities. After the customary stirring opening ceremonies, including a small parade, a hymn to freedom, and a moment of silence to commemorate the dead leaders of the socialist movement, Edouard Anseele of the Belgian party set the theme of the congress with a bold statement of socialist demands.

> The proletariat, which from today henceforward must be recognized as the herald of world peace, demands peace in the Balkans, republican autonomy of the Balkan peoples, the abandonment of alliances and diplomatic intrigues which carry with them the seed of every war. Austria-Hungary must not try to rob the Balkan peoples of the fruit of their victories, and if Russia attacks, the Russian proletariat itself will rise and support it [the international proletariat] enthusiastically and admiringly. . . . The International is strong enough to speak in this tone of command to those in power and if necessary to follow up their words with deeds. War on war, peace for the world, hurrah for the workers' International!

The address, which was frequently interrupted by wild storms of applause, set the mood for the whole congress. Throughout the first day, speaker after speaker mounted the podium to paint the horrors of war and the strength of the international proletariat. Keir Hardie, the English delegate, pointed out that the congress represented 15 million socialist voters and 45 million members of the working class. Jean Jaurès, looking up at the great bell tower of the cathedral as he spoke, closed the day's proceedings with a stirring appeal:

> In this church I heard just now as it were a call to general reconciliation—the sound of the bells that welcomed us. It reminds me of the motto which Schiller set at the head of his wonderful "Song of the Bell": *Vivos voco, mortuos plango, fulgara frango.*

His voice trembling with emotion, he explained:

> I call the living that they may defend us from the monster which appears on the horizon; I cry for the uncounted dead in the East whose odors greet us like a remorse; I shall break the thunderbolts of war which menace us from the sky.

The delegates rose in unison with a storm of applause and loud cries of "Hurrah" for the International and for peace.

The next day the congress continued on the same halcyon note. Votes for all the resolutions were unanimous, including the reaffirmation of the Stuttgart resolution and certain vague statements that the Balkan socialists should work for reconciliation, that the Austro-Hungarian armies must be prevented from attacking Serbia and menacing Albania, and that the working classes of Germany, France, and England should redouble their efforts to prevent a world war.

In the atmosphere of self-congratulation, no one paid much attention to the one pessimistic note in Victor Adler's otherwise optimistic speech: "It unfortunately does not depend on us Social Democrats whether there is a war or not."

The governments of Europe actually seemed to hear the bells of Basel. In the year following the extraordinary congress the Treaty of London ended the first Balkan War, temporarily forestalling the world war which the pessimists had predicted. The next summer saw another Balkan war, between Bulgaria and the combined forces of Serbia, Romania, Greece, and Turkey, but this one seemed more like a farce than a real threat to peace, and in time it was ended by the treaties of Bucharest and Constantinople. The arms race continued unabated, but there were theorists who could argue convincingly that the staggering expenditures which modern armaments demanded would produce a crisis in the economies of the European states, and that the crisis would not only end the arms race but also would provide the potential situation for enormous gains by the working classes. Indeed, some offered, the crisis could be the long-awaited signal for the revolution that would end the bourgeois order in Europe. In any case, most believed, there was no need to fear war anymore. In the spring of 1914 Jean Jaurès said to a friend: "Don't worry, the socialists will do their duty. If he wants to start a war, four million German socialists will rise as one man and kill the Kaiser."

Yet there were signs that supported Victor Adler's pessimism, especially in Austria, where Prime Minister Count Stürgkh had successfully pushed the two army bills past the Social Democratic opposition in the parliament. And in both the Austrian parliament and the Ballplatz, there were continued clamors for a containment of Serbia and a halt, if need be a military halt, to Serbian "aggression" in the Balkans.

But after Basel it was not difficult to ignore these pessimistic little signs. The congress, originally scheduled for the summer of 1913 in Vienna, was moved to the summer of 1914. The new date gave the Vienna congress the additional aura of the twenty-fifth anniversary of the founding of the Second International and the fiftieth anniversary of the founding of Marx's own First International. The plans called for an enormous manifestation of the solidarity of the working classes in the face of whatever renewed bellicosity the ruling classes might raise. So many delegates were expected—upward of one thousand were predicted—that a special rule had to be decreed by the Bureau of the International in Brussels, limiting even the largest delegations to 120 representatives. The agenda, decided at a special meeting of the

Bureau of the International, reflected the general optimism felt by almost everyone in the International. The three central topics for debate at the congress were to be world depression, the increasing cost of living, and imperialism. All three had been discussed at numerous previous congresses, but usually only in passing, as the parties of the International spent most of their energies on resolutions to deal with specific problems of the socialist movement. Now the leaders of the International were so convinced of the tenuous situation of capitalism everywhere that they decided to discuss the grave weaknesses of capitalist society—as if to contrast the preparation, unity, and strength of the International with the failings of capitalist governments everywhere. Two minor questions, included on the agenda because of their topicality, were the question of alcoholism among workers and the situation of political prisoners in Russia.

Perhaps the most important single item on the agenda was the Vaillant-Hardie Amendment, which called for the use of the general strike as a positive action on the part of socialists everywhere to meet the threat of war by any government. Similar motions had been introduced to congresses of the International as early as 1893. Each time they had been either shelved or defeated. But after two summers of war in the Balkans, the situation in Europe had changed drastically enough to persuade some parties to rethink their policies toward antiwar measures. Many parties, especially in Western Europe, were anxious to supplement optimistic fatalism with a positive plan of action. Advocates of the amendment, anticipating the usual objections of the Germans (who argued that "General Strike is General Nonsense"), were already explaining that the amendment was not meant to jeopardize the fighting strength of a nation, but to force nations to arbitrate their differences instead of resorting to immediate mobilization.

Fritz, as Chairman of all the committees that were to deal with the forthcoming congress, had the responsibility of coordinating the arrangements for the congress. Credentials of the delegates had to be verified, hotel and travel arrangements had to be made, drafts of resolutions had to be printed in hundreds of copies, and reservations for meeting places for the congress and the many smaller commissions had to be arranged. It was grueling labor, requiring hours and hours of administrative work which took up most of Fritz's time during the spring of 1914. And as the political climate in Austria warmed with the weather during that spring, the task of arranging for the details of the congress became more and more difficult.

In March Prime Minister Count Stürgkh had prorogued the Austrian parliament. Although it did not seem possible for the ministries to rule for any sustained period under Article Fourteen of the constitution, the absence of any parliamentary forum for complaints against abuses made the ukase of the censors and other petty bureaucrats that much more arbitrary. Newspaper articles and letters relating to the congress were repeatedly delayed and confiscated. Arrangements for meeting rooms were mysteriously held up, "awaiting further consideration," then canceled. In general there seemed to be a rather efficient campaign to frustrate the organization of the congress.

Fritz was in the midst of the final arrangements, with the congress less than two months away, when the two shots of the assassin Princip rang out in Sarajevo on June 28. No one, least of all the socialists, suspected that those shots would be the exclamation points marking the end of an era in European politics.

The new crisis in the Balkans found most of the leaders of international socialism on vacation. Karl Kautsky was in Rome, Fritz Ebert was on the island of Rügen, Philip Scheidemann was in the Alps, Lenin was hiking in the Carpathians, Victor Adler was taking another cure at Bad Neuheim. Almost alone, Fritz watched the critical situation develop in Vienna. Like most of the socialists he viewed the immediate aftermath of the assassination as simply the beginning of another long hot summer in the Balkans. There was no note of alarm in any of his communications to the Bureau of the Socialist International until July 21.

That day, a fairly routine article in the *Arbeiter-Zeitung,* reporting on the recent party convention of the French socialists in Paris, was censored. Fritz speculated that the censor had acted because the article had included a mention of the Paris debates on the general strike as a possible working-class response to a declaration of war by any of the European governments. Familiar with the ways of the Viennese police and censors since childhood, Fritz was wary. He wondered whether the gratuitous act of the censor might not indicate that the police were planning a major action against the forthcoming congress.

The next day he called a meeting of those Austrian party leaders who were not on vacation to present them with the draft of a letter he had prepared for submission to the Bureau of the International in Brussels. The party leaders met for several hours on the afternoon and evening of July 23. Fritz tried unsuccessfully to point out that there were dangerous signs of war preparations by the Austrian army and the Ballplatz, but the majority of the party leaders, especially Dr. Karl Renner, argued that his views were too pessimistic, and that the congress could probably be held in Vienna in any case. Only Friedrich Austerlitz, the gruff and redoubtable managing editor of the *Arbeiter-Zeitung,* shared Fritz's pessimism.

After hours of debate, Fritz agreed to mitigate the tone of the letter to Brussels. What he sent was mild and very conditional:

In case the peril of war persists, the dangers for the congress are exceptional. . . . We consider it impossible to hold a congress in Austria in a period of potential outbreak of war, because we could not guarantee that the government and the police would conduct themselves like those of a civilized state.

FRITZ

Less than two hours after Fritz dispatched the letter to Brussels, the correspondence bureau of the party received the text of the Austrian ultimatum to Serbia. Another emergency meeting of the party leaders was called, this time to draft a manifesto against the war that seemed promised by the ultimatum. Couched as an editorial to elude the censors, the manifesto expressed understanding for the Austrian right to demand reparations for the crime of Sarajevo and to demand an end to the Serbian government's toleration of underground plots. Then, in a more orthodox vein, the manifesto pleaded for the continuation of peaceful negotiation, warning that the German workers of Austria could not support a war of aggression. Several paragraphs which attacked Count Stürgkh for failing to convene parliament in the time of crisis were deleted by the censors before the manifesto could be published in the *Arbeiter-Zeitung* on July 25.

News of the Serbian answer to the ultimatum was made public in Vienna the next day. Most of the Social Democratic party leaders quickly moved to hide any party documents or other materials which related to the forthcoming congress. As the only large antiwar group in Vienna, they expected to bear the brunt of the government repression in the case of war. Years later Fritz recalled that he was amazed at the apparent intimidation and cowardice of the party leaders, who seemed to fear nothing more than that they might be arrested or prosecuted for the possession of antiwar materials.

On the afternoon of Sunday, July 26, another meeting of the party leadership discussed a telegram from Brussels calling for a meeting of major socialist leaders to respond to the deteriorating diplomatic situation. The consensus was that Fritz should take the first available train to Bad Neuheim, apprize his father of the situation in Vienna and other capitals, then travel with his father to Brussels where they could report to the Executive Committee of the Socialist International.

They arrived in Brussels on the evening of July 28, after the Austro-Hungarian declaration of war on Serbia had been issued. In the morning—a gloomy, rainy day—the twenty delegates from various European parties gathered in the newly built wing of the Maison du Peuple, resolved that somehow they could act in a determined and bold manner. Two items were on the agenda: the international situation and the disposition of the Vienna congress. Since Fritz was not accredited as a representative to the bureau, Victor once again had to speak for the Austrian party. He was extremely ill—many at the meeting thought he had aged ten years overnight. On the morning of July 29 he addressed the group with his appraisal of the situation in Vienna.

He began by saying that even if Serbia had accepted every point on the ultimatum, the war was inevitable. Then, to the astonishment of most of the delegates there, he assessed the preparedness of the Austrian Social Democratic party to oppose the war:

> The party is incapable of acting. To say otherwise would be to fool the bureau. It is not necessary to be duped by the news. What we see now is the result of many years of class agitation and demagoguery. There are manifestations in the street in favor of war. A new situation is being created in our country, a country already beset by problems and by nationality conflicts. What will become of the situation? No one knows.

The rest of his speech was a catalogue of the woes besetting the party:

> Demonstrations are impossible. One merely risks his life and invites imprisonment. So be it. We have already been through that. But the organization and the newspaper itself are in danger. One risks annihilating thirty years of work, without any political results. . . . We must safeguard our institutions.

Ideas of the strike, etc., are no more than fantasies. The question is extremely grave, and our only hope is that we will be the only victims, that the war will not spread.

He concluded: "Even if the war is localized, the situation of the party will be very serious."

The other delegates were appalled by the speech. Hugo Haase of the German party and Bruce Glasier of the English party spoke of the strengths of their own parties and attacked the Austrians for their weakness. Victor Adler was able to give a mocking and crushing reply to their criticisms, but in the eyes of most of the delegates Victor Adler was no longer the symbol of the International—if, indeed, there was still an International.

Later, in private, Fritz witnessed a discussion between his father and Jules Guesde, an old-guard leader of the French Socialist party. Victor admitted to Guesde that he believed that Austria would not only have a front against Serbia, but also fronts against Russia, Italy, and Romania—and that Austria would have to fight.

"And a front against the workers?" asked Guesde.

"No, no, no!" answered Victor, admitting in so many words that the Austrian Social Democratic party would not lead any opposition to the war policies of the Austrian government.

That night there was an enormous antiwar rally in the Cirque Royale in Brussels. Jaurès, despite a bad headache, addressed a crowd of thousands of Belgian workers to assure them that the socialists of the world would never permit a war. He spoke with his arm around the shoulders of Hugo Haase, the German party executive, and amid the cheers of the crowd he concluded with another of his eloquent pleas:

If in the mechanical chain of circumstances and in the intoxication of the first battles our masters did succeed in dragging the masses along with them, then, as typhus finishes off the work of the shells, as death and destruction strike, men returned to sobriety will turn on the rulers of Germany, France, Russia, and Italy and ask them what reasons they can produce for all these corpses. And then revolution unleashed would tell them: "Begone and ask pardon of God and men!"

For hours after the speech the streets of Brussels echoed with shouts of "Down With War, Long Live Peace!" and "Long Live International Socialism!"

Neither Victor nor Fritz attended the rally, much to Fritz's disappointment. The next day, when the Socialist leaders again assembled to discuss the plans for the Vienna congress, Fritz had a short private talk with Jaurès. As if explaining why he had excluded Austria from his list of nations the night before, Jaurès said that the Austrian Social Democrats should not be intimidated. No matter what happened, he urged, the party must somehow recover the courage to lead a campaign against the war.

More than two years later, Fritz could still recall the conversation in detail: "I felt ashamed by the words of Jaurès. I knew perfectly well that he was not attacking me, but I could not bring myself to disavow my father." It was the first time in his life that Fritz had been ashamed of his father.

In the session that afternoon the Bureau agreed to shift the location of the congress from Vienna to Paris and to advance the date to August 9. It was too late.

On the morning of July 29, while Victor Adler was describing the situation in Austria, the Austrian artillery was already shelling Belgrade across the Danube. From there the gears of the frightening machine of alliances, built up in years of European "cold war," began to turn of their own accord. Nothing could stop them. On July 29 the Tsar declared a general mobilization of the Russian forces, which he subsequently rescinded, then re-declared the following day. On July 31 Germany proclaimed a "state of threatening danger of war." Later that day, Austria declared a general mobilization.

For several more excruciating days, while the socialist leaders returned to their home countries, the gears kept turning. On August 1, France and Germany declared general mobilizations —the last preludes to the dreadful formalities. Later that day Germany declared war on Russia. On August 3, Germany declared war on France. On August 4, England declared war on Germany. On August 6, Austria-Hungary declared war on Russia. And on they went . . .

The First World War had begun.

9

Franz Josef Mounts His Horse

Otto von Bismarck, who had predicted that "some damn foolish thing in the Balkans" would start a world war, also prophesied that "if Franz Josef mounts his horse, all his peoples will follow him." He was right on both counts.

Most of Vienna had heard about the declaration of war against Serbia from café gossip and the newspapers on the afternoon of July 28. By late afternoon groups of demonstrators were in the streets, shouting "Down with Serbia" and "To Belgrade." The evening newspapers published the Emperor's war manifesto. Stressing the perfidious ingratitude, hostility, and faithlessness of Serbia, the Emperor somberly admitted that his fond desire to consecrate the last years of his reign to peaceful purposes had been shattered by the "malevolent opponent." Serene in conscience, the Old Gentleman told his peoples that he had "set out on the path which duty prescribed," trusting firmly in the sacrificial loyalty of his peoples and his army, so often demonstrated, and "in the Almighty to confer victory on my arms."

That night enthusiastic Viennese paraded through the streets, flaunting pictures of the Emperor and black-and-yellow imperial flags as they sang *Gott erhalte Franz den Kaiser* and the stirring *Prinz Eugen Lied*. With the orders for general mobilization, issued at five o'clock in the afternoon of July 31, companies of soldiers began to appear in the streets. Units called up from the potentially hostile nationalities—Germans, Magyars, Czechs, Croats, Slovaks, Slovenes, Ruthenians, Romanians, Poles, Italians —temporarily forgot their intermural rivalries as they marched together to the *Radetzky Marsch* and other lusty martial airs. Many of the new recruits and reservists understood no German beyond the eighty words used in command, but in the majestic light blue tunics of their imperial uniforms they marched together as one army. And the crowds cheered.

For most of Vienna enthusiastic fatalism replaced the weariness of years of "cold war" and the exhaustion of months of diplomatic intrigue. Thousands and hundreds of thousands felt what they had never felt in peacetime, that they belonged together. A city of two million, a country of fifty million, in that hour felt that they were participating in world history, in a moment which would never recur. The acrimonious discussions and arguments of the "Slav Question" and the "Balkan Question" resolved themselves overnight in an outburst of enthusiasm and trust. Even a political skeptic like Sigmund Freud could write: "For the first time in thirty years, I feel like an Austrian, and would like to try it once more with this not very promising empire. The mood everywhere is excellent."

The mood everywhere *was* excellent. In the streets differences of class, rank, and language were flooded over by the rushing feeling of fraternity. Strangers spoke to one another in the streets; people who had avoided one another for years shook hands; porters, laundresses, shoemakers, and apprentices from the tenaments in the suburbs mingled in ease with the fashionable crowds of the Ringstrasse and the Kärntnerstrasse. Only the hapless foreigners who perchance spoke a careless few words of English or French in the streets felt any hostility from the crowds.

Those who were convinced of the righteousness of the cause at hand raised paeans of thanks to the God who had matched them with the hour, while many a skeptic surrendered his critical judgment to the passions of the day. The philosophic anarchists and the pacifists became patriots, while the patriots became insatiable annexationists, until every discussion on the street ended with a platitude like "He who cannot hate cannot really love" or with coarse inculpations. Few indeed would venture the thought that the all-high ruler, Emperor Franz Josef, in his eighty-third year, would have called his people to war, would have demanded such a sacrifice of blood, unless from direct necessity, unless evil, sinister, and criminal foes were threatening the peace and tranquility of the empire. For the few who persisted in dissent, a new word was borrowed from the French—*defeatist.*

The war fever spread quickly. French and English signs disappeared from shop windows overnight. Society ladies swore they would never again speak French instead of German. The poor nuns of the convent *Zu den Englische Fräulein* had to change its name, because the public would not believe that the *Englische* applied to the angels and not to the Anglo-Saxons. Declaration of war against Russia tempered the optimism of those who had believed that the war could be localized against little Serbia, but for thousands of less sober souls the passions of Russophobia only added to the mania of war fever. Fear of the ever-dreaded cossacks justified a sacred war against that huge and dreaded power which mystically embodied the despotism and barbarism and imperialism of the East in the name of the Tsar. Men who might have once shuddered at the specter of the Russian colossus drew playful cartoons of a gorilla with the caption "The Tsar in civilian dress."

FRITZ

From the pulpit of St. Stephen's Cathedral, Gustav Cardinal Piffl, Archbishop of Vienna, thundered the blessings of the Church: "It is the voice of God which speaks through the roar of the guns." His sermon echoed the sentiments of many in the empire, who believed firmly that God and the military might of the German ally would guarantee a short and successful war. "We'll be home at Christmas," the recruits shouted laughingly to their mothers and brides as they boarded the trains for Galicia and the Balkans. And in the dining room of the Hotel Meissl & Schadn, or around the marble tables of the Café Pucher, the influential few murmured to one another: "Three short months—then peace with glory!"

Thanks to the foresight of Prime Minister Count Stürgkh, the mobilization of the Austrian forces proceded smoothly and on schedule. The armies quickly trebled their peacetime numbers to the full mobilization strength of 1.4 million men. Some shortages of equipment—rifles, machine guns, light artillery—were noticed immediately, and many of the reservists had to wear black-and-yellow armbands over their civilian coats because of a shortage of uniforms. But in all the troops looked like the great paintings in the museums, the only idea of war for many in Vienna. Chiseled into the façade of the War Ministry in Vienna was the Roman aphorism *Si vis pacem, para bellum*—who could suppose that the Emperor and his government had not heeded the challenge to the letter?

On the home front, Count Stürgkh put the provisions of the War Service Act into effect. Before the fighting actually commenced, a state of emergency was proclaimed, suspending ordinary civil liberties throughout the Austrian half of the empire. On the day of the order for general mobilization, an imperial decree instructed field commanders in areas near the fronts (Galicia, Bukowina, and parts of Moravia and Silesia) to "issue decrees, give orders, and enforce the same." On November 4, 1914, trial by jury was abolished, and where civil courts ceased to function, courts-martial were used to administer criminal law.

With no pressures or interference from the prorogued parliament, Count Stürgkh was able to establish a War Surveillance Office, attached to the Ministry of War and containing delegates from half a dozen other ministries. The War Surveillance Office undertook the supervision of those controls, including a stringent censorship, that were deemed essential to maintain the war footing of the empire. Everywhere the rights of the individuals and of private enterprise were sacrificed to the demands of Moloch. Few protested as the temporary absolutism of the spring of 1914 was converted into "absolutism for the duration." What mattered now was to win the war, to defeat the perfidious enemies of the empire. Then, in the calm of victory, Austrians of every political persuasion and every nationality could enjoy the fruits of victory.

The Habsburg armies took the field in the same colorful spectacle they had mounted for their last great military campaign almost fifty years before: the glorious Magyar cavalry massed for open charges, the cannon displaced on open ground to cover the cavalry charges, the infantry in close order formations to finish off the enemy the cavalry would dislocate. The troops, with their red trousers and light-blue coats, were paraded for the picturesque pageantry of nineteenth-century warfare.

It took less than a month for commanders and men alike to realize how drastically the machine gun and the trench had changed the nature of warfare. Before they could recover from that initial shock, the Habsburg lines were completely overrun by the panic-producing thrusts of cossack horsemen and the sheer numbers of Russian troops. Indeed, within a month all of Galicia, a rich grain-producing region the size of New York State, was occupied by Russian armies. Only the capital, Lemberg (Lvov), somehow held out until the end of August.

In Vienna the crowds continued to demonstrate in the streets, often in front of newspaper offices where they waited to read the latest news from the battlefields. But the newspapers in Vienna gave little hint of what was happening at the front. What they did report was either couched in the careful language demanded by the War Surveillance Office, or self-censored out of patriotic responsibility. Retreats were described as "a regrouping of forces for strategic purposes." The people of Vienna, trusting in the impeccable integrity of their Emperor, waited patiently for the reports of victories.

The first communiqué of the General Staff was issued after Galicia had fallen to the Russians. A masterpiece of understatement perhaps unequaled in war reporting, it began: "Lemberg is still in our hands. . . ." Many in Vienna, expecting reports of deep penetration into Russian territory, were incredulous. Within weeks, as the newspaper reports of "strategic regroupings" continued, as Lemberg was evacuated, as other areas of Moravia and Austrian Poland fell to the Russian steamroller, the optimism of Vienna collapsed, until even the policy makers at the Ballplatz and the War Ministry began to recheck the calculations upon which they had based their strategies.

The assumption which had governed the prewar strategies of the Austrian and German General Staffs was that while the Russian armies were almost limitless in numbers, they would mobilize so slowly that quick thrusts could penetrate deep into Russian territory before the great Russian bear rose up to strike back. According to the Schlieffen Plan, the Germans, faced with a war on two fronts, would use the bulk of the army in the West, against rapidly mobilizing French and English armies. Then, after achieving a quick victory with overwhelming numbers in the West, the Germans would bring their troops across Germany swiftly by train to meet the slowly mobilizing troops of the Russians. German and Austrian strategists both felt confident that the Habsburg troops, though left alone to attack the Russians in the opening weeks of the war, could capitalize on their own rapid mobilization and shorter supply lines to mount a swift thrust against the lumbering

Russians, or at least hold the front until large numbers of Germans could be brought East for the kill.

The Russian estimate of Habsburg fighting strength proved far more accurate than Austrian or German estimates. (The Tsar said, early in the war: "I attach only secondary importance to our operations against Austria.") In the opening weeks of the war, Tsarist troops were not only equal in numbers to the Habsburg troops, but were superior in equipment, training, and general supply. After learning important lessons in the war against Japan, the Russians were prepared for the slow drudgery of trench and machine-gun warfare, and using concealed artillery emplacements, tactically deployed infantry, and the fierce cossack charges, they quickly routed the unprepared Austrians.

By the end of September 1914 newspapers in Paris and London were saluting the Moscovite steamroller alongside their praise of the Anglo-French victory on the Marne. In the London *Times* Winston Churchill referred to "the collapse of Austria as a military factor . . . as the greatest feature yet apparent in the course of the war." In Vienna the cynics characterized the Habsburg strategy as one of letting the enemy tire himself by running farther and farther over the territory of the empire. But for most of Austria, the news from the front was no joking matter. As the reports of "strategic regroupings" revealed how close the Russian armies were to Budapest, serious voices began to speculate about a defense on the Danube. Fearful skeptics could picture the dreaded cossacks pouring into Prague and Vienna. Although the Germans won a surprising victory over the Russians at Tannenberg, the bulk of the great German armies were bogged down on the Marne, in northern France. The Schlieffen Plan had gone completely astray, and relief for the Austrians was no where in sight. Only the freezing winter of 1914–1915 finally halted the steady advances of the Russian armies. And when they halted, vast areas of the Habsburg empire were occupied by Tsarist troops.

Meanwhile, the newspapers carried no mention of the Balkan campaign, where more than one-third of the Habsburg armies were pitched against the puny forces of the little Kingdom of Serbia. Even without a positive report in the press, the wily followers of the war in Vienna had learned to read between the lines of the General Staff communiqués and to interpret for themselves the huge white spaces in the papers which indicated the careful pruning of the censors. If no Serbian territory was reported occupied, if the capture of Belgrade was not reported as imminent, it probably meant that the Habsburg armies were being defeated even by Serbia.

They were. Incredible as it seemed to the General Staff in Vienna, the first two thrusts of the Habsburg forces were repelled by the Serbians. These defeats were an even greater blow to the prestige and self-esteem of the Habsburg armies than the setbacks against Russia. On December 2, 1914, the Emperor's eighty-fourth birthday, a third thrust of the Habsburg armies reached Belgrade—a birthday present for the Emperor. Within days the thrust was reversed, and the Habsburgs were again expelled from the Kingdom of Serbia.

Thus, after three months, the war was not only far from over but the Habsburg armies were suffering devastating defeats on all fronts. Instead of the quick victories they had expected, Austrians everywhere had to look forward to months, perhaps years, of continued fighting. And victory seemed imminent nowhere. What the newspapers and the communiqués of the General Staff failed to report, the soldiers returning from the front told in detail, in terms so terrible that the home-fronters trembled. Wounded veterans of one month of the campaign told of whole armies being swallowed in the mud, of the unending flood of Russian soldiers who poured out of the trenches and over the steppes, of terrifying charges by cossacks which swept everything before them off the field of battle. The firsthand reports of casualties and disasters gave the lie to almost every report of the censored press.

In the first winter of the war propagandists sponsored by the government and by patriotic organizations did all they could to rally the support of the Austrians. Poets began to rime *Sieg* with *Krieg* and *Not* with *Tod*. Professors, statesmen, and men of letters joined in the effort to revive the fighting optimism with exhortations. "Why have Austrians been dying?" began a typical piece in the *Neue Freie Presse*. It answered: ". . . for a free and happy monarchy, for a country liberated from the fetters of the past. . . . They have died because they knew that their Fatherland could no longer exist under the goad of doubt and with hatred and disloyalty all around." The arguments, which had sounded so good in early August, were now tired and worn. The Viennese, skeptical in the best of circumstances, had given their last ounce of optimism at the outbreak of the war. "The three months are up," former optimists mumbled. "Where are the easy victories we were promised?"

It had been more than a century, since the Napoleonic campaigns, that Vienna had actually felt the consequences of a war. In the fall of 1914 breastworks laced with barbed wire were hastily erected around the city, and open areas such as the Prater were converted to parade and drill grounds for the training troops. At first the breastworks and the drilling troops were somewhat quaint curiosities, visited by nice ladies in what they called "patriotic outings." In the city normal activities were only slightly interrupted by parades of soldiers down some of the thoroughfares, usually to the accompaniement of "Hurrahs" from a flag-waving crowd.

Karl Kraus, the Viennese satirist, coined the apothegm that in Berlin conditions are serious but never hopeless, while in Vienna conditions are hopeless but never serious. If ever valid, which is questionable, his cynicism was woefully inaccurate by December 1914. The city was flooded with hundreds of thousands of refugees from the occupied areas of the empire. Hospitals filled so quickly with wounded soldiers that churches, schools, and aristocratic palaces had to be converted to handle the overflow. Some foreign correspondents wrote that Vienna resembled a vast hospital, the parks and streets filled with "outpatients." The women of the city, led by the Emperor's youngest daughter, Marie Valerie, volunteered as nurses to care for the wounded veterans. The one-time "companion" of the Emperor, Frau Katharina Schratt, responded to the call of Emperor and country by converting her elegant suburban villa to a temporary hospital and working there alongside aristocratic dowagers and other personal friends.

Performances at the Opera and several of the theaters and concert halls continued, usually with all German and Austrian programs and preceded by the German and Austrian anthems and the unavoidable appeals for relief funds. There were even some celebrated premieres, including Richard Strauss's *Die Frau ohne Schatten* in 1915 and a revised production of *Ariadne auf Naxos* in October 1916. But try as they might to preserve an aura of gaiety in the city, the Viennese soon began to feel the sheer drain of a world war. Schools were closed as the teachers were called up for service and buildings requisitioned as temporary hospitals and barracks. Prices on all sorts of commodities rose drastically, and the lack of raw materials closed many factories, producing some temporary unemployment in the city. As soon as the situation was ripe, speculators in dozens of commodities began to reap staggering profits, until more and more of the economy had to be brought under the control of the War Surveillance Office.

As early as December 1914, when the grain-producing areas of Galicia were occupied, bakers were ordered to cut the wheat content of bread to 70 percent, the balance to be barley and rye. Housewives were instructed in the press to economize on their consumption of strategic foodstuffs; by April 1915 these exhortations were enforced with ration cards for bread, later followed by cards for milk, sugar, coffee, fats, and even potatoes. As the grain shortages mounted, food scientists concocted new formulas for bread made of potato flour, cornmeal, rye, and perhaps a tiny percentage of wheat.

Horses and automobiles were commandeered for the armies at the outbreak of the war, driving many families to public transportation for the first time in their lives. Later, when fuel shortages became severe, the hours of public transportation were restricted. Street illumination was cut down to conserve fuel, and housewives were encouraged to ration the fuel they used for heating and cooking. The scarcity of wool led to clothes woven out of nettle fiber, and the shortage of leather made shoes of canvas a badge of patriotism.

The final straw, for many Viennese, came when chicory or roasted acorns and beechnuts were offered as substitutes for coffee. Then even the singular characters who were used to watching the world through the newspapers they read in their favorite cafés began to feel the realities of war. Dozens of armchair politicians, reviewing the policies of the Ballplatz and the War Ministry over cups of ersatz coffee as they smoked ersatz tobacco, began to discuss in earnest the vast gulf between the promises of August 1914 and the realities of the war.

10

Armaggedon

At the outset of the war, the "chief aim" of Austro-Hungarian policy, as Foreign Minister Burian put it in a letter to Chief of the General Staff Conrad von Hötzendorf, was "to get the greatest possible increase of power and security when things are rearranged." The original plans included grandiose schemes for the incorporation of Serbia and vast areas of Poland and Romania into the empire, much as Bosnia and Hercegovina had been incorporated before the war. But even in the first winter of war there were many in Vienna and elsewhere who realized that the war was being waged less to acquire territory than to preserve the monarchy itself. The beginnings of a split with Hungary had developed early in 1915, when Hungarian grain magnates began to take advantage of Austrian needs by carefully timing the release of their stocks to capitalize on the rapidly changing market. As the negotiations for the *Ausgleich* of 1917 grew closer, the Hungarians were discussing extraordinary demands, including a lower quota of the joint costs of war and a series of favorable tariffs. The Austrians, driven by the need of war materials, were at the mercy of the Magyars.

Meanwhile, many Czech troops were deserting rather than fight against the Russians, and in Geneva and Paris Eduard Beneš and Thomas Masaryk were laying the foundations for the Czechoslovak state they hoped to wrest from the moribund monarchy. The South Slavs, witnessing the debacle of the Austrian armies in the Balkans, were willing to reconsider the possibility of an alliance with Serbia. In Zagreb and other cities there was even clandestine talk of a Yugoslav state to be formed from Serbia and parts of the Habsburg empire.

It was with these problems, and the desperate situations on the battle fronts and the home fronts in mind, that Austrians looked forward to the spring of 1915, when the Russian bear would wake from his hibernation to go on the rampage again. And, as if the situation were not bad enough, the spring of 1915 brought the shock of the Italian declaration of war against Austria.

Before the war Italy had been allied with Germany and Austria-Hungary in the Triple Alliance, last renewed in 1912. By invoking a clause of the treaty which limited Italian obligations in case the future hostilities were between Russia and Austria-Hungary, the Italians in August 1914 had declared their neutrality in the expanding conflict. For months Italian diplomats sized up the relative situation of the Central Powers and the Entente, weighing the secret bids of territory and support that each side offered. For a while the Viennese joked about the situation (*Was ist der Dreibund? Ein Zweibund und ein Vagabund!*). Then, in April 1915, the Italians, following the classic pattern of their diplomacy, sold to the highest bidder. Accepting the promises made by the Entente powers in the secret Treaty of London, the Italians broke off relations with Austria-Hungary and Germany, and in May 1915 declared war on the Habsburg empire.

News of the Italian "treason" stunned Austria. The Emperor issued a manifesto condemning the "perfidy of which history knows not the like." In private he cried in despair: "This will be the end of us, I fancy." The war against perfidious Italy soon became the touchstone of national honor. The Italian front, the only front on which Habsburg armies had yet to be defeated, was the only hope for self-respect. The strategists began the task of preparing yet another campaign, stretching the Habsburg armies still thinner, while they awaited another season of devastation and despair.

At the time of the fall of Galicia the Austrian General Staff had made repeated requests to the Germans for extended help in the East. By the spring of 1915, with the war in France hopelessly bogged down, the Germans were able to send substantial reinforcements of infantry, artillery, and supplies. With the new troops bolstering the faltering spirits of the Habsburg veterans, on May 2, 1915, the combined Austrian and German artillery opened an enormous barrage between Gorlice and Tarnow, beginning a campaign which in four months would see the Russians swept out of all the occupied territory in Galicia, Bukowina, and Russian Poland. German troops also fought alongside the red-trousered Habsburg troops in the Balkans, leading in the fall of 1915 to staggering victories over Serbia and Montenegro. These victories, accomplished with the help of the well-trained and well-equipped German troops, seemed to avenge the appalling defeats of the previous year. Indeed, as the war entered its second year, Hapsburg troops had regained almost all the territories lost to the Russians and had occupied all of Serbia and Montenegro and most of Albania. The dreams of the war policy seemed within hand, and much of the Russian army was so devastated by the rapid advances of the Germans and the Austrians that it was widely believed that the Russians could never mount another offensive.

In Vienna the propagandists went to work to rally the pessimistic public. For some, the news from the front brought cheer and hope. But for many others, more than a year of censored reports in the newspapers and the communiqués of the General Staff had hardened indifference and incredulousness. Families were still hungry, the streets were still dark, homes were still without fuel. For those who had expected a war of three months' at the most, the victories were too late.

Moreover, on the Italian front, the field of honor, the war quickly settled into a standstill. The snow-covered Alpine passes, as one soldier wrote, were "more the setting for an opera than a battlefield." Heroic thrusts and counterthrusts by Austrian and Italian troops failed to secure decisive victories for either side.

As the war ground through its second year, the fronts everywhere began to stabilize into a long, gruesome war of muddy trenches, useless infantry charges, and dreaded artillery bombardments. After the initial successes against Russia and in the Balkans, the advance of the Central Powers had stumbled to a halt in the East as in the West, and through the winter of 1915–1916 the troops of both sides held their positions in a protracted war of attrition. Things did not change until the summer of 1916, when in response to a plea from the Italians the Russians launched a tremendous attack along the entire Austrian front. Known by the name of its commander, the Brusilov Offensive was not halted until October 1916. In what temporarily looked like a repeat of the opening weeks of the war, Russian troops poured across the plains and up to the Carpathian passes. Once again German help was able to stem the tide, but this time the Germans demanded over Austrian objections that a joint command be established in the East. On September 6, 1916, Kaiser Wilhelm II was named Generalissimo of the Eastern front.

The Brusilov Offensive, the last heroic attempt by the Tsarist forces, marked the end of offensive operations by the Russians. But the Romanians, who had hovered in neutrality since the beginning of the war, were induced by the Brusilov Offensive to join the Entente, bringing six hundred thousand fresh troops into the war against Austria. The untrained and inexperienced Romanians were no match for the Germans or even the Austrians, and with the collapse of the Brusilov Offensive in late September 1916, the Central Powers began to roll hard against the Romanians, driving close to the important oil fields of Ploesti and the enormous grain-producing Romanian plains that could replenish much-needed supplies. By the middle of October, the defeat of Romania seemed imminent.

Indeed, by October 1916, as the war entered its third year, Austrian victories seemed to be piling up on every front. The Russians were apparently defeated, the Balkan belligerents were out of the war and occupied, Romania was close to falling. Only Italy remained, and it was widely assumed that with the stabilization of the broad Eastern front, additional Austrian and German troops could be brought down into the Italian campaign to bring the long-awaited decision there.

On paper, the situation in October 1916 looked impressive. In fact, it was desperate. Although Vienna, Prague, Budapest, and most of the other cities of the empire had not witnessed fighting, they lived as though under siege. Foodstuffs were becoming more and more scarce, rationing more strict, and starvation so widespread that food riots broke out in many cities in 1916. Fuel was now so scarce that regulations permitted the heating of only one room in any dwelling. In the severe winter the new regulation led to hundreds of frozen water pipes and long queues in front of communal water pumps for housewives who no longer had running water in their homes. Fuel shortages and the commandering of horses and motorcars reached such proportions that public transportation was limited to a few hours each day and in many cases stopped completely. Picturesque teams of two to four dogs pulling low carts provided almost the only transport. Women had to walk to the butcher shops and the bakeries, where they waited in interminable queues for a few grams of indescribable meat or a loaf of the soggy indigestible black concoction which passed for bread.

Many of the windows that had gaily displayed black-and-yellow flags and bunting at the beginning of the war now showed only black, as the casualty counts for Austria reached figures that would have once been unimaginable. By the fall of 1916 more than 7.5 million men had been called up for service in the armies, over five times the original mobilization and equal to 15 percent of the entire population of the empire. Army standards had been lowered so drastically that mere boys and old men were being called up, given the briefest possible training, handed a rifle, and sent into combat. More than 1.5 million men had been reported captured by the enemy, and almost as many had been killed or wounded.

Newspaper vendors still shouted the headlines in the empty streets—VICTORY IN RUSSIA! SUCCESSES IN ITALY! MAJOR ADVANCES AGAINST ROMANIA!—but few in Vienna believed or even cared about the newspapers anymore. As the lists of captured, dead, and missing were posted in Vienna and other cities, as the thousands of wounded soldiers were hauled through the streets on jerry-built ambulances to the makeshift hospitals, Austrians from the breadlines to the Ballplatz began to realize the truth about the war: It was hopeless. Without the support of the German armies, the Habsburg forces had been helpless. They had been overrun by the Russians and held to a standoff by the tiny Serbian army. Their complete inability to defeat even the Italians spelled the end of Austria-Hungary as a great power.

It was only with the aid of large numbers of German troops and supplies that Habsburg armies had won the tremendous campaigns of 1915 and 1916. And when books and newspaper articles began to discuss plans for a postwar *Mitteleuropa*, including economic and cultural integration of Austria with the German empire, even the optimists of 1914 could see the price of the Pyrrhic victories of 1915 and 1916. The German armies had protected the empire from annihilation at the hands of the Russians, the Serbs, and the Italians. But the price of protection was high, for in the process the Habsburg empire had become an unwitting partner to the German bid for the mastery of Europe.

Victory was now impossible, for no matter what happened in the war, the empire was doomed. If the Entente managed to defeat the seemingly invincible German armies, England and France would help Masaryk and Beneš and every other visionary schemer dismember the empire into small nation-states. If the Central Powers won, they would emerge as a single great Central Power. The Habsburg alternative to German rule would be doomed, and the citizens of Austria and Bohemia would either become second-class subjects, forever beholden to their German saviors, or would find themselves outcast subject peoples, denied even the few rights they enjoyed under the many compromises that had made up the policies of Austria-Hungary.

The only hope was peace. After the first disastrous year of war, peace with a remnant of honor might have been possible. Now even a disgraceful peace, quietly suggested by some, was impossible. With the acceptance of German aid, the Emperor and his advisers had lost the initiative in formulating any kind of policy. The once proud Habsburg army had been forced to accept the supreme command of a German Generalissimo, the diplomats in the Ballplatz now danced to a tune called on the Wilhelmstrasse in Berlin. Even the proud old Emperor may have realized that he enjoyed the continued occupation of his throne only because Wilhelm II had a tiny streak of sentimentality and respect.

Powerless to act, the men who tried to guide the Habsburg empire were desperate. In the fall of 1916 a caller asked Count Stürgkh whether advocacy of peace was a mark of madness.

"Mad?" said Stürgkh. "Every hour of the day and far into the night men come through that door and say to me, 'We want more men for the trenches—we want more guns—more ammunition—more money.' Mad indeed? You are the only sensible person that has passed through that door in a long time."

Sensible and possible were never synonymous in Austria-Hungary, and peace, though sensible, was not possible. As a nobleman and a loyal servant of his Emperor, Count Stürgkh knew the empire had no choice but to fight on. Stürgkh and his bureaucrats, the Emperor and his General Staff, Premier Count Tisza of Hungary and his gentry officials—these few men took upon themselves the awesome responsibility of directing the destinies and lives of the fifty million people of the empire. Fortunately, although the war had strained Austrian society precariously, widespread faith in the Emperor and his government had kept the strains from breaking into civil war. Again and again Austrians whispered reassurances to themselves. Again and again the Emperor spoke to his subjects, the father encouraging his unruly but brave children.

The few weak souls who did crack under the strain were quickly silenced and controlled by the courts and the censors. The courts, for all practical purposes, had become instruments of the High Command for use against dissidents. Many would-be critics of the war, of the Stürgkh System, or of Habsburg policies, were interned, imprisoned, or sometimes, after farcical trials, executed. The censors, too, did their share toward crushing any dissent which might undermine the war effort. With parliament prorogued, the newspapers were the only possible outlet for criticism, and although they were generally faithful to government policy, periodically it became necessary for the censors of the War Surveillance Office to remind them of their responsibilities to the Emperor and the nation. Opposition papers were supplied by the government with patriotic articles and with hints at the wisdom of printing the articles—and they printed them.

Even in peacetime an enormous proportion of the work

force of Austria had been servants of the state, either in the vast civil service or the army. In wartime still vaster numbers of men were called up for the armed forces or otherwise impressed into sometimes unwilling service of the state. With the activation of the War Service Act, railways and many private industries were put under state control for the duration of the war. Workers in these industries effectively became civil servants, and as such were subject to government pressure to maintain high production and to put up with the strict discipline that war demanded. Moreover, these vast numbers of workers were placed by the War Services Act under the jurisdiction of the harsh military courts, even for civil offenses.

In spite of the obvious efficiency of the Stürgkh government, which had somehow managed to keep the state functioning through more than two years of war, from 1915 on there were persistent clamors in Austria for a revival of the parliament. The Viennese press, public personalities who were not intimately identified with the ministry, and a vast collection of political groups of almost every persuasion demanded a return to constitutional government and an end to absolutism. The *Neue Freie Presse* devoted a series of editorial leaders to the theme, arguing that for the political health of the country many urgent problems—food supply, civil liberty, foreign policy, postwar reconstruction—required full and frank discussion in the legislative forum. In the fall of 1916 the militancy of the articles led the censors to delete several paragraphs, leaving enormous white spaces on the pages. Parliamentary leaders of every party, from the Social Democrats to conservative Right-wingers in the House of Lords, joined in urging the immediate reconvocation of parliament. The Mayor of Vienna reported that the City Council, following the demands of public opinion from all sides, had resolved itself in favor of the convocation of parliament. The censor struck out part of the Mayor's amplifying remarks.

FRITZ

To many it seemed absurd to deny the Austrian Parliament the right to meet when legislative bodies were convening regularly in Hungary, in the allied lands of Germany, Bulgaria, and Turkey, and even in Russia. But Count Stürgkh, remembering the parliamentary sessions of the prewar period better than most, remained adamant in his cavalier disregard of his critics. "Absolutism for the duration" had proved its utility in the first months of the war, and for better or for worse Count Stürgkh was determined to carry on to the end. Arguing that the tenuous situation of the empire could not permit the irredentist explosions which the convocation of parliament would invite, he reminded his critics that Austria was threatened by enemies on three fronts; the last thing the empire needed was a fourth front within. With the rumors of the activities of Masaryk and the other seditious schemers drifting willy-nilly through the empire, and the negotiations for the new *Ausgleich* at a very critical stage, a renewed clamor by the nationalities in the parliament could be the last straw for the beleaguered empire. War taxed the empire enough, without the filibusters, flying inkpots, cavalry bugles, and the rest. Supported by the High Command and by his close inner circle of advisers, and upheld in his stand by the rapidly aging Emperor, whom he diligently tried to protect from the exhausting necessity of occupying himself with the problems of innovation, Count Stürgkh publicly lumped those who cried for parliament with those who cried for peace, as defeatists.

One day, as he walked past the House of Parliament with Jean Gignoux, the Secretary of the Swiss Legation in Vienna, Count Stürgkh gestured at the building. "The greatest work of my period of office has been to transform this building into a hospital," he said. "My work will not be complete until I have converted it permanently into an asylum for incurables."

In the isolation of high office it was an easy statement to make. From his office in the Hofburg, or from the dining room of the Hotel Meissl & Schadn where he lunched on beefsteak, Count Stürgkh could not see the breadlines in the streets or the women who trudged home through darkened streets to their unheated houses, where hungry children and black flags in the windows told the truth about the war.

11

The Imperial and Royal
Social Democrats

Despondent and a little ashamed, but hopeful for the future, Fritz left Brussels for Vienna on the evening of July 29, 1914. Before his train left he wired Friedrich Austerlitz, the managing editor of the *Arbeiter-Zeitung,* that the International congress planned for August 23 in Vienna had been rescheduled to August 9 in Paris.

At the station in Vienna Fritz picked up a copy of the *Arbeiter-Zeitung* to find that not one word of his report from Brussels had been printed. His first thought was that government censors had intercepted his telegram; later a party comrade told him that Austerlitz had received the telegram and had decided not to print it.

Fritz was outraged. Writing out the report exactly as he had telegraphed it from Brussels, he confronted Austerlitz with the text that evening at the editorial offices of the *Arbeiter-Zeitung.* Austerlitz argued that he was sure the International would not want the newspaper endangered by printing what the government might consider inflammatory material, especially at the outbreak of the war. They fought late into the night, until Fritz, failing apparently to convince Austerlitz that the shift of the congress was a matter of overwhelming importance for the party and for the working class of the empire, stormed out of the office. Although Austerlitz finally recanted and printed the report the next morning, Fritz did not speak to him for over a year after the incident.

More decisive for Fritz than the break in his association with Austerlitz, whom he had known since the founding of *Gleichheit,* was the indication of just how "cowardly" the members of the party could be—how afraid they were of the government censors and the police. Already in the July 28 issue of the *Arbeiter-Zeitung,* the editors had wafted a sentimental "first kiss" to the workers called to the colors, cautioning those comrades who were on the home front that war would fashion a new Austria and that the most important duty of the party was to maintain its organization for the postwar period. More and more workers were pouring into the streets to take part in chauvinistic celebrations in support of the war, and the *Arbeiter-Zeitung,* instead of condemning the cries of "Down with Serbia!" or "Hurrah for the Emperor!" came close to echoing them.

The news from other capitals was as depressing as the situation in Vienna. Reports from Brussels, Berlin, and Paris told the same story of crowds in the streets, of workers demonstrating —not against the war, but in support of the war. On July 31, just after he had met with government officials to urge restraint on their part, Jean Jaurès was gunned down by a hysterical self-proclaimed "patriot" as he dined in a favorite café. His death robbed the International of its most eloquent antiwar spokesman at the moment when he was most needed.

After the run-in with Austerlitz, Fritz wired his father,

who had gone from the exhaustion of the meeting in Brussels to rest again in Bad Neuheim. Despite their differences in Brussels, which they had not discussed, Fritz was convinced that his father could somehow bring Austerlitz and the rest of the staff of the *Arbeiter-Zeitung* back to reason and restore the momentum of an antiwar campaign.

But when Victor arrived in Vienna on August 2, he was too busy to talk about the *Arbeiter-Zeitung*. He set himself the task of arranging transportation and visas for the foreign socialists who were caught by the war in Vienna. Leon Trotsky, who had been in exile from Russia since the Revolution of 1905, came to the headquarters of the Austrian Social Democratic party on August 3 for advice. Victor drove him directly to the police prefecture, where he hoped to use his influence to get Trotsky an exit visa. On the way there, Trotsky pointed out the festive mood of the streets.

"It is those who do not have to go to war who show their joy," Victor said. "Besides, all the unbalanced, all the madmen now come out into the streets; it is their day. The murder of Jaurès is only the beginning. War opens the door for all instincts, all forms of madness."

The prefect encouraged, indeed insisted, that Trotsky leave for Switzerland that night.

Lenin, also in exile, was on vacation in the Austrian Carpathians. Torn between the double threat of the advancing Russian armies and the building harassment of the Austrian authorities, he wired Victor Adler for help. Victor went to the Minister of the Interior, pleading that Lenin was neither an ordinary Russian citizen nor a spy, but rather "a determined opponent of Russian Tsarism who has devoted his life to the struggle against the Russian government." The Minister asked if Lenin was still an opponent of the Russian government.

". . . He is its enemy and he will be its enemy when Your Excellency may again have become its friend," Victor answered.

Lenin was also granted permission to leave Austria.

While Victor worked on behalf of the exiles, Fritz, through sheer inertia, continued to busy himself with books, papers, and stamps for the International congress still scheduled for August 9 in Paris. Now that the declaration of war against Serbia had awakened the Austrians and the International, he reasoned, there was still time to forestall a world war. The agenda for the forthcoming congress had been narrowed to a single item—War and the Proletariat. Fritz hoped that another massive demonstration of solidarity against the war, like that in Basel less than two years before, would be enough to urge or force the European powers into peaceful negotiations. After all, four times since 1907 (at Zurich, Copenhagen, Basel, and Brussels) the International had ratified the Zurich Resolution. Was it possible now, when the "threat of an outbreak of war" was felt in every European capital, that the working classes and their parliamentary representatives would not fulfill their duties?

A whole age was to elapse between August 1 and August 9. From the end of the extraordinary meeting in Brussels until well after the declarations of war, the Executive Committees of the different socialist parties met in interminable sessions to decide what their official positions would be toward the war. Everywhere the socialists were quick to disclaim any responsibility for the war and to accuse the imperialist governments of pitching humanity into the maelstrom. *Vorwärts,* the influential Berlin daily of the German Social Democrats, wrote on July 25, after the Austrian ultimatum:

> No drop of German soldier's blood must be sacrificed to the Austrian despots' lust for power, to the imperialist commercial interests. Comrades, we call upon you to express immediately in mass meetings the unshakable will for peace of the class-conscious proletariat. . . . The ruling classes, who in peacetime oppress you, exploit you, want to use you as can-

non fodder. Everywhere the cry must ring in the despots' ears: "We want no war! Down with war! Long live international brotherhood!"

The rhetoric was fine. But what would the socialists do to fight against the war? Would the workers take to the streets and refuse to fight? Would the parties be willing to lead a general strike or to go underground if their respective governments moved against them? And could the socialists refuse their patriotic duty against aggressors? A vote against the war in Germany or Austria could mean defeat by the forces of Tsarism. Could the socialists invite the invasion of their own lands or even its defeat by a more reactionary nation?

The most agonizing deliberations came in Germany, where the Reichstag was scheduled to vote on the question of the war credits—the financing of the war—on August 4. The caucus sessions of the Social Democrats were continuous and acrimonious (one delegate repeatedly burst into tears) until moments before the historic vote. Then, after days of soul-searching statements and counter-statements, desperate improvisations and resignations, Hugo Haase, the Chairman of the delegation, read their final statement. He began by disclaiming all responsibility for the war, proclaiming that the Social Democrats had worked with all their strength for peace. But, he continued:

> . . . its efforts have been in vain. For our people and its peaceful development, much, if not everything, is at stake in the event of the victory of Russian despotism which has stained itself with the blood of the best of its own people. Our task is to ward off this danger, to safeguard the culture and the independence of our own country . . .

All 110 Social Democratic votes were cast in favor of the war credits. (In the final vote of the delegation in caucus there had been 14 dissenting votes but out of a sense of that "democratic discipline" which had long been the pride of the party, the 14 agreed to make the vote unanimous.) One member of the party walked unnoticed out of the hall while the vote was being taken, but as far as the party, Germany, and the world knew, the German Social Democratic party had voted for the war credits.

The French socialists, after attending the funeral of Jean Jaurès in the morning, also voted for war credits on the afternoon of August 4 (in order to defend their country from the dreaded and backward *Boche,* they argued). Somehow their vote was less of a shock. For while all the Great Powers had been gearing for a war, it was Austria and Germany which had chosen the time and the way to precipitate the debacle. And the German Social Democratic party was the party of Marx and Engels, the model and inspiration of the parties in the International. They were the party that had always been apart from the state, the party that had said "Not a man and not a penny to this system," the party that had always refused to participate in the traditional cheer of "Hurrah for the Kaiser" at Reichstag sessions, the party whose consistent opposition had earned the infamous sobriquet of "Fellows without a country" from the Kaiser as the German state all but disowned them. With 110 Reichstag deputies, more than a million members, 2.5 million trade-union followers, and a strength at the polls so great that one soldier out of three who answered the call to arms in Germany was a Social Democratic voter—this was the party on which all hopes rested and toward which all eyes were turned. Their vote for the war credits meant the certain cancellation of the International congress and the almost certain end of the Second International.

Within weeks the *Burgfrieden* in Germany and the *Union sacrée* in France ended all effective opposition to the war by the largest socialist parties of the Second International.

Because the Austrian parliament was prorogued, the socialists in Austria were spared the soul-searching of their German and French comrades. The war credits in Austria were an academic question, as Count Stürgkh and the General Staff had already put many of the provisions of the War Service Act into effect. Yet ties of language, culture, and politics bound the Austrian Social Democrats with the German party, and if only vicariously, many of the Austrians shared the agonies of the Germans. Moreover, the party did have to exercise its role of giving guidance to the masses in lieu of parliamentary activity. They too had to ask whether they should risk the wrath of the government by placing themselves at the head of an antiwar movement, or whether they should resign themselves to the defense of their country against the forces of barbarism from the East.

In the *Arbeiter-Zeitung,* Friedrich Austerlitz had already given tentative answers to these questions. On August 5 he announced the historic vote of the German Social Democrats in a leading article: "In the struggle for national honor, Germany is united and will remain united until the last drop of blood. . . . Never has a party handled itself greater and more nobly than the German Social Democrats," who despite the accusations of the ruling classes that they are enemies of the empire, "stand ready to defend their Fatherland," and "to lend to the state the property and the blood of the working masses."

For Austerlitz, the vote for the war credits marked "The Day of the German Nation"—as he titled his article—a day "on which was displayed the dignity, grandeur, and sublimity of the German spirit . . ." But there were many members and followers of the Austrian Social Democratic party who were not German, and who traditionally had looked to the party as the only group in Austria which seemed somehow to transcend the struggle of the nationalities in the Habsburg empire. Now Austerlitz' article plunged the multinational Austrian party into the ranks of the "hurrah" patriotism of the German bourgeois parties. In a tumultuous meeting at the party headquarters on August 5, several members of the party raised serious questions about the German nationalism of the article. To their surprise, Victor Adler defended to the word the article and the spirit of chauvinism it conveyed.

Victor's attitude toward the war was implicit in his early background, which he and the other leaders of the party had tried to forget in the years when his leadership had forged the Austrian party into the third largest socialist party in the world. Before he became active in the labor movement, Victor had been active in the German nationalist movement, including the group around Georg Schönerer which drafted the Linz Program, a political platform that later received the highest praises of Schönerer's infamous political heir, Adolf Hitler. And even as he became the spokesman of internationalism in Austria and in the International, Victor Adler remained something of a German nationalist, proud of his German *Bildung* and convinced that only the Germans could provide political and cultural leadership for Central Europe.

With the war, Victor, still the redoubtable leader of the party and perhaps of the International, revealed the depths of his German nationalism, as he urged the party to support the war against the threat of Tsarist imperialism. "Today," he said, "we are faced with the question whether the Russian armies will march into Brünn, Budapest, or Vienna. In such a situation . . . if I feel the knife at my throat, I must first of all push it away." There were more than enough statements in the writings of Marx and Engels to support Victor's viewpoint. In 1860 Marx had written:

> The only circumstances which legitimize the existence of Austria since the middle of the eighteenth century is its resistance to the advance of Russia into Eastern Europe . . . a resistance helpless, inconsequent, cowardly, but tough.

Yet Victor realized how fully the question of war credits became the whole dilemma of Social Democracy in Germany and

Austria, and indeed in the International: "I know they have to vote for them; I simply don't know how I might force it through my lips, but it has to be. . . . There is only one thing worse than war, that is defeat."

For no one was the shock of the German vote, Austerlitz' article, and Victor's defense of the vote and the article as great as for Fritz. During Victor's speech, Fritz said nothing. (After only three years with the Austrian party he was still reluctant to voice his views against the leadership, and this, after all, was his father.) But as he listened to his father's rationalizations and justifications, he realized that the remarks in Brussels had not been the lapses of a sick man. After twenty-five years of leading the Austrian Social Democratic party and the Second International, twenty-five years of continuous efforts to stave off the imperialistic wars that would cost the blood and property of the workers of the world, Victor Adler was now supporting a war that would pit the workers of Europe against one another in an unparalleled bloodbath. All the wonderful rhetoric of "War on War!" the whole struggle against war and oppression, the very idea of the International—were suddenly abandoned. His father, whom he had worshiped since childhood, the man whose exemplary strength and leadership he had tried so hard to emulate, was suddenly reneging on everything that had gone before.

That evening, feeling as though his "whole life plans and life work had been wrecked," Fritz took the train home to Brunn. As the train rolled through the low hills of the Vienna woods, through the fields where the armies of Napoleon had once stalked toward Vienna, Fritz carefully thought through his views on war and peace and the International. There was no alternative now but to resign from his duties as Secretary of the party and his editorship of various party publications. "In the great world-shaking events through which we now live," he wrote, "the first decisive defeat has struck us. *The International is destroyed,* the work of twenty-five years is in ruins. *This defeat I cannot crowd out of my*

FRITZ

conscience, rather I must keep the facts in plain view." It was difficult to accept the impotence of the International after the massive display at Basel, even though it was apparent that there was little the International could do to halt the mechanical march of the mobilizing troops. But what was worse than the powerlessness of the International was the fact that "as far as we can see, in every land, the Social Democrats have not been carried away by the war as an insuperable destiny—rather, more or less, they have made the war rhetoric of the states their own." The vote of the German Social Democrats was the last straw. That vote, and the defense of that vote by the leaders of other parties, proved that internationalism had been abandoned in the hearts of its founders.

In such an era, Fritz wrote, he could not belong to the movement any longer. He could not lend his name to articles in a newspaper like the *Arbeiter-Zeitung,* which actually filled him with shame. For him, he concluded, there was no choice but to quit the movement and to work alone, if necessary at the tiniest secret press, where he at least could say and write what he believed. Then he could at least have the hope, "that sometime, perhaps only in many, many years, the cry might ring out: The International is Dead, Long Live the International!"

Kathia had heard about the vote and seen Austerlitz' article before Fritz arrived. Without mentioning a word about either, she asked Fritz, "What else is there to do, except to shoot ourselves?"

For Fritz there was something else to do. A meeting of the entire leadership of the Austrian party was planned for the next week. Fritz polished his letter of resignation and a memorandum explaining his views, hoping that the two documents would provoke a good debate on the editorial policies of the *Arbeiter-Zeitung* and the war policies of the party leadership.

At the meeting Victor Adler again spoke in defense of the newspaper and the support of the war. One after another the other leaders of the party—Austerlitz, Seitz, Ellenbogen, Pernerstorfer

—found reasons to justify support of the war. Only one speaker, Karl Renner, his voice trembling as he spoke, urged a return to the spirit of internationalism and a condemnation of chauvinism. Finally Fritz rose to argue that because Austria had started the war it was doubly important to fight the war in Austria, and to point out that the war cause could not be explained as a struggle for democracy in Europe, because the Austrians and Germans were fighting not only the "Oriental barbarism" of the East, but the more democratic nations of the West, like Belgium and France. But Fritz and Renner were alone in favor of internationalism, and while many others in the party remained bitter because of the Austerlitz article, the majority were clearly in favor of supporting the war. After hours of debate and discussion, the meeting closed inconclusively. Fritz's resignation was not discussed at all.

After the meeting Victor and Fritz took up the matter of the resignation between themselves. For both it was a return to a battle they thought had ended four years before. Only this time the positions were reversed.

"It is better to be wrong with the working class than to be right against them," said Victor. For the workers of Austria, chauvinism and Russophobia had proved more compelling than any arguments of internationalism. The duty of the Social Democratic party was to support the workers and to prepare for the future, after the war, when the workers might make great gains. There was nothing they could do to oppose the war anyway, and if they tried a futile protest they might jeopardize the whole structure of the party.

It was the kind of argument that had made Victor the most popular leader of the masses in Vienna. Pointing out that two of the four Secretaries had been conscripted, Victor begged that Fritz not give up his post at such a critical moment.

But for Fritz, war and peace and the International were not matters for temporizing and compromise. The arguments of

Marxism on these questions were as certain as any arguments of physics. Wars between nations were imperialist wars, foisted on the workers of the world by the greed of the ruling classes and paid for in the blood of proletarian soldiers. It was the duty of the workers, led by the Social Democratic parties, to fight war with every last ounce of their strength. How, he asked, could he continue to work for a party that violated this most sacred of Marxist precepts? How could he lend his time and his name to work that for all practical purposes was actually aiding the war effort?

The argument was not settled easily. Father and son had often fought over whether or not Fritz should work in the labor movement, but never before had they argued the theory, or as Fritz would put it, the morality of the issue. As always it was Fritz's uncompromising and absolute *truth* against Victor's flexible and realistic *necessity*. But this time there was a tragic dimension to the argument, for in Fritz's eyes his father was suddenly a fallen idol, a traitor to the most sacred of causes. Father and son might still need and love one another, but the magic bond of respect which had made Victor the most important man and hero in Fritz's life was broken. Even love could not transcend the absoluteness of a moral imperative.

Fritz finally agreed to stay on temporarily in the Secretariat, but only to handle routine administrative duties.

At the end of October, when the privations of the war were already noticeable in Vienna, Fritz and Kathia had a long discussion about where Kathia and the children should stay for the duration of the war. Both thought the war would end soon, but Kathia, who had never liked life in Fritz's Vienna, took the war as the perfect excuse to return to Zurich and her mother. Fritz, realizing that he would need every minute for the struggle against the war, gave in without much struggle. Kathia moved with the children to Unter-Aegerie, near Zug. Her mother moved in with them again.

Alone now, Fritz moved to a flat in Vienna which he shared with a colleague named Bruno Frei. He took his meals with Victor and Emma. With Kathia gone, Fritz grew close to his mother for the first time. Emma, who had seemed so strange in the years of her melancholia, when she grasped at her children as Kathia did, was now the only island of neutrality in a stormy household of constant arguments. Every evening Emma would stand by helplessly as Fritz and Victor argued late into the night. Each political move Victor made, each article he wrote for the *Arbeiter-Zeitung,* each speech exhorting the workers to maintain their unity and to push toward the conclusion of the war—provoked a new round of fighting between father and son. Emma was left to pick up the pieces of her family.

At the end of November Victor wrote to Karl Kautsky:

The political conflict with Fritz is not so bad *personally.* He is and remains my most intimate friend. But I cannot bear to see him dragged under by fantasies, and I cannot help fearing that he will not be able to do all for the party that I expect of him. My hope is that in a more peaceful period he will regain his sense of reality and that the idolatry of absolutism, which he calls "principle," will somehow soften. A "family tragedy" it is not. For that I have no talent, and it is only those people for whom no situation is piquant enough and who are used to seeing everything in *personal* terms who will call this a family tragedy.

Victor, desperately ill and weak, did all he could to conceal the pain of fighting with his son over what seemed no more than words. What good did it do to argue principles when the war would go on anyway? he would ask in desperation. For Fritz, desperately alone, Victor was the only one to whom he could turn—Victor, who had in the end always understood, but who could not understand a word anymore.

FRITZ

One night, as the battle reached a crescendo, Victor said, "In spite of everything, what keeps us together is much more than what tears us apart." Father and son cried together then, as they had cried when Victor, after describing his visit to the brickworks to eight-year-old Fritz, promised that Fritz would one day serve the movement and change all of that.

12

Two Choices

At the beginning of October the entire Executive Committee of the party (about 150 men after the decimation of conscription) gathered for an eight-day conference of closed meetings to discuss the policies of the party and the editorial stance of the newspaper. The conference began with a resolution by Victor Adler in support of the war effort. Although most of the party had been won over to his views before the conference, there was still enough dissent to produce debates of a copiousness and intensity unknown in the meetings of the Austrian Social Democratic party. On the second night of the conference, Fritz made a ninety-minute speech attacking the policies of his father and the other party leaders. It was only the second time he had spoken out publicly against the leadership of the party, and the first time that he had crossed verbal swords with his father in a public meeting.

Emma, at the conference as a correspondent for the youth

supplement of the *Arbeiter-Zeitung,* reported what happened in a
letter to Karl Kautsky:

> Fritz spoke like the Lord God! . . . For me it was terribly
> sad—nine-tenths of those present were prejudiced against
> him. What was even more painful for me was that such an
> unselfish, pure man should remain so misunderstood. The
> people there are absurd—not for an instant can they forget
> whose son he is and compare—as if each could not be a differ-
> ent man, sound in his own way. . . . Willy Rothar [Wilhelm
> Ellenbogen*] got up on the podium like some wise prophet
> and treated the thirty-five-year-old man like a little boy who
> needed someone to blow his nose. Then I understood what
> he has told us for years, that for all these years he has always
> been regarded as a young newcomer. . . . [Austerlitz] an-
> swered him so boorishly, so ignorantly and so pettily, that he
> appeared a nobody to me. He put down this unselfish man as
> a stickler for principles and a "witless" crank. . . . The sad-
> dest thing is that no one understands Fritz and no one will. . . .
> It is ironic that I am slowly sliding toward Fritz's political
> views. As he stood up in the midst of those hostile agitated
> men, I went to him and wished him luck for his speech, and
> told him that I agreed with him on every point. . . . As a rule
> I am no authority for Fritz, but he was nonetheless immensely
> pleased. My hand still hurts, he squeezed it so hard. . . .

What Fritz vainly tried to argue at the meeting was exactly
what the party leadership had argued for years—that no amount
of rationalization could justify the support of a barbarous and
imperialistic war. But in the fall of 1914 his arguments fell on
deaf ears. Along with the rest of war-crazy Austria, the rank and
file of the Social Democratic party had responded to the appeal of
the Emperor and the quickening tempo of the martial music.
Crowds of workers in the streets were ready to greet any speech

---

* Code names were used in letters to dispel the suspicions of the censors.

about the International with catcalls of "Traitor!" or "Coward!" or "Defeatist!" The party leadership avoided the question of possible opposition to the war so carefully that the annual police report for 1914 noted: "The position of the Austrian Social Democratic party has remained thoroughly loyal."

Unable to explain his views even in party meetings, let alone to the masses in the streets, Fritz searched for a forum where he could argue his case. The *Arbeiter-Zeitung,* of course, was out, even if he had not felt qualms about lending his name to its columns. In the early days of October he wrote a few short articles for the *Volkstribune* and the *Sozialdemokratische Korrespondenz,* two socialist weeklies with rather limited readership. Few readers, if any, responded to his pleas of "Have we forgotten our internationalism?" His own little journal, *Das Volk,* was disallowed by the censors at the beginning of the war, for no ostensible reason. That left only one outlet, *Kampf,* the theoretical journal, of which he was still Co-Editor.

At the outbreak of the war, Fritz shared the editorship of *Kampf* with Karl Renner and Otto Bauer, both dynamic young intellectuals in the party leadership and renowned authors on the nationality problems of the Habsburg empire. Bauer was conscripted at the beginning of the war, and taken prisoner by the Russians in the early weeks of the campaign, leaving Renner and Fritz to edit the journal. The situation was in many ways ideal, since they were the only advocates of internationalism in the party leadership.

Because of difficulties with the censors and the printers, the issue scheduled for August 1914 was scrapped. In its place Fritz sent a short, printed phamphlet to the subscribers, detailing and documenting his own position and the official position of the party before the outbreak of hostilities. For December 1914 a double issue was planned, which Renner and Fritz built around an attack on the "nationalism" of the party leadership and the editorial stand of the *Arbeiter-Zeitung.*

FRITZ

The publication of the double issue of *Kampf* led to an enormous furor at the party headquarters. Victor especially up-braided Fritz and Renner for endangering the very existence of the party by printing such harsh criticisms of government policy. Fritz answered that there was nothing in the issue that had not been traditional party policy before the war, but Victor was insistent, even suggesting that a third editor be appointed for the journal, ostensibly to fill in for Otto Bauer. Victor first suggested Austerlitz (Fritz was sure he meant himself). When Fritz refused the sugges-tion, Victor offered the compromise of Wilhelm Ellenbogen.

Fritz and Renner then announced that if the party insisted on appointing a new editor, they would both resign. The ulti-matum led to a fresh round of arguments, but in the end they got their way.

Throughout the spring of 1915, while government-spon-sored propagandists tried to rally public opinion in Vienna for the imminent renewal of hostilities against Russia, Fritz struggled to gain a foothold for his views in the party. He had little chance among the rank and file. The workers were still infected with war fever and Russophobia, which the defeats of the fall had done little to soothe, and the only forum at Fritz's disposal, *Kampf,* had little audience among the workers, even in peacetime. The real audience at which Fritz aimed was not the public but the party leadership, whom he hoped somehow to recall to reality. What made his situation even more difficult was that in the early months of 1915 positions within the party began to shift. Austerlitz, who had been the strongest advocate of war and the spokesman of the extreme German nationalist stand at the outbreak of the war, began a gradual slide toward the advocation of a peace without annexations by either side, a position which Victor was also will-ing to support by Easter 1915. Neither, however, was willing to venture a public stand against the war by the Social Democrats. Meanwhile, Karl Renner, who had been one of the few advocates of internationalism at the outbreak of the war, joined the editorial

142

staff of the *Arbeiter-Zeitung* and began more and more to advocate a position that called for the exploitation of the war to realize what he called the positive goals of the socialist movement.

In time Renner began to argue for a temporary *Burgfrieden*, an armistice in the struggle between classes until the end of the war. Fritz then realized that Renner's "internationalism" was very different from his own, and in the April 1915 issue of *Kampf* Fritz published a strong attack on Renner's idea that the "international of fact" (his euphemism for the Habsburg empire) had replaced the international of ideology.

The break with Renner left Fritz almost completely alone in the party. A few members agreed with his views, but no one of the stature of Renner, who was a recognized authority on the nationality problem and had been a member of parliament since 1907. When he broke with Renner, Fritz also jeopardized the only forum where he could express his views, for while they were Co-Editors, Renner was the senior figure of the two, and with the backing of the party he could easily triumph in a showdown.

Over Easter 1915 Fritz visited Kathia and the children in Switzerland. On the way back to Vienna he stopped for a few days in Zurich to talk with old friends at *Volksrecht* and at the Swiss party headquarters. He attended several formal meetings in the few days, and even got into a debate with an anarchist, which he handily won. The idea then occurred to him to stay in Switzerland. The editor of the newspaper had recently been fired (for advocating German nationalism), and when the Swiss party leaders sensed that Fritz might be interested, they offered him his old job as Editor-in-Chief. The details were quickly worked out, and Fritz asked only that he be allowed to return to Vienna to discuss the plan with friends and colleagues there, and to submit his resignation from his party and editorial posts in the Austrian party.

In Vienna Fritz found that while no one was willing to

listen to his views on the war yet, the party leaders were anxious that he not quit his position. Not only Victor, but Seitz, Renner, and even Austerlitz urged that Fritz remain in Vienna. They were willing to go so far as to guarantee that he could continue to have complete freedom of expression in *Kampf*. Only Victor Adler's childhood friend, Engelbert Pernerstorfer, who had never outgrown the German nationalist movement and who was now calling for National Socialism (an ominous portent of the future), argued that in the newly oriented socialism there was no room for anyone with Fritz's views.

Ultimately it was not the urging of the party leaders but the pleas of Fritz's few remaining sympathizers that convinced him to stay on in Vienna. Like him, they were convinced that the war would end soon, perhaps within three months, and that the imminence of peace made it imperative for the opposition wing of the party to be well-represented in meetings. Also, Hugo Haase, who had become the leader of the Left in the German Social Democratic party, was in Vienna for a meeting of German and Austrian socialist leaders. He privately urged Fritz to stay on in Vienna and to fight on for an internationalist antiwar stance in the party. Fritz finally decided to stay. He organized his supporters into the Karl Marx Association, which attempted, generally unsuccessfully, to hold lectures and antiwar discussions.

In May 1915 another all-party conference was scheduled in Vienna, giving Fritz a further opportunity to state his positions to the entire party leadership. After what had happened the month before, Fritz was sure that his views would at least be heard out as a legitimate opposition to the majority position.

In the debates at the conference, two resolutions were introduced: the majority platform which supported the war of "defense" against Russia, Serbia, France, and England, and the temporary *Burgfrieden;* and Fritz's resolution calling for an immediate end to the war and a return to the revolutionary struggle for the liberation of the working class. Again father and son alternately took the podium in a public spectacle of the family fights. When the final vote was taken, there were eleven votes for Fritz's resolution. There were more than a hundred votes in support of the majority resolution.

Although it pointed the way to a long uphill struggle, the vote was a minor victory for Fritz. But the trip to Switzerland and the debates had been so exhausting that he suffered a relapse of his myocarditis. To recuperate he went for five weeks to the spa at Edlach, accompanied by his father. They were both there during the decisive weeks of the Italian declaration of war against Austria and the reopening of the Austro-German offensives against Russia and Serbia.

At Edlach Victor and Fritz spent their days strolling back and forth through the garden promenades, engaged in endless political discussions. From a distance the two of them looked like brothers. They dressed alike, in sloppy coats, their pockets bulging with books, papers, pencils, and in Fritz's case even an inkwell he carried for emergencies; both had the great manes of hair which the Germans call a *Lowenkopf* or lions' head; both walked with their shoulders hunched and their hands clasped behind their backs, as if together they bore the woes of the world.

To another guest at the Spa, Sophie Lazarsfeld, the wife of a Viennese lawyer, they resembled two brothers she knew from a market. When Sophie mentioned the resemblance to her husband, Dr. Robert Lazersfeld, he immediately identified Victor Adler, whom he had long admired. A few days later Sophie met Fritz in the library, beginning a friendship which Fritz was one day to recall as a "wonderful miracle . . . like a fairy tale."

Sophie, who knew nothing of politics, was a breath of fresh air in that stultifying summer of political frustration. She and Fritz were almost the same age, and they soon found there was much they could share. They began to discuss books and music, to walk in the gardens, to listen to *lieder* or chamber music. Sophie reminded Fritz that there was more in life than the political strug-

FRITZ

gle, that he had once loved books and opera and songs, especially Richard Strauss:

> *Und morgen wird die Sonne wieder scheinen*
> *Und auf dem Wege, den ich gehen werde,*
> *Wird uns die Glücklichen sie wieder einen*
> *Inmitten diesen sonnenatmended Erde . . .* *

It did not take long for the relationship to become what Victor called a "pleasant summer acquaintance." And in time Victor came to the Lazarsfelds to thank them for rescuing his son (jokingly he called him *Steinesel*, "stubborn mule") from the sump of overwork.

When he had regained his strength enough to return to Vienna, Fritz took up his old administrative work in the party Secretariat. He also returned to his typewriter to begin anew the struggle to recall the party to reason. All summer long he wrote articles in *Kampf* and in the *Volkstribune* to clarify and defend his position. Backing up his arguments with carefully selected quotes from Marx, Engels, Bebel, and from the prewar writings of Otto Bauer and other Austrian socialists, Fritz answered the arguments and justifications of the party point for point.

The party had argued that it supported the war because it was a war of defense. Fritz asked whether the German invasion of neutral Belgium or the Austro-German plans for the future partition of Poland were defensive acts. The party said that the war was necessary to protect Germany and Austria from Tsarist barbarism. Fritz asked whether the "defensive" war of England and France and Belgium—to protect themselves from Prussian militarism—was not also justified. The party argued that it was the

---

* Tomorrow's sun will rise in glory beaming
  And in the pathway that my foot shall wander,
  We'll meet, forget the earth, and lost in dreaming,
  Let heaven unite a love that earth no more shall sunder . . .

146

duty of politically advanced countries like Germany and Austria to defend themselves from reactionary nations like Russia. Fritz asked whether any nation could be more reactionary than Austria, where the parliament was prorogued and the entire country run under a strict military dictatorship. The party said that certain annexations by Austria and Germany could be justified to protect the Central European economic federation and to permit the advance of capitalism which would finally lead to socialism. Fritz asked whether the French demands for Alsace-Lorraine could not be justified by the same argument. The party said the war was a struggle for national emancipation. Fritz asked what had become of the struggle for the international emancipation of the workers of the world. And when the nationalists in the party shouted *Deutschland, Deutschland, über Alles,* Fritz asked what had happened to the old cry of *Sozialismus, Sozialismus, über Alles, über Alles in der Welt.*

By the end of the summer his articles had become so direct and venomous that several fell under the heavy hand of the censor, who had taken to protecting the Imperial and Royal Social Democrats in their loyal defense of Austria-Hungary. Although Fritz never abandoned the theoretical tone of his articles, more and more he began to single out particular figures as the real advocates of the treasonous position of the party. Pernerstorfer, the "social patriot," received a special attack in one article. On the whole, Fritz concentrated his efforts on Renner, who had all but taken over the editorship of the *Arbeiter-Zeitung,* and had became the chief advocate of support of the war. For Fritz, the treason of Renner, who had opportunistically shifted positions, was equal even to his father's treason. And it was easier to attack a surrogate father than to strike where it hurt most.

Fritz saw Sophie often in Vienna. His roommate had married and moved, and her husband had been called to the front, leaving both of them alone. They went to concerts or the theater together, or just walked and talked, anything to fill that vast vacuum left by Fritz's alienation from party and family. In time Fritz grew close to Sophie's children, fourteen-year-old Paul and his younger sister, Elizabeth. He would play games with them, discuss their schoolwork, take them to concerts or theater— always with a gentleness that told of his hunger for family. Yet even after months of seeing the Lazarsfeld family, Fritz kept a very proper distance from them. Sophie he always called *Frau Doktor,** and with the children he used the somewhat stilted *Sie* instead of the informal *du*.

Sometimes, when the situation was unbearable, Fritz would explain his political woes to Sophie.

"Why do you tell me these things?" she would ask. "You know I am ignorant of these things."

"I tell you because you do not understand," he would say. "It clears my mind."

Sophie, who could not understand, was the only one who even listened to Fritz's arguments anymore. Month after month, through the summer and fall of 1915 and the winter of 1916, Fritz continued his unavailing campaign to gain converts among the party leadership and followers among the rank and file of the party. And month after month his bitterness built, as his articles were disregarded, his careful positions ignored, his attempts to influence party policy rebuffed. Because of the efficiency of censorhip in Austria and the isolation of the Austrian party from every other socialist party except that of Germany, Fritz scarcely realized that elsewhere in the world there were other socialists who had also never abandoned their belief in international socialism.

In September 1914 the Italian and Swiss parties had tried

---

* A form of address which designates the wife of someone with a doctor's degree.

to organize an extraordinary conference in Lugano to carry on the work of the International. In the spring of 1915 the youth and women's sections of the International followed up the Italo-Swiss initiative with a meeting at Bern. Led by women like Clara Zetkin and Angelica Balabanova, the conference drafted an appeal to the working women of the world:

> Where are your husbands, your brothers, your sons? Why must they destroy one another and all that they have created? Who benefits by this bloody nightmare? Only a minority of war profiteers. . . . Since the men cannot speak, you must. Working women of the warring countries, unite!

Soon a small group of dedicated men responded to the appeal of the women. In early September 1915 a conference assembled in the tiny alpine village of Zimmerwald, near Bern, to take up the long-unfinished business of the Second International. The Zimmerwald meeting, held in strict secrecy, brought together internationally minded socialists from Germany, France, Italy, Russia, Poland, Hungary, Holland, Switzerland, Sweden, Norway, Romania, and Bulgaria (the English delegates could not get passports at the last minute). It was not a very impressive gathering. As Trotsky recalled, "Half a century after the founding of the First International it was still possible to seat all the internationalists in four coaches." Few of the great leaders of the Second International were there. The Bureau of the Second International, which had been moved to The Hague after Belgium was overrun by the German armies, bitterly opposed the Zimmerwald gathering as a potential cleft in the socialist movement. The majority parties in Germany and France did all they could to sabotage the meeting.

Despite the opposition, the Zimmerwald conference brought together the whole spectrum of antiwar opinion, from moderates like Karl Kautsky to the far Left, led by Lenin, who wanted to declare open civil war with the majority, and use the world war as a pretext for a world revolution. After much debate, in the true spirit of the International a compromise resolution was passed which, in rhetoric at least, satisfied everyone:

> The warmakers lie when they assert that the war will liberate oppressed nations and serve democracy. In reality they are burying the liberty of their own nations as well as the independence of other peoples. . . . To you, men and women of labor, to all those who suffer by and for the war, we say: "Above the frontiers, above the battlefields and devastated countries, Proletarians of the World, unite!"

So effective was the censorship of the War Surveillance Office in Austria that Fritz, who would have readily represented Austria at the Zimmerwald conference, did not even know about the meeting. Indeed, Austria was the only one of the belligerents to be totally unrepresented at the meeting. It was not until a month after the conference, when he went to Switzerland to visit his family, that Fritz heard about the Zimmerwald meeting from friends in Zurich.

In December Fritz answered the Zimmerwald group in a manifesto of his own entitled "The Internationals in Austria to the Internationals of All Lands." Reiterating all his previous arguments against the war, and against the policy of the socialist parties which supported the war, Fritz called out, in the name of the suffering and hunger and death that the masses were enduring on account of the war, for "the declaration of war by the international proletariat against all the powers which made the war."

The manifesto could not be printed in Austria, but after it was smuggled to Switzerland it appeared on December 3, 1915, in *Volksrecht* in Zurich, *Tagwacht* in Bern, *Avanti* in Milan, and Trotsky's exile paper, *Nasche Slovo* in Paris. Fritz's detailed indictment of the horrors of the situation in Austria created something of a sensation in foreign socialist circles. When someone tried to smuggle a copy of *Volksrecht* with the manifesto into Austria, the military authorities issued a special censorship order forbidding all criticism of the "patriotic" stand of the Austrian Social Democratic party.

In late December 1915 another of Fritz's inflammatory articles caused a renewed blowup at party headquarters. Fritz said that the government censors were bad enough, and that he really did not welcome party censors as well. But the party's leaders were annoyed by the publicity that Fritz's manifesto had attracted, and Victor in particular demanded that Fritz act responsibly toward the party. Fritz answered with another offer of his resignation, and the ultimatum that if he could not have absolute editorial freedom with *Kampf*, he would refuse to cooperate with the party in any way.

The bluff worked. Renner quit his co-editorship of the journal, and Fritz, freed from the constraints of checking things with Renner, turned *Kampf* into an even more critical opposition journal, with articles attacking Renner's politics and ideas, the policies of the nearly defunct Bureau of the Socialist International in The Hague, and indirectly, at least, every "treasonous" act of the Austrian party. Still, in order to pass the Austrian censors, the articles had to be couched in the most abstruse theoretical language, and since the audience of *Kampf* was steadily declining, Fritz picked up little or no support for his views.

Indeed, the virulence of his attacks on the party leadership increased his isolation within the party to the point where many were calling for "measures to silence the Left," meaning Fritz. In speeches and in the party press, his views were repeatedly attacked as "divisive" and "heretical."

In mid-February Fritz had heard from a Romanian socialist leader named Rakowsky, who was on his way home from Switzerland, that a sequel to the Zimmerwald conference was being planned for April in the remote Swiss hamlet of Kienthal. Ostensibly traveling to visit his family for Easter, Fritz set out for Switzerland in late March. At Salzburg he was stopped and detained indefinitely because of preparations that were being made for an offensive in Italy. Fritz debated wiring his father and asking him to use his influence at the War Ministry to get the required special visa, but before he sent the telegram he realized that if the authorities found out about the Kienthal conference, his father would be compromised with the government. Reluctantly Fritz returned to Vienna.

Not until months later did Fritz find out what happened at Kienthal. A minor Austrian party functionary named Koritschoner had "represented" Austria without the knowledge of the Austrian Social Democratic party. He was so unknown to the group at Kienthal and so undistinguished in party circles that it was as though Austria were unrepresented in the work that advanced the preliminaries of the Zimmerwald conference. Only months later, when Fritz was finally able to visit his family in late July, did the leaders of the Zimmerwald Commission find out that there was indeed at least one voice against the war in Austria.

In April 1916 the second all-party conference of the Austrian Social Democracy took up the question of opposition within the party. Fritz made a resolution calling for support of the Zimmerwald program of opposition to the war. At the end of two and a half days of debate, Victor Adler summarized the majority resolution, which supported the party's war policy and condemned all dissenting opposition within the party. "We vote for the Social Democracy," explained Victor. "For a strong and unified Social Democracy." Fritz's resolution received sixteen votes to the more than one hundred fifty for the majority position.

Afterward the reports of the conference made no mention of Fritz's resolution or of the discussions of the opposition within the party. The report instead stressed the unanimity of the party in support of the policies of the leadership. Fritz then wrote up the text of the resolution he had introduced and the record of the votes, and sent it off to the *Arbeiter-Zeitung*. It was not printed.

The final blow for Fritz came in July 1916, when the Executive Committee of the party met to decide what to do about the Hammerbrot bread factory which the party owned. Fritz argued that it should be sold. In peacetime it lost money, and in wartime, when it was being run by the War Surveillance Office, it was costing the party even more. Ownership of a factory run by a military dictatorship, Fritz argued, made the party a direct accomplice of the government. The rest of the leadership opposed any decisive move, which they argued might provoke the government into taking some measures against the party. When Fritz introduced a motion in favor of selling the factory, it got only four votes. Many delegates who had been wavering during the debate voted with the party leadership rather than risk identification with the "renegade" opposition of Friedrich Adler.

That night, July 8, 1916, Fritz told his father in private that he could not continue to work within the party. He said he no longer felt morally bound to it in any way, and that while he had previously refrained from following through with his plans to give up his post because he sympathized with the problems of personnel shortage, he could no longer carry on his duties, even the purely administrative chores. As soon as the right opportunity presented itself, he announced, he would leave the party and carry on the struggle he knew was right.

The trip to Switzerland at the end of July provided the perfect opportunity to mull over the details and possibilities of the future. For three months Fritz was to weigh the alternatives.

One possibility was to stay in Switzerland. The Zimmerwald Commission offered the possibility of working with men who shared his interest in the International, and if he worked with *Volksrecht,* he could write whatever he wanted about the situation in Austria, exposing the fallacies of the policy of the Austrian party and the wretchedness of life under the war dictatorship in Austria. He wrote to Kautsky and Haase in Berlin for their advice. They pointed out that while he would have complete freedom to say almost anything in Switzerland, his writings would have little or no influence in Austria, and that after a prolonged exile he would lose any chance of returning to Austria to influence the future direction of party policy. The prospect of losing his "legitimacy" in Austria weighed as a real liability of the Switzerland plan.

A second alternative was to accept an invitation Kautsky had extended to come to Germany and to work on the *Neue Zeit*. Writing for the *Neue Zeit* had been a dream of Fritz's youth, and the present position of the journal was very close to Fritz's own views on war and the International. But there were problems with the Germany plan too. For one, it was too easy to abandon active party work for theoretical work. Theory came easily to Fritz, and he was comfortable working in theory, whether physics or politics. But in a period of such revolutionary potential as a world war, it was escapist to take the easy road into theory.

The real problem with both the Switzerland and the Germany schemes was that they finessed the central issue: *Austria*—the bulwark of reaction, the military dictatorship where thousands of soldiers and workers and women and children were dying from bullets and hunger every day. *Austria*—a nation of fifty million people ruled by a tiny camarilla of bureaucrats and warlords, a nation where parliament had not met since the start of the war, where the slightest criticism of official policies was attacked with censorship, detention, prison, or even execution. *Austria*—a nation where the Social Democrats, instead of leading the workers and the downtrodden in a struggle against the government, had joined the government against the people.

There was no answer to the horrors of Austria in Switzerland or Germany.

13

The Third Choice

In November 1914 the Austrian army authorities called Friedrich Adler up for a medical review. His examination was probably much like that given the Good Soldier Schweik, for despite his obviously incapacitating heart condition he was declared fit for active service. In February 1915 he was conscripted into the National Guard. It took the army physicians, in their customary bumbling manner, thirteen days to discover Fritz's myocarditis and to cancel his induction orders. Those thirteen days were enough time for the sergeants at the training center to get a uniform on the new man, cut his hair short, thrust a rifle into his hands, and assign him temporary duty in the stable with the cavalry horses.

For Fritz, who had never before held a gun, that rifle prompted some serious reflections about war and killing. "Could I shoot someone?" he asked himself. The answer came easily: "In war I would not shoot anyone." If the situation ever came to shooting, he decided, he would rather shoot the enemies in his own country, who were closer and more oppressive, than the "enemies" of a foreign land. But still he wondered, could he ever shoot someone? He discussed the thoughts with no one, not even Sophie or Victor.

The question was still nagging a month later when Fritz got into one of his periodic arguments about censorship. Someone was arguing that there was really nothing that could be done about censorship, that the only hope was to use little tricks and to sneak as much truth as possible past the heavy hands with their blue pencils. Fritz wondered to himself why it was always necessary to deal with the authorities by little tricks. Why not attack force with force? What would he do if *Kampf* were disallowed? People always said, "There is nothing that can be done." Why not? wondered Fritz. Why not shoot the censor?

For weeks, every time he came up against the authorities or a reference to the power of the government as the excuse why he should not write or say the truth, or as a justification of the attitude of the party leaders, Fritz reacted by pondering the possibility of a political assassination. The idea remained a sporadic thought, though, neither considered nor planned; Fritz was not a man to act on spur-of-the-moment instincts.

Whom would he shoot? The first man he thought of was Count Tisza, the Premier of Hungary. With the support of the Magyar gentry, Count Tizca ruled Hungary with an iron hand, and by threatening to withhold strategic Hungarian supplies from Austria he made himself in many ways the most powerful man in the whole Austro-Hungarian monarchy. But the assassination of Count Tizca might be misconstrued, especially abroad, as an act in the interest of Austrian independence and not as a blow for freedom. Then there was Hochenberger, still the Minister of Justice in Austria. The real problem in Austria was injustice, and in 1915 as in 1911 it was the Minister of Justice who was the obvious symbol of injustice. But with Hochenberger too there were problems. As everyone could remember, Victor Adler had been speaking in parliament during the first attempt on Hochenberger's life. That coincidence alone had been enough to convince public and government alike that the Social Democrats were behind the assassination. It would serve no purpose to be part of another set of false accusations against the Social Democratic party, since that would do no more than raise the old specter of a "Red" scare. What about the censor himself? The most obvious manifestation of the repression of the government was censorship—why not shoot the symbol? Yet hardly anyone even knew the chief censor's name, and a man whose identity and activities were so shrouded in the secrecy of the operations of the War Surveillance Office would attract little attention to the total situation in Austria. Count Stürgkh and Foreign Minister Burian were possibilities, but neither seemed significant enough. In the spring of 1915 Count Stürgkh seemed no more than a figurehead, a pawn of the military authorities. The Foreign Minister was unfortunately an inadequate substitute for Count Berchtold, his predecessor, who as Foreign Minister in July 1914 had signed the ultimatum to Serbia which began the whole bloodbath. The association of the office was not enough. No one was really the right person.

The legality or illegality of an assassination was not a problem. Since childhood Fritz had been convinced that "quite simply, the struggle against the police and the government authorities was an obvious duty." Laws, or at least "bourgeois laws," were tools of authority of the ruling classes, used whenever convenient to oppress their potential enemies and to maintain their own strength. *Of course* an assassination was illegal, *of course* it was illegal to kill someone. But did the question of legality or illegality mean anything in the middle of a war, when thousands and hundreds of thousands of soldiers and civilians were dying violent deaths every day, when whole armies were sent into the fields with orders to kill all men who wore a certain color of uniform or who spoke a certain language? Bourgeois legality was not a real issue to a revolutionary.

What was a problem was the questionable theoretical validity of an individual revolutionary act. Was it justifiable for an individual to act on behalf of the masses of the working class? To do so was, in the words of the anarchists, to "propagandize by the deed." The anarchists, enchanted by the vision of a stateless society, without government, without law, and without private ownership of property, had propagandized efficiently. In the twenty years before 1914 their deeds had accounted for the deaths of six heads of state: President Carnot of France in 1894, Premier Canovas of Spain in 1897, Empress Elizabeth of Austria in 1898, King Humbert of Italy in 1900, President McKinley of the United States in 1901, and Premier Canalejas of Spain in 1912. They had also accounted for the deaths of numbers of government officials and industrial captains. None of their targets had been true tyrants. Rather, the anarchists attempted to dramatize their dream and their ideals through singular bold acts. Themselves without heroes, unless their vision itself could be called a "hero," the anarchists struck out for a leaderless and classless society by striking down the symbolic leaders of the world they rejected.

But the Social Democrats had always been irrevocably opposed to the tactics and theory of the anarchists. Although in the 1880s and even in subsequent decades the governments of many countries had lumped the two groups together under strenuous laws of censorship and repression, often using the pretext of an assassination or an attempted assassination to move against the Red Terror, the anarchists and the Social Democrats usually regarded each other with as much suspicion as they reserved for the bourgeois government. In most of the Social Democratic parties, and in the International itself, the anarchists were viewed as heretical renegades and by the turn of the century they had been purged. In the subsequent polemics of International congresses and in the theoretical journals, "anarchist" or the corollaries, "anarcho-syndicalist," "anarcho-socialist," and "opportunist," became the worst epithets a Social Democrat could fling.

Fritz's own involvement with the labor movement was contemporary with the purge of the anarchists. He had often debated, with success, against anarchists, using his own familiarity with Marxist theory to show that an individual action could not substitute for a mass action, that an individual act could not make a revolution. Revolution, like every other great change in history, had to grow and evolve through the inexorable flow of the great forces of history. For a revolution, a true revolution, the great force of the proletariat would have to rise, by itself, and in a concerted action overthrow and replace the bourgeois governments—as the first stage on the path toward a classless society. To offer a simplistic solution, such as the anarchists offered, to suggest that removing the head of state would change the body, was not only heresy, it was foolishness.

Yet there were verses in the vast Scripture of Marxism that were not so certain. Before he elaborated his views in the *Communist Manifesto,* Marx wrote:

> The question whether objective [*gegenständlich*] truth can be attributed to human thinking is not a question of theory, but is a *practical* question. In practice man must prove the truth, that is, the reality and power, the this-sidedness of his thinking. The dispute over the reality and nonreality of thinking which is isolated from practice is a purely *scholastic* question.

In the same scribbled notebook Marx had also written the line which today graces his tomb: "The philosophers have only *interpreted* the world in various ways; the point, however, is to change it."

"In practice man must prove the truth . . ." How much of the world knew the truth about Austria and the war? In Austria Fritz had tried to write the truth and the censors had disallowed his magazine or mutilated his articles. In the Social Democratic party he had tried to speak out with the truth and he was censured like an errant and mischievous little boy. Even his father refused to listen to the truth—the very truth for which he had struggled throughout his life. Somehow, theorizing about the effectiveness of an individual act could seem meaningless in the face of the awesome and silent truth about the war in Austria.

". . . the point, however, is to change it." An assassination might have no direct effect on the government in Austria, but it could prove the catalyst that would awaken the working class and the party from the temporary insanity of war fever. If only the party and the masses would realize that the government was not invincible, if only they would realize that the leaders of government were fallible, mortal men, then perhaps everyone could return to the true struggle for the liberation of the masses.

In theory Fritz had always opposed the provocation tactics of the anarchists and the radicals and the Social Revolutionaries. But even as he thought through the theoretical arguments on individual action, he could remember how excited he was in July 1904 when he heard that the newly appointed Russian Minister of the Interior, Plehve, had been blown to pieces with a bomb thrown by a Social Revolutionary named Sazanov. Despite every theoretical argument, that assassination had filled the socialists of Europe with excitement. Victor Adler and the other leaders of the Austrian party, no less than Fritz, had the feeling of spring with that news. And in Russia it was spring, for within a year the revolution had become a reality. Could Austria be so very different?

Practical details and theoretical questions about assassination drifted through Fritz's sober mind in April 1915 when he visited Kathia and the children in Switzerland. Though serious and weighty as ever, Fritz's speculations were still unreal. He had held a gun once in his life, he had never shot at anything, he had never even harmed a living thing, and he was far from sure that he could shoot anyone.

On the way back from Unter-Aegerie, in Zurich, Fritz stopped in a gun shop. He had already decided that he should own a gun, if not for an assassination, then at least for protection. After all, he was a revolutionary, and if the only revolutionizing he had ever known had been with a typewriter, in time of war the future was still uncertain enough to make violence a very real possibility. He would be ready.

Fritz knew next to nothing about guns, but he had heard of an effective small pistol called a Browning automatic, which was illegal in Austria. After a short discussion with the gunsmith Fritz decided that the little pistol would be perfect for his purposes. The gunsmith explained the mechanism of the pistol, letting Fritz try a few practice shots at the target in the back of the shop. Fritz squeezed the shots off timidly, a little amazed after each shot that he could actually fire a gun. He bought the pistol and six bullets, enough for one full load.

On the trip back to Vienna Fritz took the pistol with him, carefully concealing it because he knew that the customs authorities would be sure to seize an automatic pistol if they ever found it. In Vienna he hid the pistol in his desk, telling no one about it.

Some months later he decided that he should take the pistol from his office to his flat, because living alone as he did he was a potential victim of a robbery. He took the gun home in his briefcase and hid it in his washstand.

From the end of April 1915 to July 1916 Fritz remembered the pistol only in moments of extreme depression and pessimism, when the ukase of the censor or the obstinance of party members convinced him that there was no future for the politics of deliberation in the party or in Austria. For a moment, or even for a few days, he would think of the pistol, of the candidates he had potentially selected for assassination, and of the many arguments for and against the act. He would carefully evaluate what the possible reactions of the party leadership and the editors of the party press might be. The assassination would have to be a spark in a highly flammable situation. If the spark did not convince the party leaders and the editors that their policies toward the war had been wrong, then surely the masses of the working class would also remain unconvinced. The only consequence then would be that Fritz would quickly be prosecuted and executed. The government would move against his colleagues in the Karl Marx Association as potential enemies of the state, and the antiwar effort would actually suffer a setback.

Usually Fritz thought either of the censor or the Minister of Justice as targets for an assassination. They were the two men closest to the real problems of injustice and dictatorship, and they were the two men who could best be connected with the horrible situation of the war in Austria. But every time he thought about an assassination, Fritz found that within a few days or weeks the crisis with the party or the censor would pass. Pessimism would give way to qualified optimism, and with the passing of the crisis and the pessimism, the thoughts of assassination would pass as well. Life would return to the stalemate of fighting a war against war, without the weapons of war.

In late March 1916, after the second all-party conference of the Austrian Social Democracy, the party leadership voted to communicate the text of their resolution on the war and the role of the party to the Prime Minister. It was regular procedure in Austria for any parliamentary representative to have open access to the Prime Minister's office, so no one assumed there would be any problem in asking the Social Democratic parliamentary delegation to convey the resolution to Count Stürgkh. But when they attempted to secure an appointment, they were rebuffed; Count Stürgkh wrote that he would not confer with party officials, and that if they wished to communicate to him they could avail them-

selves of the mails. His brusqueness was an unprecedented chas-
tisement of the party and the parliamentary delegation.

Fritz was by no means in sympathy with the final resolution of the party conference, which had been passed over his own
resolution of support for the Zimmerwald peace efforts, but he did
join the other members of the party in a sense of outrage at the
callousness of Count Stürgkh and his government. It was well
known that the Prime Minister was immune to criticism of his
policies. To disregard even a message of support was unprecedented arrogance—the mark of the tyrant.

It was the first time that Fritz understood the role Count
Stürgkh played in the government of Austria. Count Stürgkh was
not the figurehead or pawn Fritz had thought him a year before.
He was the head of the bureaucracy, the instigator of the war
policies. He was not following the military camarilla, he was leading them, using the enormous imperial bureaucracy to serve the
needs of the war.

Suddenly everything was clear. Count Stürgkh had pushed
the Army Bill and the War Service Act through parliament to
prepare for war. He had prorogued the Bohemian Diet and the
Austrian parliament to silence all potential criticism of an imperialist war policy. Count Stürgkh had been one of the cloistered
few individuals who had seized upon the pretext of the assassination of Archduke Franz Ferdinand to impose an ultimatum and
thus to force Europe into war. And when the war started, he had
established the War Surveillance Office to maintain a war dictatorship in Austria. He had ordered the police state regime against all
critics of the war or the government. He had ordered the incredible prison and death sentences for men whose only crime had been
a harmless poem or a casual joke about the war in a letter home
from the front. It was Count Stürgkh who had masterminded the
net of censorship and secrecy which kept Austria isolated from the
whole world, making it impossible for an ordinary burgher in a
café to read any newspapers from enemy countries, or even from

some of the allied countries. And worst of all, it was Count Stürgkh who had masterminded the destruction of political life in Austria, who had made Austria the only state in the civilized world with no representative legislature. Ignoring the interests of all of Austria, he was discussing a twenty-year *Ausgleich* with Hungary, an arrangement which would make every possible concession to the Hungarians—all to prolong the war effort at the expense of the workers and women and children of Austria, who were already starving in the streets.

The more Fritz thought about Count Stürgkh's role in the government, the more the whole nefarious plot became clear. Count Stürgkh had replaced the Council of Ministers, for all practical purposes, by the War Surveillance Office, removing from any influence or power all those ministers who in any way disagreed with his policies. Disregarding every entreaty of his critics and the pleas of responsible voices in Austria, he had placed himself even between the Emperor and the people, so that the President of the parliament, Sylvester, was not allowed an audience with the Emperor.

After March 1916 there was only one man Fritz ever thought of assassinating. Whenever he finished another screaming telephone battle with the censors, he told himself that the censor was only another of Count Stürgkh's bureaucrats, another cog in the gears of the great war machine Count Stürgkh had built. When hungry women came to the offices of the Social Democratic party to plead for ration cards or for help in keeping their last sons out of the army, Fritz thought of Count Stürgkh, whose vast war machine needed more and more human fuel to carry on its rampages. When Fritz heard that another group of Czech dissenters had been executed for protesting the dictatorship in Bohemia, or that a middle-aged insurance clerk in Silesia had been sentenced to death for publishing a translation of the American antiwar song "I Didn't Raise My Boy To Be a Soldier" in a provincial newspaper, he thought of Count Stürgkh and his network of police agents.

When Fritz saw photographs of the dozens of women and men who, after summary proceedings, had been hanged as alleged spies, he thought of Count Stürgkh's desperate efforts to rid the country of "traitors" and "defeatists"—an effort which cost the lives of hundreds of unsuspecting and innocent Austrians and foreigners. And when Fritz suddenly felt ashamed to be an Austrian, ashamed to be part of a nation which had thrown morality and sanity to the winds in a fever of chauvinism, he thought of Count Stürgkh, who had callously disregarded every shred of morality or humanity in his efforts to forge and maintain an absolutist state in Austria.

And yet, as much as Count Stürgkh controlled this horrendous absolutism, Fritz knew that killing Count Stürgkh alone would change nothing. Like Count Tisza and Hochenberger and Burian and the censor and the generals and even the Emperor, Count Stürgkh was only a part of the great machine of bourgeois government. If he were killed, a replacement would be found, and with the silent acquiescence of the parties and the people of Austria, the replacement would rule as Count Stürgkh ruled, oblivious to the laws of history and the rights of man.

The problem was not to kill Count Stürgkh, but somehow to call the party and the people back to their historic tasks and away from the madness of war. And that was an enormous mission for one man.

14

The Assassination

When Fritz returned from a visit with Kathia and the children in August 1916, he knew he would not work any longer than necessary within the strictures of the Social Democratic party. Although he was still not sure what he would do after he quit the party, he had sorted out the alternatives pretty carefully: Switzerland and the sanctuary of the editorship of *Volksrecht* seemed the most likely choice, Germany and a position with *Neue Zeit* was a poor second. The idea of the assassination still haunted the recesses of his mind, but only as a desperate third choice, too risky and contingent on too many intangibles to be a real alternative. Fritz advised many of his colleagues at the party headquarters, including Seitz, that he planned to resign from his duties. He explained as well as he could that he felt that he could no longer fulfill any useful function as a constrained opposition within the party. Seitz assured him that the party would not stand in his way.

What remained was to tell his plans to his father who, until the beginning of September, was resting at Bad Neuheim. When Victor returned to Vienna his condition was much worse, as bad as it had ever been. To avoid aggravating his father's health, Fritz decided to hold off telling him that he was leaving for Switzerland until the last moment. There followed several tense weeks, while Fritz tried to make the necessary visa and travel arrangements for a move to Switzerland without letting his father find out. When Fritz finally raised the subject with his father, on October 10, he was afraid to press the point for fear of provoking a relapse of his father's heart condition. The discussion ended inconclusively.

The situation gradually became intolerable, as Fritz could not stand facing his one-time colleagues at the party offices any longer, and could not bring himself to respect them enough to stand up as a responsible opposition within the party. They were immune to his arguments now. Victor was so ill that Fritz could not discuss politics with him at all. Yet, until he received final permission to leave Austria and an exit visa from the War Ministry, which was reconsidering his military status, Fritz had no choice but to remain at his post, reporting daily to his still arduous administrative tasks. The only forum where his ideas received any hearing at all was in the weekly meetings of the Karl Marx Association, now a group of about 120 members who subscribed more or less to Fritz's views. They met to discuss matters each week, usually devoting the evenings to long critical discussions of the editorial policy of the *Arbeiter-Zeitung* or the speeches of various party leaders.

The one other possibility of expressing his views was in the series of lectures to workers that the party sponsored each winter. The dates for the 1916–1917 series were announced in September, and Fritz signed up for the first available date, October 23. His topic was to be "The Past and the Future of the International."

Week after week slipped by while Fritz awaited the action

of the War Ministry, and as the weeks passed, the possibility of working either in Switzerland or Germany diminished. The editors of *Volksrecht* and the *Neue Zeit* could not be expected to wait interminably for Fritz.

At the same time, the situation in Austria was worsening at a frightening rate. The battlefront victories of the summer and fall of 1916, which were moving triumphant Austrian and German armies farther and farther into the territories of Serbia, Russia, Romania, Montenegro, and even Italy, gave the governments of the Central Powers room to plan for more aggression and more grandiose imperialistic schemes. Rather than using the victories to bring the war to an end, the reports from every source indicated that the German and Austrian General Staffs were planning for a longer war, hoping to extend their victorious fronts even farther into the territories of neighboring countries. What it meant was that the killing and the starvation would go on for months, perhaps even years more.

On the home front, Count Stürgkh had followed up the victories on the battlefields with a new wave of repression and censorship. Harmless protests about the failure to reconvene parliament were regularly censored, and hundreds of alleged spies, traitors, and defeatists were being arrested. The censorship was becoming so strict that completely harmless articles Fritz wrote for *Kampf* were held up, "awaiting further consideration," for over a week in various offices, long enough to delay the publication of an issue on purely technical grounds. These episodes were such blatant acts of political repression that Fritz could not help thinking again of political assassination. "If the newspapers are going to be outlawed by the government," he would say to himself, "then there is no choice for us except to outlaw the government." The idea occurred to him that for every newspaper suspended, a member of the government should be killed—until the system was recalled from degradation and despotism.

Within the Social Democratic party the situation was also

worsening. Members of the leadership were openly distrustful of the members of the parliamentary delegation, many of whom were somewhat to the left of the official line of the party. The delegates had been excluded from exercising any parliamentary voice for so long—more than two and one half years, since the proroguement in March 1914—that no one in the party was really sure how far they would go in voicing a protest to the war if the parliament were to reconvene. When Fritz tried to point out the levels of mutual distrust within the party, he was rejected on both sides. With what seemed to him a rather paranoid fear, the leaders of the party were afraid to have anyone point up the slightest crack in the supposedly unified front of the party. They were not only hostile to criticism, but also hostile to the suggestion that the entire party was anything less than 100 percent united in their stand of "loyally" supporting the war effort and awaiting the future.

Demands for the reconvocation of the Austrian parliament reached something of a crescendo in October 1916. Count Stürgkh, backed up by a fearful minority of German nationalist parties, adamantly and successfully resisted every entreaty by influential individuals and by groups, but the demands continued, until finally, through the Ministry of Justice, Count Stürgkh ruled that all public assemblies and meetings to discuss the question were out of order and illegal.

In October a group of university professors, many of whom were highly respected scholars, organized a closed meeting to discuss the question of the parliament. A noted authority on parliamentary bodies, Professor Bernatzik, was scheduled to give a theoretical lecture, and the two co-presidents of the parliament were scheduled to make brief addessses. The meeting was scheduled for Sunday, October 22, and open only to invited guests. Since closed meetings—"by invitation only"—had always been permitted in Austria, even during the worst days of anti-socialist measures in the 1880s, the organizers of the meeting did not expect any trouble with their plans.

On Monday, October 16, Fritz learned that there was a possibility that the conference of professors would be forbidden by police order. With that news he realized for the first time that no free exchange of opinion would ever be tolerated in Count Stürgkh's Austria. Count Stürgkh had made himself into a virtual dictator. The one element which had been lacking in all of Fritz's plans for an assassination—the correct psychological moment—was set.

Since it was impossible for the Social Democrats to point out the situation in parliament, because there was no parliament and because the Social Democrats were not ready to attack the system, the time had come to demonstrate the truth to the people of Austria and the whole world by unparliamentary means. A parliamentary session might have as its agenda the simple program: "Point Number One: The Impeachment of the Stürgkh Ministry." That was impossible now. Fritz would have to rely upon himself. He substituted a new agenda, equally simple: "Point Number One: The Assassination of Count Stürgkh."

That evening Fritz was scheduled to give a speech in Graz. On the long train ride he began thinking about the assassination, going through the theory and the timing in his systematic, thorough way. He also thought of Kathia and the children, wondering what would happen to them. A ballad of Heine kept going through his mind:

> *Was schert mich Weib, was schert mich Kind,*
> *Lass sie bettln gehn, wenn sie hungrig sind,*
> *Mein Kaiser, mein Kaiser gefangen!**

---

* The hell with wife, the hell with child,
Let them beg if they are hungry.
My Emperor, my Emperor is in chains!

FRITZ

He had never liked Heine, although his father had read the poems aloud often. But these lines said what he really felt about Kathia and the children. They would be all right. He had put enough money away in Switzerland at the beginning of the war to provide them for a while. If the worst were to come, Victor would surely watch out for them.

The rest of that evening Fritz thought about the motto of the old radical faction of the labor movement in Vienna: "We dedicate our lives to those high goals, for which generations have been only sacrifices, only martyrs." When Fritz was a child Victor had often told him how those brave men of the early movement had been ready to sacrifice themselves, to risk their last drop of blood for the movement. Maybe, Fritz thought, the time had come for a new generation of men willing to sacrifice themselves.

He knew he would be sentenced to hang if he were to carry out the assassination, and he decided—even before he was sure about the assassination—that he would not plead for mercy. What good would it do to rot for years in a prison? If it was right to kill Count Stürgkh, then it must be right enough to be worth the life of one socialist. To make his point, to the party, to the people, and to himself, he would have to be ready to die. As he realized, he was proving himself as much as any point of politics.

On Wednesday and Thursday, October 18 and 19, rumors were rife about the conference of professors. A report from the police station would say that it looked like the conference would be allowed, then someone with a contact in the Ministry of Justice would report that it was certain that the conference would be canceled. With every new rumor Fritz changed his plans. During the mornings, while he plowed his way through the incredible administrative work which piled up at the party headquarters each day, he would daydream about how and where he would carry out the assassination. He did not know where to find Count Stürgkh, let alone how he could get close enough to shoot him.

On Friday morning Fritz was working as usual when he

received a phone call from a friend at the university, Professor Ludo Hartmann, who relayed the news that the conference of professors was definitely canceled by personal order of Count Stürgkh.

Fritz decided: "It must be now." As soon as the thought entered his mind he became nervous. He knew that he would have to keep working as though nothing were the matter, and that he would have to keep every appointment, so that no one would suspect that he was planning something.

Dutifully, he reported the news of the cancellation to his colleagues in the office. Then he went up to the editorial offices of the *Arbeiter-Zeitung* on the second floor of the party building to tell Austerlitz the news. In a long discussion about Count Stürgkh and politics in Austria, they agreed on almost everything. Austerlitz remarked that the situation was actually incredible, because it was not the Emperor who was exercising the tyranny, but a petty, narrow-minded Philistine. In fact, he added, Stürgkh was not really a despot, but a nobody who was petty enough to go to the pub every day and order a portion of meat. Any despot would be intelligent enough not to eat meat in public in the midst of mass starvation and severe rationing.

Surprised, Fritz asked if Count Stürgkh really ate at a pub every day.

Austerlitz answered that as far as he knew Stürgkh ate at the Hotel Meissl & Schadn.

"Everyone knows that," someone else said. "He eats every day at the Hotel Meissl & Schadn."

It was mid-afternoon when Fritz left the office to go to his parents' flat for lunch. On the way he kept thinking about the lucky bit of information he had picked up that morning. In his life Fritz had seen Count Stürgkh once, in a parliamentary debate a good four years back. He could not remember exactly what Count Stürgkh looked like anymore, and he knew nothing about his daily schedule. Somewhere he had heard that Count Stürgkh spent evenings in a café, but he did not remember which café, and he was afraid to ask such a leading question of anyone.

"He eats every day at the Hotel Meissl & Schadn." It would be the perfect place to shoot him, Fritz thought. And Sunday, the scheduled day for the conference, would be the perfect day for the assassination—a kind of poetic justice. Then he decided that there was too much chance that on Sunday Count Stürgkh might vary his daily routine. It would be better to make it Saturday—*tomorrow*—he thought. The Saturday newspapers would carry the reports that the conference had been canceled, the final proof of Stürgkh's dictatorship and tyranny, and people would be certain to associate the cancellation with Fritz's deed. It was too bad though; he had tickets for himself and Sophie to attend the opera on Sunday night, a new production of Strauss's *Ariadne auf Naxos* which had gotten excellent reviews in the *Neue Freie Presse*.

When Fritz told his father that the conference was going to be canceled, Victor said that he had already called the Police President to protest. Fritz answered sarcastically that it was stupid to protest with the authorities, since they would do nothing. As he and his father argued, Fritz could not help laughing to himself at the irony of the situation—that his father would now worry about protesting the actions of a man who would be dead by that time the next day.

Later Fritz called to see if Sophie was free for the evening. She explained that she could not break a previous engagement with an important army official who might be able to relieve her husband's assignment at the Italian front. There was no way Fritz could let her know how important the evening was.

That night a meeting of the Executive Committee of the party was scheduled at the Railway Workers Home. Fritz went to fend off any suspicion about his actions. At the beginning of the meeting the Chairman announced the cancellation of the professors' conference, opening debate on what the report of the cancellation in the *Arbeiter-Zeitung* should say. Fritz demanded that the report carry a critical commentary on Count Stürgkh's government. When someone suggested that any critical commentary would be censored, Fritz answered that the censors' report could be printed with the notice of the cancellation of the conference.

Fritz was nervous and excited, and before long he became so adamant in his demands that Seitz, who was chairing the meeting, asked him to assuage the tone of his remarks. Ignoring Seitz, Fritz went on with his criticism of the *Arbeiter-Zeitung*. For a long time, in the meetings of the Karl Marx Association, he had been preparing a new scheme for a press commission representing all viewpoints in the party, which would serve as a watchdog commission over the various party publications. When he introduced the idea at the meeting, voices from all sides shouted him down. Several speakers insisted that the idea was ridiculous, since the various publications already represented the viewpoint of the party. With that, Fritz became furious. For the first time ever he made a passionate verbal attack against individuals in the party. In particular he singled out Karl Leuthner, who for years had been on the editorial staff of the *Arbeiter-Zeitung*. Leuthner, Fritz said, had discriminated against everything Fritz ever wrote for the paper, on personal and ideological grounds. Fritz went on with a list of occasions when articles he had written were refused by the *Arbeiter-Zeitung*.

Many of the delegates to the meeting had seen Fritz argue with other party leaders over politics or ideology; a few had been witnesses to the passionate quarrels of Fritz and Victor. But no one had ever seen him break his icy composure at a party meeting. Even when discussions had reached a screaming pitch, Fritz had always argued in a precise scientific tone. Now he was hurling accusations at people, many of whom were not even there to defend themselves. As people in the audience began to hoot and boo, he added to the list of those whom he accused of monopolizing the press and excluding dissent. The arguments became so heated that someone ran to the telephone to get Austerlitz, who was not at the meeting, in the hope that he could straighten things out.

Austerlitz arrived in minutes. As he took the podium to try to restore order, Max Winter hurled the worst of all insults at Fritz: "Party traitor!" When Fritz stood to answer, his remarks were drowned in a chorus of rancor.

Austerlitz finally brought the meeting to order. When everyone sat down to take up the agenda again, Fritz was alone on one side of the room and the rest of the committee together on the other side. Austerlitz was not alone in thinking how much the situation represented Fritz's position in the party.

In the tram that most of the delegates took home from the meeting, the conversation was mostly about Fritz and the "affair" he had caused at the meeting. No one had ever seen him behave like that before. A metalworker named Fischer said simply: "He is a fool!"

Fritz took a different tram home, arriving at his flat around eleven o'clock. He worked for about an hour answering letters and cleaning up various matters on his desk, then went to bed around midnight. From his student days he had learned to sleep well, even when he was nervous. As he fell asleep he thought to himself, "This is the last night I will sleep here."

On Saturday he woke up an hour earlier than usual, and dressed in his good suit so that he would not look out of place at the hotel. Taking the pistol out of the washstand, he noted that it was still loaded with the bullets he had put in at the gun shop in Zurich. He stuffed it into his coat pocket. Then he went to the party headquarters, where he still had a half day's work to finish before lunch time.

At the office he worked hard, both to clear up the business on his desk and to allay any suspicions about his behavior. He was responsible for the tangled protocol of the previous night and the agenda of the next meeting.

Before he got down to work Fritz called Sophie's husband's office to leave a message that he would not be able to attend the opera on Sunday. He promised that he would send the tickets over so that they could be used.

Fritz's Co-Secretary, Skaret, was going through the final proofs of the invitations for a workers' rally planned for November 5. When they spoke briefly of the cancellation of the professors' conference, Skaret said: "Now it is superfluous. If the conference is canceled, there is nothing we can do for the workers' rally."

"We shall see," Fritz answered. "Put them through anyway."

Later in the morning Fritz went up to the editorial office of the *Arbeiter-Zeitung* to pick up some papers. Pernerstorfer was standing in the waiting room with his coat on. They said hello and exchanged a few words about the next issue of *Kampf*. Then, as Fritz started downstairs, he heard Pernerstorfer mumble something like "anarcho-socialist."

"I prefer that to your views," Fritz snapped back.

"To each his own," answered Pernerstorfer.

It was a normal working day, at least for everyone else, and in the course of the morning Fritz managed to see most of the party leaders, including Ellenbogen, Seitz, and even Max Winter. He tried to be as cool as he could with all of them, hoping that he would draw no attention to himself and that no one would notice how nervous he was.

Seitz, coming into his office, said: "What you did was really insane." He was talking about the night before.

"There is still more to be said about that," Fritz answered.

Around noon Fritz called his mother to say that he would not be coming there for lunch. Emma said he seemed in a bad temper. She asked if something had happened at the office: Had he gotten into another fight with Victor? Fritz answered that he was just in a bad mood and did not feel like lunch. When he hung up he thought how much better his mother knew him than anyone else. She was the only one who noticed the state he was in, and she noticed from his voice alone.

A few minutes before one o'clock he left the office. He was about to get on the tram for the Neue Markt and the hotel when he remembered that the housekeeper had the key to his flat. It would be better if he had the key when he was arrested, he thought, so that she would not be involved with the police.

It took a few minutes to get the key. Then Fritz took the tram back into the city. Neue Markt was the last stop. As he got off the tram he wondered if it was too late to catch Count Stürgkh at lunch. That would be horrible, since today had to be the day. On Sunday Stürgkh might not eat in his usual restaurant. Monday would be too late for the assassination to have the right association with the conference. It had to be today.

In the hotel he walked straight into the ground floor restaurant and looked around. There was no one who looked like Count Stürgkh. Fritz stood and thought for a moment before he remembered that there was another restaurant on the mezzanine.

He bounded up the stairs, hung his hat and coat in the foyer of the dining room, and went in. The first person he saw was Count Stürgkh. A shock came over him—*he was going to kill this man.* "What must I do? Shoot now?" he wondered. "No, I must pull my self together and do everything carefully." He realized then how little he knew about Count Stürgkh. The only thing he was sure of was that Stürgkh was not married.

Walking quickly from one end of the room to the other, Fritz finally took a seat two tables from Stürgkh's corner table. There was a clock on the wall directly in front of Fritz. It was one thirty when he sat down. When the waiter came over to take his order, Fritz remembered an old family trait of the Adlers—hunger made them nervous. It was true of his father and it was true of his uncle. Maybe the nervousness would go away if he ate, he thought. Anyway, he could not be sure what would happen afterward, how long it would be until he ate again. Hastily he ordered a big meal—soup, a main course with vegetables, and a plum pastry. His voice trembled as he ordered, and he noticed how quickly he was speaking.

When the wine steward came to take a beverage order, Fritz asked for mineral water. He had never drunk any alcoholic beverage since he was nineteen. A busboy brought the water, and Fritz asked him: "Isn't that the Prime Minister?"

The busboy, somewhat condescendingly, assured him that it was.

Fritz ate quickly, hoping that the food would quiet his nerves. While he ate he felt in his right coat pocket, where the pistol was. Carefully he removed everything else from the pocket and disengaged the safety on the pistol.

When he finished eating Fritz asked for coffee and paid his bill. Then he began to think about the task ahead of him. When should he make his move? Should he say something? What should he say? It had to be soon, and there were so many details to work out.

There was one big problem. A woman sat at the table behind Count Stürgkh, and if Fritz were to shoot from where he was there was a chance that he would hit the woman, or that his bullet might ricochet off the wall behind the woman and hurt her or another innocent bystander. He decided to wait. To leave Count Stürgkh would have to walk by Fritz's table. That would be the perfect moment.

Fritz wondered whether people would find it strange that he lingered so long over empty plates. To look less suspicious he picked up the copy of *Neue Zeit* which had been in his pocket and tried to read. He was actually interested in one article about the last party conference of the German Social Democratic party, wondering whether the article might have been intended as an answer to his own article about the conference in *Kampf*. He was too nervous to concentrate. Instead he kept wondering what he should say when he shot Stürgkh. Nothing? Then people might not understand his act. For a long time he composed various phrases until he settled on a formula that combined the two concerns: "Down with tyranny! We want peace!" No sense confusing the matter with references to the party now; that could all come later, at a trial or a hearing. For now the point was to shock, to make people think about the situation in Austria, to say what they should think: "Down with tyranny! We want peace!"

While Fritz composed, two men came to Count Stürgkh's table and sat down. Now there were three innocent people to watch out for, the two men and the woman who sat behind Stürgkh. But how much longer could Fritz wait? Weren't people already staring at him, wondering why he sat there after he had clearly finished his lunch?

Finally the woman got up and left the room. Fritz looked at the clock. Two fifteen. Before he could put his hand into his pocket for the gun, before he could even put down the newspaper, a steward came between him and the Prime Minister's table. Other people were moving in the dining room. People were standing by the buffet along the wall by the door. Fritz kept watching the steward, who was serving a glass of liqueur to Count Stürgkh. When the steward finished and moved away from the table, Fritz said to himself: "It must be now. If not now, I will lose the chance."

Once more he looked at the clock. Two thirty. There was no one near Count Stürgkh's table.

The next few minutes went so quickly that it was not until he had fired the three shots and forced out the words that were sticking in his throat that Fritz realized it was done. The shots had gone off almost automatically, one after another, almost before he could release the trigger.

Fritz's only thought was: "Now my life is over!" He saw what looked like blood spurt from Count Stürgkh's left cheek, but before the Prime Minister had fallen from the chair Fritz turned toward the door, thinking that he had to get to the foyer of the room before the officers at the table next to Count Stürgkh's table pulled their sabers and cut him down. He realized that his arm with the pistol was still extended straight out.

In moments Fritz was pressed on all sides by pushing and shoving people. "Throw him down!" shouted someone. Someone else screamed, "You sonofabitch, you!" A saber was swinging wildly over his head. His glasses were torn off. Fritz's gun fired again. Fritz thought he would be lynched.

"I want to be tried in a court," he said. "I am Doctor Friedrich Adler."

Finally there was a clear space. A man stepped forward. "My name is Police Officer Müller."

"Please," answered Fritz. "I will go with you peacefully."

The agent took him by the arm and escorted him to a small room, the office of the hotel cashier. There other officers searched Fritz and took the contents of his pockets and the pistol which was still in his hand. One officer took away the small box of bonbons he carried to soothe his throat after speeches.

Fritz protested: "Can't I keep these?"

"Certainly not," the officer answered. Fritz wondered why for a few minutes, then realized that the officer probably believed there was poison in the bonbons. They thought he would commit suicide. How little they understood. How difficult it would be to explain everything to them.

For almost a full hour Fritz was questioned in the little office, first by the police officers, then by a special agent named Schober, and finally by the Police Commissioner, Baron Gorup. As the questions and his mechanical answers droned on, Fritz's nervousness subsided, until he heard a police agent in another room call for an ambulance.

FRITZ

"There has been an attempt on the life of the Prime Minister," the voice said.

For the first time Fritz thought about the possibility that he might not have killed Count Stürgkh. What if the Prime Minister had only been wounded? He would stay in office, and as a martyr he would be able to strengthen his dictatorship. Or what if he were badly wounded? He might suffer for a long time before he died. That was not Fritz's intention, to cause more suffering in Austria. Fritz was afraid to ask whether he had killed Count Stürgkh.

When the police wagon was ready to leave the hotel with Fritz inside, the Police Commissioner said: "I always took you for such an idealist, and now this!"

Fritz answered: "If you cannot understand it now, Herr Commissioner, there is nothing I can say."

When the wagon started to move, Fritz pushed aside the curtain over the back window to look out. Neue Markt was the last station on his tram line. He thought to himself that this was the last time in his life that he would see the Neue Markt.

15

The Assassin

By the middle of the war Victor Adler was unable to work for more than a few hours at a time. Usually he would spend the morning on party business, then go home for lunch and a long nap in his armchair before the late afternoon editorial meetings of the *Arbeiter-Zeitung*. To assure his much-needed rest, the telephone was removed from his room during the naps.

On the day of the assassination the phone in the Adler flat rang at three o'clock. Victor was sleeping soundly. When Emma answered the phone, an unidentified caller said: "Have you heard yet? The young Adler has tried to shoot Count Stürgkh."

She froze. Unable even to answer the caller, she could not bring herself to wake Victor and tell him the news. Instead, she called Friedrich Austerlitz at the nearby office of the *Arbeiter-Zeitung*.

Beneath his gruff façade Austerlitz had always been rather sentimental toward Fritz. He could remember the days when Fritz

FRITZ

ran around the offices of the newspaper asking if he could help or begging for stories of the early days of the labor movement. Indeed, for Austerlitz, Fritz was always that excited and clever little boy. When Emma said that she had heard about the shooting, he tried to comfort her in his own way. "Fritz always does such things," he said. Emma was too distraught to understand the irony.

Minutes later Austerlitz arrived at the Adler flat, bringing Seitz along for moral support. Emma led the two of them into Victor's room and gently woke the sleeping man.

Victor, seeing his two friends in front of him, greeted them warmly, or as warmly as he could in the midst of a fit of coughing.

Then Austerlitz told him what had happened. He had already checked with the police and found that Fritz had killed the Prime Minister.

Victor, still sleepy, smiled indulgently. As though he were still waking from a dream, he said, "Oh, go on, that cannot be . . ."

It was only after Austerlitz and Seitz had left the room that Victor grasped what they had said and what it all meant. Without a word he took Emma in his arms. They wept together.

For Victor the assassination turned a recurrent nightmare into reality. There had always been only one reason that he opposed Fritz's entry into politics, only one reason that he had fought to keep Fritz in chemistry, physics, or epistemology. Fritz's sister had been in a mental institution since 1897. Fritz's mother had been in and out of various institutions for years. Fritz's brother, although he had passed muster and was serving in the army at the front, had never had sufficient powers of concentration to hold down a real job. And now, Fritz . . . With his training as a psychiatrist, Victor could readily discern the pattern he had always feared.

At six o'clock, as usual, Victor came into the office of the *Arbeiter-Zeitung*. The group of party leaders who had been discussing the assassination in Austerlitz' office stood up when he walked into the room. Although the same questions were in everyone's mind—How would this affect the party? What position should the paper take?—no one said anything.

Victor walked over to Anton Huebner, whose son had been killed in the battle of Halicz. "This is the time when fathers lose their sons," he said.

Unsure whether they should extend some kind of condolences or raise the questions on their minds, the men stood nervously, waiting for Victor to say something else. They did not wait long.

"I believe that Fritz's deed will not really harm the party," he said. Then he turned to Max Winter. "Is it true, Winter, that potatoes are again more expensive today? Check on that and report back to us."

That evening Victor and Austerlitz wrote a report on the assassination for the *Arbeiter-Zeitung*. Victor had already decided that the only reasonable defense of the action, both for the protection of the party and in anticipation of Fritz's trial, was a plea of temporary insanity. The details of the legal defense could be worked out later. For the newspaper, Fritz's act was explained as the result of an uncontrollable mental derangement. "For all who knew him," read the article in the Sunday edition of the *Arbeiter-Zeitung*, "there remains only one explanation—that his already mad soul was driven to this decision through a precipitous disordering of the senses, of which there were no sure signs even in the last hours before the act. The horrible decision seems to have surfaced in his mind all of a sudden . . ."

Rumors and gossip about the assassination were rampant in Vienna by Saturday evening. Professor Josef Redlich, one of the eternal hangers-on who waited in the wings of the Austrian political stage, took a walk through the streets of the city at five o'clock. "Among the people," he wrote in his diary, "the news was received with the overwhelming sentiment of a kind of gloomy spite . . ." Count Stürgkh had always been a remote figure. Few people outside government circles even knew what he looked like. Many people had heard of the War Surveillance Office, most realized that the controls of that bureau had something to do with the harsh life of wartime Vienna. Everyone knew that the prolonged proroguement of parliament was part of the Stürgkh System. Beyond that, people outside the government knew little about this man. And they cared little. Men and women who worried where the next meal would come from could no longer worry about a prime minister. They could only trust. A new prime minister would be appointed. Things would go on. Only if a miracle would somehow end the war would real change come. Otherwise the great machine would just keep running. If one gear were substituted for another, it would change nothing.

A cabinet official told the Emperor about the assassination early Saturday evening. He said something to the effect that the tragic death of the Prime Minister was incomparably worse than the loss of a great battle, Then, although he was almost too ill to work, he set himself the task of searching for a new chief for the great bureaucracy.

In the almost vacant ministries and government buildings, and in the cafés where the influential of Vienna still gathered, the conversation of an idle bureaucracy turned quickly from hasty obituaries to speculation about who would be appointed to fill the vacancy. Two days after the assassination Redlich wrote in his diary: "In the city a gloomy apathy reigns. I dined yesterday with Frau Fraenkel-Ehrenstein, and numerous ladies of the official circles were there. All said that the people showed no anger over the assassination."

For two days the press dutifully reported every available detail of the assassination on the front pages. The bourgeois papers were unanimous in a chorus of indignation that such a fanatic should be able to roam the streets, but with the exception of a few evasive hints in the extreme Right-wing papers, none of the editorials upbraided the Social Democrats for "harboring" the murderer.

The argument of temporary insanity in the *Arbeiter-Zeitung* was received with general skepticism, even in the party. Most party members had never known very much about Fritz, outside of his official duties and the fact that he was the son of Victor Adler. He had rarely spoken in public meetings, and most of his writings were in the theoretical journals which the rank and file rarely read. Since the outbreak of the war he had been vocal in the meetings of the Executive Committee of the party, but with the exception of his latest outburst, only a day before the assassination, his speeches had been in the tone of his writings—cold, hard, and logical, without the slightest trace of excited or emotional appeal. Yet he had been enough of an embarrassment to the party that members who knew him were glad to have the easy explanation of temporary insanity available, if only to dissociate the act from the party. After two years of carefully avoiding any dispute with the government, the Social Democrats were wary lest any incident become the provocation for government action against the party.

In fact, the only overt action of the government was a series of house searches in the residences of members of the Karl Marx Association and others who had been associated with Fritz's views. Apparently finding nothing that would indicate a conspiracy, the authorities contented themselves with an order disallowing the Karl Marx Association.

On October 25, after lying in state at the Chancellery for two days, Count Stürgkh's body was buried in a quiet funeral. The proper people were there, including Pernerstorfer and Seitz on behalf of the Social Democratic party, but the funeral could attract no more interest than small articles on the third pages of the *Neue Freie Presse* and the *Arbeiter-Zeitung*. After a day or two of flurry about the assassination, public concern had shifted back to the steady news of the war. Headlines went back to battle reports from the Romanian front, rumors about new plans for the future of Poland, gossip about the health of the Emperor, and speculation about the outcome of the election campaign in the United States, where both candidates had declared themselves neutral in the war. In the cafés and the ministries, aspiring candidates for new appointments suddenly remembered that it had been almost five years since they last jockeyed for positions in a new government. With so much to worry about, few people thought too much of the young man who was undergoing questioning at the police headquarters in Alsergrund.

On the first day of interrogation Fritz was questioned for eight hours. A stenographer took down every word directly on a typewriter, which was enough to convince Fritz that the government was trying to rush his case. It was common procedure for the wartime courts to expedite "justice" with summary trials and summary executions, so that protests over cases could be minimized. Knowing that a summary proceeding, held under the almost complete secrecy of heavy censorship, would rob him of the full use of the political situation and the historical moment the assassination was meant to create, Fritz determined to delay the proceedings. Only if the proceedings could be dragged out over a period of months—instead of the two weeks which he imagined as the government goal—would the impact of what he was trying to say to the party and public be felt.

After the first day of interrogation Fritz did all he could to procrastinate, filling the eight hours of each day with rambling childhood memories, with catalogues of his experiences in the early days of the labor movements in Austria and Switzerland, and with detailed explanations of theoretical and organizational disputes in the party and in the International. When his narrative reached the period of the war, he elaborated his descriptions with comments on the policies of the government, and with an extensive list of instances and episodes from the history of the empire and the Social Democratic party. It was really the first time since the outbreak of the war that anyone, outside of his close colleagues in the Karl Marx Association, had listened to his views. Telling his story to the interrogators was not the same as telling it to the public, but it was a chance to try out his views, to explain to someone the desperation that had forced his act and the consequences he expected.

After Fritz had told the entire narrative of the assassination, Dr. Jacobs questioned him for several more days to ask his views on murder, religion, anarchism, and other issues which the government might use in its case. The interrogation lasted until November 7.

Kathia, still living with the children in the Swiss Alps, heard about the assassination from a family friend named Otto Lang. From her experience with the Austrian government before the war, she knew that any letter she wrote to Fritz would be intercepted and probably confiscated. Instead she wrote to Victor and Emma:

If I could be with you . . . perhaps it will still be possible. For now, go to him and tell him that we are strong and that that should be a consolation to him. Tell him also that I am with him as I was in the old days, and thank him for all the beauty that we have lived through together and for all the good that there is. Bring him this greeting and say that the children will grow up to be like him, and that he should be content with regard to the children. He has given us the best, now he should think only of what is imminent for him.

Not until October 28, a full week after the assassination, was Fritz allowed to answer Kathia's letter:

FRITZ

My dearest Kathinka,

Finally I have a pen and paper and the first letter that I shall write is of course to you. That I think of you, of the children, and of Mama and everyone else in Zurich, you know without my writing. Today the only message is that things are fine here in every way. I am bearing up under the stay here better than expected: physically I am in fine condition, my appetite is excellent, I fall asleep easily and I sleep better than in the best of times. My heart condition, you will have peace of mind to hear, is altogether normal, and my general health is at least as good. There is no hint of any nervousness; on the contrary, I feel an extraordinary contentedness and peace of mind which in general I seldom, and in wartime never, have felt. I have been reading, with the greatest of pleasure, Riehls' *Der philosophische Kritizismus*, which for a long time I have been saving for a moment of peace and quiet. You should also read it sometime. Also I have been reading *Faust, Hamlet,* and a few novels, so that I do not miss the newspapers (which I have not seen for a full week) at all. Father has been here twice, and yesterday he was here with mother. He is rather confused that I have not at all lost my composure and that I am so often in a mood for joking. I believe that you can understand me better, as I am sure that you understand this whole thing, that you will remain the all-understanding one that you have always been. I received your greeting and I was overjoyed that we have such empathy with one another. About the thing itself, as long as I am here, I dare not write. . . . I would give anything to see you, but we must be prudent and keep our heads up. Kiss the children, whom I will write as soon as I can, give Mama a warm greeting and greet all our friends and acquaintances. And the most heartfelt kiss from

Your Fritz

From scanty information and a fertile imagination Kathia had already pieced together an elaborate version of Fritz's relationship with Sophie. She and Fritz easily convinced themselves, in a rather formal correspondence, that the difficulty of travel made a visit to Vienna by Kathia impossible for the time.

What troubled Fritz in jail was not family but the outcome of his act in the political situation of Vienna and the empire. Would the party and the public understand what he had done and why he had done it? Would the party leaders realize the necessity of taking up the cause of immediate peace and a rededication to the goals of the social revolution? Would the public take up his cry and demand an end to absolutism in Austria and the war in Europe? With no newspapers and no visitors except immediate family, Fritz had no source for the answers to these questions except his mother and father. At each visit he begged them for political news.

To Fritz's chagrin, his mother and father had no time to discuss politics when they visited him in jail. Their main concern seemed to be his health, and the only terms they ever used to discuss the assassination (or the "case" as they were already calling it) were pathological. It was as though they were no longer political people, but only a mother and father.

Emma tried to be stoic about what had happened, and somehow she managed to sleep at night. She viewed the episode with a kind of Old Testament self-righteousness. What Fritz had done was another plague that had befallen the family, another curse that Emma could accept, but could never understand or forgive. She had lost one daughter in an institution, one son was weak-minded, now her eldest son had committed a murder. The sentence for murder was death by hanging. And so Emma would look at Fritz, shake her head, and weep.

Her visits so distressed Fritz that he wrote her a long letter to explain himself:

Dear Mother,

Yesterday, as you were here for the visit, I again had the feeling that you see my whole situation and everything that concerns me very differently from what it actually is. . . .

FRITZ

You regard me as unfortunate, which I am not and have never been in my life. My life might naturally have taken a completely different course, but I am not at all distressed that it came out as it did. To me it was never the length, but the content of life that mattered. And I am completely satisfied with mine, with the way it has been used. Man can live but one life and must decide many times. I perhaps might have been very successful in theoretical epistemology, and it is clear to me that this study might have fulfilled my whole life and made my entire life happy. But I felt it as the highest duty to work in the movement, and I have given up my studies for six years with complete clarity of conscience. I was and am convinced that everything which can be discovered there—as fascinating as it is for the researcher—can wait for that later time when a more fortunate society can clarify and discover things. This "sacrifice" of my purely scientific interests is not to say that I accept my party activities only as a "duty" or that I have not always been happy to perform them. On the contrary, I have always been at my work with every passion and enthusiasm, which has enabled me to work as I do. . . . Man cannot experience every possibility, but of those I have experienced, I am fully content. I was never an "unfortunate" man, rather, the words of Lynkeus

> *Ihr glücklichen Augen,*
> *Was je ihr gesehn,*
> *Es sei, wie es wolle,*
> *Es war doch so schön!**

for me were always the most living reality. I have gone through much that is difficult in life, and actually, since we

---

* From *Faust*, Part II, Act v, 1. 11300 f.
You blessèd eyes,
What you saw everywhere,
Be it as it may,
It was, oh, so fair!

---

were children, my life has always been at the decisive moment. I never knew whether I would make it over the next material or psychological snag, and always I held it as possible that my life would run aground. But I also knew always that I never wavered a hair's breadth from the pattern of life as I understood it, that I would always search out the best of all conditions for it. Whatever happened throughout these years, in the final instance I was always satisfied, because I always knew that it was the best that was possible. It is probably superfluous to ask what might have happened "if . . . ," but I know for sure that there was little that I wanted which did not happen. . . . Above all it has been that way with Kathia. Whatever difficulties might come along, she was always the highest thing that I could ever know. I can imagine nothing else in my life and never for an instant wished that it had been otherwise. She was always everything to me that a person can ever be to another person, and we have always understood each other completely in every meaningful matter.

In your explanations you are always quick to seize upon pathology and I see now intimations of what you must think that you would search out such explanations. There cannot be a quarrel over this, but I hope that the time will come when you will accept me as a healthy person. . . . At least I have not the slightest symptom of regret. That does not mean, however, that I have not sensed the painfulness of your lot. I have learned to understand you better in the last two years than ever before, and I have loved you more than when you could not always see my raw externals. I also know all too well that you have nameless difficulties which you must bear. But I cannot commiserate with you or pity you for my sake. "A man's will is his Kingdom of Heaven," they say, and they are not wrong. Whoever follows his will, whether he lives or dies, is not to be pitied. On the contrary. In these times things go badly for most mothers with sons. But anyone whose son follows *his own* will, who goes into the war on account of *his own* conviction, is far less to be pitied—even when the sons have fallen—than those whose sons become sacrifices without knowing why and what for. Life is not the highest good—of that I have always been truly convinced. For me, grasping-for-life has always been directly unsympathetic. On this my opinion is neither depression nor pathology, but simple reality. To live seriously and to die serenely is all that a man can really wish for. This fortune I have in full measure and thus there is no ground on which to pity me or to be sad. On the contrary, the only thing which I would truly want is that you would accept my destiny with peace and strength, without sentimentality and exaggeration of any kind—as I have. I know that to want that of you is the most difficult and painful of all. In spite of everything I beg you as your loving son,

Fritz

There was little else Fritz could say or write to his mother. And while he could hope that she would somehow understand what he had done and why, it was from his father that he really expected the understanding that had been denied him for two and a half years. Victor, for Fritz, had always been the model of the political man, the one man who could always understand a situation, no matter how complex. And now, after Fritz had "proved" the validity of what he had been arguing for these two long years, after he had demonstrated to the world that the situation in Austria could be changed and should be changed, he expected his father to understand, to follow his reasoning and arguments with sympathy if not with complete agreement. If he could not convince Victor, could he really expect to convince other party leaders and the public?

Every effort of explanation met a wall of incomprehension. To Victor the only possible explanation for Fritz's act was psycho-pathological, and every argument Fritz offered seemed to confirm Victor's opinion. Even Fritz's apparent euphoria, his light and almost joking mood, which he insisted was proof that he fully accepted the consequences of his act, seemed to Victor a pathological symptom. Why else would a man who was almost certainly going to be sentenced to death be in a joking mood?

From the end of October, Victor began to spend almost all of his time on preparations for Fritz's defense. He first hired two distinguished lawyers, Dr. Gustav Harpner and Dr. Sigmund Popper. Harpner was an eminent barrister who had often defended the Social Democratic party and various members, including Victor, in civil and criminal (political) proceedings. Popper was less well known, but he was a personal friend of Fritz's, and Victor hoped that his participation in the case might assure Fritz's cooperation with the defense. To supply the lawyers with psychiatric material, Victor dug up his old psychiatry texts, many of which he had not looked at for forty years. Within weeks he would write to friends like Kautsky that he was "immersed" in the texts. It left him little energy for regular party activities.

Fritz rejected his father's ideas about the defense completely. When he found that his father not only would not or could not understand his motives for the assassination, but also would not abandon the idea of a defense on the grounds of insanity, Fritz did all he could to thwart his father's preparations. As a regular part of the pretrial investigation procedure the court ordered a psychiatric examination to determine whether the accused was competent to stand trial. With ease Fritz convinced the examiners that he was quite able to stand trial. They were not eager to prove otherwise.

Victor then requested that the court convene a faculty medical commission, hoping that their findings would confirm his own diagnosis and thus be admissible as evidence for the defense at the trial. Most of the psychiatrists from the university were close to Victor's age, and many had gone through the same psychiatric curriculum at the university as he had. Victor thus had every reason to believe that they would share his views.

FRITZ

The central question of forensic psychiatry is the dispute between environmental and hereditary factors in the causation of mental disorders. Before the 1870s the idea that criminal insanity could be hereditary was shocking in many circles, since it implied that an individual might not be "accountable" for his actions. Then, beginning in Vienna in the 1870s, when Victor was a star pupil and First Resident in the psychiatric clinic of Theodor Meynert, the psychiatrists and the courts began to recognize the concept of inherited criminal psychopathic personalities. Gradually the idea spread to courts in other countries, until by the mid-1880s the concept was well established in European courts.

The question remained moot, however. By the turn of the century, most American courts were still reluctant to accept the concept of heredity in psychiatric testimony. Meanwhile, psychiatrists in Austria and other European countries were beginning to come full circle. Although Vienna had slipped from the vanguard of psychiatry to some rather conservative positions ("Vienna did all it could to take no part in the development of psychoanalysis," wrote Sigmund Freud, who was still unrecognized in the official circles of Vienna psychiatry), there were many experts there who by the first decades of the twentieth century were leaning toward the idea that heredity could do little more than weaken a patient or perhaps predispose him to mental illness. Moreover, it was difficult to predict the temperament of the public or the courts in cases of political assassination. Many infamous political assassins have been given the crudest caricatures of trials as the courts gratuitously waived normal procedures and criteria in the wave of widespread public hysteria which often accompanies the trials.

Fritz's trial was set for May 1917, mainly to give the psychiatrists from the University of Vienna time to interview the accused and to formulate their expert judgment. When he realized that his case would not be decided within two weeks, and that the immediate response to the assassination had apparently been nil,

Fritz shifted his hopes from the immediate situation to the trial. At the trial he would have the opportunity to air his views on the war, the party, and the people. The infamy of the case was sure to attract public attention, even if the government tried to censor all news of the trial. Events between November and May were sure to change enough to prove that he had not been wrong. Perhaps the changes would not be immediate, but people were sure to begin to understand the situation of the war and of the absolutism under which Austria lived. Then his explanations in the trial would fall on ready ears.

Meanwhile, Fritz had almost seven months to wile away in the Vienna city jail. It was the first time in twelve years that he had time to think, with no pressure of articles to write, administrative chores, party meetings, or lectures. The food in jail was mediocre, the cell small and dark, the only fresh air a daily walk in the enclosed courtyard. But Fritz had never been overly sensitive to physical comforts. Indeed, for the true scholastic, the monastery is a kind of paradise.

Fritz's link with the outside world was Sophie. He began writing to Sophie and her children the first week, and the messages he could not squeeze into double entendres he put into an illegal correspondence that the lawyers would smuggle out to a secretary and thence to Sophie. Sophie willingly defied Victor's orders to help Fritz with his defense and with his work by sending the books and articles which he requested.

No visitors except family and the lawyers were allowed, but when Sophie got the idea that she wanted to see Fritz, she went to the warden and explained how she and Fritz had met when they were sick and at the same spa. Although in a slip of the tongue she said *Strafanstalt* (jail) instead of *Kuranstalt* (spa), the warden was affected enough by the story and the combination of persistence and feminine wile to allow a visit.

Sophie thought Fritz would be as overjoyed as she when they met in the little visiting room. In fact, he was so embarrassed to be seen unshaven and in his prison clothes that they said almost nothing for ten minutes until, to Fritz's relief, the guard ended the visit.

In the solitude of his cell, Fritz turned back to the philosophical and mathematical problems he had been working on in 1904—as if the twelve-year hiatus in politics had never occurred. Much had been written since he first worked on the theories of Mach and Ostwald, but with nothing to distract him, not even daily news, and with plenty of books sent by Sophie and allowed by the guards, Fritz set to work. His only interruptions were the occasional visits of his parents, the lawyers, and the psychiatrists. Otherwise he was alone with his books. It was not long before he was so engrossed in his studies that he complained to his father that there were not enough hours in the day for his work.

It is said that men never think more clearly than in the moment before their death. For Fritz there was a six-month interlude before the trial and the sentence of death by hanging he was sure would follow. It was a long "moment," but Fritz was convinced that in the quiet and solitude of his cell he could think more clearly than at any point in his career.

In 1905 Fritz's schoolmate Albert Einstein had unobtrusively published a treatise on the Special Theory of Relativity that revolutionized the work in the field of the epistemology of physics. The theory was followed with other new work, culminating in Einstein's General Theory of Relativity of 1916. Fritz worked hard with the new materials, and with texts of Ernst Mach's lectures at the university, using his talmudic concentration to wade through pages of very difficult theory. By mid-February his concentration had paid off with an extraordinary discovery. As he described it in a letter to Kathia:

. . . I woke Saturday with the solution to a tiny problem which has bothered me for more than a year, namely the

Foucoult pendulum problem. In the course of working through the consequences of my little insight I have arrived at a generalization about the Newtonian principles—an elementary law which until now has simply been overlooked.

He did not elaborate the discovery in that letter, except to say that it was a "decisive critique of the relativity theories of Mach and Einstein."

In a letter to Victor and Emma, Fritz described the new discovery in a little more detail. It was a new system of basic laws which could replace the old Newtonian system of mechanics. "What Mach searched for, I have found. . . . Like all great discoveries," he explained, it was simple, yet pregnant with consequences. His pen would not write fast enough to get it all down on paper.

Although Fritz and Victor still disagreed sharply on the question of the assassination and Fritz's defense at the forthcoming trial, Fritz's new discovery greatly pleased his father. "He is passionately engrossed now in his studies of epistemology and Machism," Victor wrote to Karl Kautsky. "He believes he has made a discovery, which I am going to rely to Professor Einstein for his final opinion."

Victor sent a manuscript of Fritz's work not only to Einstein, whom he had met in 1911 when Fritz brought him home for a visit, but also to several other renowned physicists. With the manuscript he sent a covering letter asking whether the discovery had any validity, or whether it could be used as additional evidence to show that Fritz was deranged.

Victor's letter and the manuscript put many people in a compromising position. The physicists who received it had known and admired Fritz for many years, and as Einstein's friend Philipp Frank put it, to say that the theory was the work of a madman "would necessarily be highly insulting to the author, since he believed that he had accomplished an excellent scientific achievement. Moreover, speaking objectively, there was nothing in any way abnormal about it except that his arguments were wrong."

The physicists avoided the dilemma by delaying their reaction to the manuscript until after the trial. But Einstein was too much of a friend not to respond to Fritz's situation in some way. On April 13, 1917, he sent a postcard from Berlin to Dr. Fritz Adler, Alserstrasse 1, Vienna. (It was typical of Einstein's tact that he would use the street address instead of writing Vienna City Jail.)

Dear Adler,

Hopefully you have received my message. I want to ask you for something special: When your case is brought to court I would like to appear as a witness. Would you propose this? Don't think the idea senseless: The testimony of witnesses must not only make the circumstances of the episode clear, but must also shed light on the personality of the perpetrator.

A postscript came closer to what Fritz wanted to hear:

How much I would like to discuss the theory of relativity with you! Hopefully this can take place afterward. I am curious about your exposition. . . . With best wishes, I am your
A. Einstein

Neither the trial appearance nor the discussion could be arranged, and Fritz continued to work on the elaboration of his new theory without the benefit of professional opinion. In his science, as in his politics, he had become increasingly oblivious to the criticism of colleagues.

Sometimes Fritz thought about the trial. In April 1917, one month before the trial, he got the idea that he might not have the freedom to say all that he wanted in the courtroom. To assure that the world got his message, he wrote a fifty-six-page letter to

Sophie with the explanation that he wanted to be sure his motives were in good hands. Harpner and Victor intercepted the letter because they feared that it might present circumstantial proof of Fritz's sanity. "It might contain a bomb!" Harpner said. Victor did not open the letter, but he delayed its delivery to Sophie until after Fritz's trial, when the contents no longer mattered.

16

The Old Gentleman
and the New

By the beginning of November 1916 it became increasingly obvious that Emperor Franz Josef, already sixteen years past the scriptural allotment of three score and ten, was nearing the end. For two and a half grueling years he had followed the fighting, trying to the very end to maintain a hold on his faltering empire. He harbored few illusions about the war. "This struggle is beyond our strength," he mourned in the second year of the war, and in July 1916 he remarked in private what no one would admit in public: "Things are going badly for us, perhaps worse than we expect. The starving people cannot stand much more. It remains to be seen whether we shall get through the next winter. I mean to end the war next spring, whatever happens. I cannot let my realm go to helpless ruin."

Through the weeks of November, Austrians kept a daily death watch on the only ruler most of them had ever known. The Emperor, the press would report daily, was eating sparingly, drinking a little wine, and still smoking his customary cigar as he toiled away on public papers. Despite his steadily worsening bronchial catarrh, the Emperor still rose at four o'clock, still dressed in an old blue uniform, still worked at his desk from early morning to late evening.

On November 21, exactly one month after the assassination of Count Stürgkh, the Emperor rose early as a matter of habit and set about his duties. After a few hours he grew fatigued. At first he asked that an armchair be placed at his worktable; later, gasping for breath, he was placed in bed. "Wake me at four-thirty, as usual," he called to his valet. "I am not finished with my work." Falling into a coma, the Emperor received extreme unction from the court chaplain and died at nine in the evening.

A special edition of the *Wiener Zeitung* announcing the demise of the ruler was soon selling on the streets. In the midst of a cold and depressing winter the news brought surprisingly little reaction. Late that night Josef Redlich recorded impressions in his omniscient diary: "The whole town is surrounded by a deep and intense tiredness; neither sorrow for the dead ruler, nor joy over his successor, can be felt."

The funeral arrangements were left to the venerable Grand Master of the court, Prince Alfred Montenuovo, and that wrinkled old stickler saw to it that every detail of the pageantry of Habsburg tradition was honored. For six days the body lay in state at Schönbrunn Palace. Then a funeral procession led by the great imperial hearse, pulled by eight huge black horses, their hoofs muffled with rubber shoes, wound its way to the Hofburg—preceded, flanked, and followed by hundreds of mounted torchbearers in a cavalcade which included life guards in medieval costume, soldiers in modern military equipage, ministers of state, and imposing dignitaries in exotic carriages. Thousands of curious Viennese lined the streets to watch the procession. Few knew it was the last time so much European royalty would be gathered in Vienna, but the sight of the kings of Bulgaria, Bavaria, and Saxony, the Crown Prince of Germany, the heir to the throne of Turkey, the Crown Prince of Sweden—in all there were over one hundred royal personages—was enough to convince many that they were witnessing much more than the passing of a man. The great age of security, already the world of yesterday for many, passed by in that procession. Without the Old Gentleman, without the awesome dignity which he represented, the empire and Europe would never be the same.

For three days, while the body lay in state in the Hofburg, the public filed by for a last look at the man who for so long had ruled over the ramshackle realm. In the chapel Masses droned on without halt; twice daily the bells of the city rang out in melancholy lament. Finally, on November 30, a brief service of consecration was said in St. Stephen's Cathedral, and the procession wound its way to the Church of the Capuchins which contained the family crypt of the dynasty. There Montenuovo followed the ancient ritual to the letter. Banging twice on the door with his staff he demanded admission.

From within the Guardian Father, as though taken unaware, boomed in a sepulchral tone: "Who is there?"

"His Majesty, the most sovereign Emperor, Franz Josef."

"I know him not."

"The Emperor of Austria and the Apostolic King of Hungary."

"I know him not."

After a third knock of the staff, the Guardian Father boomed out again: "Who demands to enter?"

"A man of sin, our brother Franz Josef."

With that reply the door was opened and the coffin was carried to its final resting place in the subterranean crypt.

When the door closed, the attentions of the empire shifted to the three figures who marched at the head of the funeral procession—the new monarch, Karl, his consort, Zita, and four-year-old Crown Prince Otto, who presumably would one day rule over the strangest realm in Europe.

For many a young progressive in the empire the accession of Karl was like the coming of spring after a very long and hard winter. The younger brother of Franz Ferdinand was kindly, if somewhat nervous in his behavior. He had pursued a rather democratic education, including a short spell at the Schottengymnasium (where Victor Adler had been graduated). He was well read, especially in history, and he had a fair acquaintance with the many languages of the empire. His first proclamation, after extolling the virtues and achievements of his august predecessor, promised that he would do everything in his power "to put an end to the horrors and sacrifices of the war at the earliest possible moment, and to restore the sadly-missed blessings of peace to my peoples." Even before his accession, Karl had let it be known that he would spend a bare minimum of time with paperwork, and would concentrate instead on familiarizing himself with, as he put it, "all sorts of men." That he did, conferring with spokesmen of the nationalities, with socialists and industrialists, with intellectuals and ministers of state, with anyone in fact who had views to offer. His flexibility was a relief to many in the empire, for whom Franz Josef had always been the aloof and distant Emperor, secluded away in his Spartan study and oblivious to all but his inner circle of advisers. Yet there was a danger that Karl was too flexible, for without a firm idea of his own policies he could easily become the pawn of successive pressure groups who would buffet him to and fro.

Karl began with a grand shuffle of personnel. Since he was planning to depend on his bureaucrats to supervise the daily administration of war and government, he needed people who were his appointments. Prime Minister Körber, the experienced oldtimer whom Franz Josef had named as his final appointment, was replaced by a prominent Bohemian aristocrat, Count Henry Clam-

Martinic. Supposedly he would be able to rally public opinion among the now openly dissident Czechs. The doddering Montenuovo, the final caretaker of old traditions, was supplanted as Court Manager by Prince Conrad Hohenlohe, who was reputed to have a sense for democratic ideas. In the other ministries and in the Supreme Command, Karl shuffled personnel around carefully, though nowhere near enough to stop the grinding gears of the bureaucracy from turning in the usual way.

Then, with his new officials, Karl set out to fulfill his promise by making peace. He thoroughly distrusted the Germans, not from the haughty pride that kept Franz Josef a notch above the parvenus in Berlin, but from a simple fear that Germany would absorb the Habsburg realm through the Mitteleuropa schemes which everyone discussed so freely. He was so reluctant to see his empire dragged into the grandiose schemes of the Germans that, unlike Franz Josef, he was willing to seek a separate peace, even if it meant leaving the German allies in the lurch.

Yet the Germans were not easily bypassed. In December 1916 the policy makers in Berlin shared Karl's desires for peace. Although the Austrian forces had been no more successful in the ninth battle of the Isonzo on the Italian front than in the previous eight, on every other front the Austro-German forces were flush with victories. Romania was finished and awaiting complete occupation; Russia, Serbia, Montenegro, and Albania were all apparently out of the war; and on the Western front, the horrid war of attrition at Verdun was going as well as could be expected. The situation seemed perfect for an overture of peace.

The reelection of Woodrow Wilson on a platform of continued United States neutrality in the war provided the opportunity for a long series of offers and counter-offers by the various belligerents. In a Senate speech Wilson called for the famous formula of "peace without victory" to settle the war. But peace without victory would not satisfy the policy makers of the Wilhelmstrasse or the War Ministry in Berlin any more than it would satisfy Britain or France. Austria and Russia were exhausted enough to beg for any peace, but Germany decreed that the only acceptable conclusion to the war effort of the Central Powers would be a "just peace," which meant nothing less than a German peace. Since the Allied powers were unwilling to concede what the Germans demanded (at the very least considerable extension of German power in Eastern Europe and the subjugation of Belgium as an economic "client" of Germany), the highest military and civil officials in Germany met to consider another way out of the impasse.

The problem was difficult, for while the German armies were victorious on all of the Eastern fronts, they were nowhere near a decisive victory in the West, and from all forecasts it did not seem possible for the German armies to triumph over the combined Anglo-French forces in the near future, even if large numbers of troops could be brought to France from the East. Meanwhile, Germany and Austria were increasingly feeling the effects of the strangulating English blockade, and as starvation set in among sectors of the civilian population which sorely lacked grain and other imports, there were fears that the war effort might collapse. The German military experts argued that there was only one way that the English could be brought to their knees, and that was if the submarines could be used to enforce a comparable blockade on England by sinking all ships bound for the British isles. Without steady supplies from the United States, the generals argued, the English would be forced into starvation in months. "By the fall," said Secretary of State Karl Hilferich, "the island kingdom will sprawl like a fish in the reeds and beg for peace." Other civilian officials pointed out that unlimited submarine warfare would almost certainly bring the United States into the war on the Entente side. "From a military point of view America is as nothing," rejoined Foreign Secretary Arthur Zimmerman. Even if the United States could raise an army, which he doubted, they could not transport it to Europe through the U-boat defenses.

On January 8, 1917, the fateful decision was made to proceed with unlimited submarine warfare. A delegation was later dispatched to Vienna to explain the decision to Karl and his officials. Most of the Austrians were firmly against the idea, fearing that the entry of the United States would make a separate peace with the Russians impossible and doom the Austrians to follow the Germans to an uncertain and terrible end. But as Foreign Minister Czernin lamented in his reminiscences: "We knew that Germany had definitely made up her mind to start the unrestricted campaign and that therefore all our arguments could have no practical value." In fact, even before the conference in Vienna, the German government had sent a note to Washington announcing that unlimited submarine warfare would commence on February 1. Angry beyond words when informed that the U-boats had already been posted to battle stations, Karl protested bitterly. The protest went unanswered. Finally Karl pitifully wired Wilhelm that they must jointly trust in the help of the Almighty.

For a while it seemed as though the Germans would not need the Almighty as an ally. Although the United States severed relations with the Central Powers on February 3, it was not until two months later, after the sinking of the *Lusitania,* that President Wilson addressed the Senate to call for a declaration of war against Germany. By then the U-boats were sinking more tonnage than even the most optimistic naval experts had predicted. In April alone 875,000 tons of shipping were torpedoed to the bottom.

Because Wilson still hoped that the conflict with Austria-Hungary could be mediated, and because none of the U-boats in the Atlantic flew the Habsburg standard, it was technically possible to postpone a declaration of war between the United States and Austria-Hungary for eight months after the declaration of war against Germany. But simply avoiding a wider war was not enough to fulfill Karl's promises to his subjects. That Germany alone might suffer the consequences of the submarine warfare

campaign was a partial consolation, but to begin negotiations for a
separate peace Karl determined to use channels which would not
be subject to German meddling.

In March 1917 the Emperor contacted his brother-in-law,
Prince Sixtus of Bourbon, who was serving in the Belgian army,
and invited him to make a secret visit to Vienna. Using the Prince
as a secret courier, Karl made overtures to the Allied powers, even
going so far as to promise that he would use his influence to
support "the just French claims relative to Alsace-Lorraine"—in
other words, that he would compromise his German ally.

Simultaneously, with the urging of Foreign Minister Czernin, the leaders of the Social Democratic party were informed that
they could attend the international socialist conference on peace
that was scheduled for the end of May 1917 in Stockholm. Representatives of almost all the warring powers were scheduled to be
at the conference, and there was a possibility that the loyal Social
Democrats would be able to serve their government in arranging
some negotiations.

With two peace feelers out, Karl and his officials waited
for the slow returns. Even though they saw no real signs, they
hoped for a possible turning point in the war.

Change came slowly in the Social Democratic party, even
after it was given new responsibilities of dealing for the government. At the beginning of November there had been another all-
party conference, only a few weeks after the assassination. The
speeches and debates went through the usual rhetoric, concluding
with Victor Adler's resolution on "The Proletarian and Peace":

> . . . the international unity of the proletarian will be stronger,
> surer, and clearer after the war than before. Fear not, you
> who call yourselves the "Left," that the class struggle will be
> mislaid by us. On the contrary, our entire endeavor must be
> to remain the fighters for the class struggle, until it is kindled

again, and until the struggle is taken up again by our side, in the old forms and in new forms, and with renewed strength.

It is probably fortunate that Fritz did not hear the speech, for it was the same line the party had followed for two years. Action was still left for the vague future, after some miracle ended the war, when the same miracle would somehow grant gains to the workers. As in the Second International, Marxist logic, with all its strange convolutions, was still the substitute for direct action.

On the day after the conference, November 5, one thousand workers met in a rally to hear speeches by the leaders of the socialist parties of Austria, Germany, and Hungary. Pernerstorfer's speech characterized the changed situation: "This is the first time in twenty-seven months that there has been a public meeting where men could speak freely." He was right, but the Stürgkh System still outlived its founder, for all reports of the rally were censored in the newspapers.

For the soldiers at the front and the people who manned the home front—for those who knew no more of politics than what they read in censored newspapers or what they heard in constant spurious rumors, which seemed to nourish more than food—the winter of 1916–1917 was cold and hard and long. Food was more scarce than ever, transport was all but nonexistent, wounded and sick were everywhere, and morale was abysmal. By March attitudes were summed up in the sign an anonymous fatalistic philosopher hoisted over a trench somewhere on the Eastern front. "Do not be angry, only wonder," the sign read. For many, it was all they could do.

Then March brought the surprise everyone awaited. It came from the least expected direction. On March 8 large-scale strikes and riots broke out in Petrograd (the name had been changed from St. Petersburg at the beginning of the war). A provisional government was established March 12, and on the ides of March the Tsar abdicated for himself and his son in favor of his brother, who in turn abdicated in favor of the provisional government.

The provisional government announced to the world that it planned to continue the war aginst the Central Powers in concert with its allies until they reached a "victorious end," but even so there was a vast change in the situation in Central Europe. For even as it proclaimed its intention of prosecuting the war, the provisional government announced a series of decrees which called for the granting of full civic liberties to all citizens and the independence of Poland, Finland, and Estonia. They also announced a proposed program of social reforms, including the distribution of land among the peasantry.

The news leaked only slowly into Austria and Germany, but even the scanty rumors of March were electrifying. And as the first reports of the revolution in Russia reached the Vienna newspapers, Austrian soldiers at the front began to hear rumors about the other development of the revolution—the efforts of the Petrograd Soviet of Workers and Soldiers, which even in mid-March had become a rival of the provisional government. While the provisional government called for the continuation of the war, the Soviet issued the famous Order Number One, depriving all officers of authority and entrusting the administration of the army to committees by both men and officers. Through an efficient propaganda network the Soviet denounced the war plans of the provisional government, calling instead for a "general democratic peace," without annexations or indemnities. The provisional government issued a long series of counter-orders to nullify the decrees of the Soviet, but to soldiers and civilians who were exhausted with almost three years of war, promises could not equal peace.

In Austria the downfall of the Tsar meant that the biggest reason for fighting the war—the defense of the cherry orchards and the acacia-shaded beer gardens of the Vienna woods against the Tsarist hordes—was meaningless. Now, instead of death and destruction, the East seemed the promise of peace. Against that promise the Austrian government could offer not milk and honey, but pittances of black bread, scarce mouthfuls of bad mutton (which Austrians have always hated), and tobacco that smelled and tasted of beech leaves. The news quickly set off a clamor for reforms, especially for an easing of the harsh military regime in the cities. No one yet cried out for what was really needed—peace.

In Austria, too, at least some of the authorities realized that the revolution in Russia meant almost certain changes for Austria. In a public address the Emperor said that what had happened in Russia proved that the whole range of Austro-Hungarian public affairs had to be infused with a democratic flavor. And the changes came. First an imperial ordinance revised labor conditions in the war industries. Then the big step. Despite strong opposition from the German nationalists and the military authorities, Karl issued an imperial rescript announcing that parliament would reconvene at the end of May.

How far Austria had slipped from the world of democratic nations could be measured by the steps required to prepare the parliament building. After two years as a military hospital, the building had to be cleared of patients and beds, cleansed, painted, and shined—just to receive the same body that had been prorogued three years before. And after almost three years of war and the death of the Old Gentleman, no one could predict what the new parliament would do, whether they would simply legitimize the government which had been carrying on since proroguement, or whether they would try to institute badly needed and long-postponed reforms. Nor could the rumors of Vienna decide whether the Emperor and his ministers would allow real reform during a war.

In the midst of rumors and speculation, Austria waited. Early April brought the declaration of war against Germany by the United States. The middle of April brought Lenin's long train ride across Germany and his portentous arrival at the Finland Station in Petrograd. May brought Kerensky's desperate efforts to rally the Russian armies.

May also brought the attentions of much of the world back to Austria, for on May 18, 1917, Friedrich Adler went on trial for the murder of Prime Minister Count Karl Stürgkh, in the first public trial of a political criminal in Austria since the outbreak of the war. To accommodate the large audiences that were expected, the trial had been scheduled for the largest courtroom in Vienna, the Jury Trial Room of the Vienna courthouse.

17

Friedrich Adler *v.* Austria

The opening of a criminal trial can be a very dramatic event. The law demands only that justice seem to be done in a trial, but tradition and public instinct insist upon much more, for trials must serve the function once assumed by public executions. Indeed, the trial is often expected to evoke the passions of a tragedy, as if the criminal act could be purged only in a catharsis of pity and fear. Thus the courtroom becomes a stage, the lawyers and judges appear in costumes, and everyone is expected to follow the stylized gestures and formalized speech that convention prescribes. And as in all good theater, reality is intensified by the rituals of the mummers' fiction.

The most familiar form of this drama is the adversary trials of British and American courts. In the Anglo-American legal tradition, which derives from the ancient Germanic rituals of trial by combat, the courtroom is an arena of contest and disputation. The lawyers of the prosecution and the defense elicit evidence in a verbal duel of examination and cross-examination, argument and counter-argument, using every weapon in a vast arsenal limited only by the rules of evidence. Even with the subtle refereeing of the judge, the clash of personality and sympathy often raises passions that are not wanting in comparison with the knightly jousts of the medieval predecessors. Finally, when the contest has brought out the "truth," a verdict by the judge or jury declares a victor between the lawyers who have championed the contestants, and the defendant is either condemned or acquitted.

By contrast, the inquisitorial procedures of most European courts can seem sinister. Their method, which is derived from Roman law and canonical procedure, substitutes an inquest for the contest of the adversarial trial. The results of a preliminary inquiry are summarized in the indictment; other evidence is submitted in prepared briefs. Then, with the evidence before them, the court begins its inquiry by questioning the accused and other witnesses. There is little cross-examination and almost no clash of the lawyers. Instead, the subtle prodding of the court is expected to somehow evoke the "truth" which justice demands. The drama of the trial thus is a drama of revelation. Audience and participants watch with conflicting emotions of fear, joy, and horror as the court plunges deeper and deeper into the dark secrets of the case. When the facts are finally in the open, the lawyers enter their pleas on the basis of the evidence before the court, and the court renders a judgment (instead of a verdict) which decides the fate of the accused.

The trial of Friedrich Adler was ideal for the stage. The characters included important and noble figures, the roles were prepared and learned well, and there was much that could be revealed in dramatic surprises and turns of plot. To please the critics the drama even offered the innovation of Sophocles: instead of two main characters there would be three—the state, the defense, and the accused himself, who was by no means willing to accept a second billing.

Most important of all, the drama opened to a highly receptive public. For almost three years Vienna had been forced to substitute the drama of war for the drama of the stage. Food shortages and other hardships could be dismissed with the lines of *Die Fledermaus*:

> *Glücklich ist,*
> *Wer vergisst,*
> *Was doch nicht,*
> *Zu ändern ist.**

Theater Vienna would always need.

"The matter before the court is the case against Doctor Friedrich Adler for the crime of murder." It was nine forty-five when the court recorder raised the curtain on the drama. He faced a courtroom that had been filled since the doors opened at nine. The crowd outside had been so large that even those with special tickets, including the press, had waited in long lines to get through the doors. Hundreds who were left outside remained there after the doors closed, hoping to hear the proceedings through the windows of the courtroom.

The six robed judges, all distinguished jurists from important courts of the empire, sat on the raised dais behind the recorder. *Hofrat* Dr. von Heidt, a Vice President of the Court of Assizes, was the presiding officer or President, as he is called in Austrian courts. In front of the dais, the lawyers sat at the counsel tables on either side of the aisle: State Prosecutor *Hofrat* Dr. von

---

* Happy is he who forgets what cannot be changed.

Höpler with his assistants on one side, and Drs. Gustav Harpner and Sigmund Popper, the defense counsels, on the other side. The defendant sat next to them.

Fritz was wearing his good suit (the one he had worn the day of the assassination). His clothes were clean and pressed, his grooming unusually careful. To the correspondent of the *Neue Freie Presse* he looked like a "typical man of letters." Before the proceedings began Fritz turned around in his chair and carefully scanned the faces that filled the gallery and the stalls. As one reporter described it, Fritz seemed to stop and stare at every face. His powerful eyes, outlined by the little gold-rimmed glasses, seemed to put every person in the room on trial. Everything about him radiated confidence, from his careful gestures to the obviously prepared sheaf of papers in his hand. With seven months to study the script, he had learned his part well.

The galleries were filled to the last row. Kathia, who had come to Vienna especially for the trial, was there. Sophie was also there. (They did not meet.) In the last row of the gallery Paul Lazarsfeld sat with his friends, admirers of Fritz Adler who sympathized with the program of the old Karl Marx Association. This trial was the biggest event of the war for them.

The courtroom was so warm and fetid in the sultry May weather that the tall windows which looked out onto the street had been opened, and the audience inside could hear the agitated crowd outside. When those in the street finally quieted down, they discovered that they could hear the proceedings within almost as well as if they had been in the galleries. Hundreds remained there all day.

On the side of the courtroom opposite the windows was the jury box—empty. Although it had not been used for almost three years, no one had bothered to remove the rows of chairs, the only empty seats in the crowded courtroom.

Before the indictment was read, the defense introduced a motion questioning the competence of the court as a special tribunal, that is, as a court without a jury. Harpner argued that it had been unconstitutional for the Emperor and the ministries to use the powers of Paragraph Fourteen of the constitution (the emergency powers clause) to suspend the right of jury trial. Since the only valid trial would be a jury trial, he argued, the court should disqualify itself from trying this case.

Höpler, for the prosecution, did not deign to answer the defense argument. Instead he reminded the court that the trial was taking place in the middle of a war. Certain expediencies, he said, were essential. Rhetorically he asked what would happen if every court in Austria were to question the constitutionality of imperial decrees.

The judges left the room to deliberate on the motion. Apparently the dilemma of ruling on their own competence did not trouble them, for within minutes they returned and the President announced their decision: "The court has decided to affirm its competence as an exceptional tribunal. Will the recorder please read the indictment?"

By Austrian standards the indictment was mercifully short and straightforward. The prosecution missed none of the details Fritz had so willingly revealed in pretrial interrogation: how he had considered the idea of an assassination as far back as January 1915; how he had made careful preparations for the murder, including the purchase of an illegal gun which he smuggled into Austria; how he had methodically narrowed the choice of a victim to Count Stürgkh; how he had planned the date and time of the murder on the basis of his knowledge that Count Stürgkh lunched every day at the Hotel Meissl & Schadn. From the confession of the accused alone, the indictment argued, the facts showed a clear case of premeditated murder, to be punished according to the law by the sentence of hanging.

Dismissing Fritz's avowed political ideals in a sentence, the indictment argued that the murder was obviously the act of an anarchist:

FRITZ

Friedrich Adler denies that he is an anarchist "in the old sense." His goals may be different from those of the anarchists, but in his views of what is allowed as means, he is certainly one with the anarchists of the old school. Whether anarchist, anarcho-socialist, or Social Revolutionary is the correct label for the accused is beyond the reach of this court. But the reprehensibility of murder as a political means cannot be a subject for debate among moral men in an orderly society.

A brief biographical sketch stressed Fritz's long exile from Austria and the fact that not until 1911, at the age of thirty-two, did he decide to work in the labor movement. His estrangement from the Social Democratic party at the outbreak of the war was thus a natural consequence of his development:

To his painful surprise he found that in Austria, as in the German empire, that natural feeling of being part of a Fatherland, with which every man is born, casts away in the first charge whatever internationalism he might hang onto by a thread. When the general will rallied all forces in defense of the Fatherland, smoothing over all political differences, it was incomprehensible to him, since he had lost all feeling for the Fatherland in years of exile. It is thus not surprising that he has taken up all the slogans of the enemy press about Austria, that he has willingly and uncritically taken as his own the lies and misrepresentations of the enemy propaganda.

Quoting Fritz's own pretrial testimony, the indictment showed that he was a completely isolated figure in the Social Democratic party, that his views were so abhorrent to his party colleagues that he was viewed as a "party traitor." His deed, thus, was the act of a frustrated and lonely outcast:

. . . the defendant came to the compelling and inexorable realization that his political career had run its course; that he

220

had become contemptible to his supporters, tolerated in the organization only because of his personal relationships; that people had ceased to pay any attention to this outcast, indeed, even to take him seriously. That which he had mistakenly considered his life work was fully and irrevocably wrecked. Even from his absurd perspective, with the illusions of an armchair revolutionary, he saw himself directly menaced; his words calling for a great revolution would remain only words, the deeds to realize these goals would never come. If Friedrich Adler, as another political gesture, would argue that his deed was the act of a fighter for freedom who has coolly and deliberately followed through with the conclusion of his convictions, then he has given himself up to a cruel self-deception.

Two forces have worked together in equal strength to bring him to his criminal decision. Not his political delusions alone but also, with equal power, the consciousness of political failure have consolidated his thought of a powerful deed into the commission of a murder. The man who has lost his goal yearns for a good exit. But what appeared to him as political heroism was in the final instance only the desperate end to a life which even he saw as useless and worthless.

When the indictment had been read, von Heidt leaned over the bench to ask the telling question of the trial: "Herr Doctor Friedrich Adler, please step forward. Do you plead guilty?"

For seven months Fritz had waited for that question. He had planned and prepared, indeed, his act itself had been committed all for the purpose of answering that one question. Standing so that the audience and the court could see and hear him, Fritz answered loudly and precisely: *"I am guilty to the same degree as every officer who has killed in a war or who has given the order to kill—no less and no more!"*

That one sentence turned the trial topsy-turvy. Until then the trial had been for a simple case of murder, a case where the court had the task of deciding the straightforward question of "guilty" or "not guilty." But for Fritz, guilt or innocence was not the central issue of the trial. The real question was whether his act had been justified, and the answer to that question required a trial of the whole ruling class of Austria, the men who had made the war and the men who perpetuated the war. If they were "guilty," then Fritz's act was, in his terms, justified, and while he could still be convicted and sentenced, he would have made his point to the court and the world.

There was no tradition of civil disobedience in Austria, and no history of men who had defied laws which in conscience they considered bad in order to call attention to the inequity or injustice of the law. What Fritz proposed demanded even more toleration from a court, for he had purposely broken a law which he fully accepted and acknowledged. He had murdered, not to challenge the law against murder, but to have his day in court, to use the courtroom as a podium from which he could address Austria and the world. There was certainly no provision in the law for what Fritz proposed to do with his trial.

It remained to be seen whether the court would permit Fritz's tactic. Would von Heidt allow testimony and argument on the policies of the Austrian government? Would he allow testimony that was obviously political, that was linked only tenuously with the facts of the case, and that was irrelevant to the questions of fact and law which were within the competence of the court? Tradition in the Austrian courts indicated that he would not, but von Heidt was not a traditional judge. Widely admired as one of the fairest members of the bench in the empire, he had the distinction of being praised even by critics of justice in Austria for his moderation and his impeccable judicial record. If anyone in Austria could guarantee a fair trial, it was thought, it would be von Heidt.

When the murmurs in the courtroom subsided, von Heidt

asked Harpner: "Are you ready to present your own version of the facts of the case?"

It was customary for defense counsel to respond to that question, but Fritz, still standing, took up his thick sheaf of notes, walked to the middle of the courtroom, and addressed the bench. As he began, the crowds outside pressed toward the windows, and the audience in the galleries hushed.

Fritz started with the delicate task of dissociating himself from his own counsel. Even before the assassination, he said, he had known that there would be some people who would try to explain his act by saying that he was insane. He could understand that his own counsel would use that argument because in the circumstances it was the only chance, and a slim one at that, of getting him off with his life. Still he argued, he had no choice but to reject that defense:

> The defense counsel, from the responsibilities of his office, has the duty of seeking to save my life. I have the duty of standing up for my beliefs, which are more important to me than whether during this war in Austria one more man will be hanged or not. For me there is a much more earnest and deeper question than that with which the defense counsel is concerned.

Indeed, Fritz continued, since it was not to be expected that the court would render any verdict except guilty or any sentence except death by hanging, he had no intention of contesting the verdict. ". . . as long as you are willing to hear me out," he addressed the bench, "I beg you to believe that I will not say one word to dissuade you from the sentence you will undoubtedly return as a special tribunal." With a jury trial, Fritz suggested, he might expect a different verdict. But of course there were no longer any jury trials in Austria.

Fritz shifted quickly to the question of war government in

Austria. His trick was to turn the phrases of the murder indictment around, to use the assumptions of the prosecutor's case as a foundation for attacks on the political and social situation in Austria. The facts of the indictment he did not contest. It was the assertions which the indictment had slipped out almost casually that Fritz picked up.

The indictment had argued that "the reprehensibility of murder as a political means cannot be a subject for debate among moral men in an orderly society." Fritz agreed. But, he qualified, "the assumption that must be tested here is whether we live in an orderly society." And what better test for that was there than the state of justice in Austria. With a sweeping gesture toward the empty jury box Fritz reminded the court that if he indeed belonged in that room because he had violated the law, the law also compelled them to remember the name and true purpose of the room. It was the Jury Trial Room, the room where juries were supposed to hear criminal proceedings and proceedings for crimes like treason, lese majesty, disturbances of the public order—in short, all of the political crimes which for almost three years had been tried in secretive summary proceedings by special tribunals acting under the direction of the military authorities. Was this clear violation of the constitution an indication that Austria was an orderly society?

Even before the declaration of war against Serbia, Fritz continued, "the declaration of war against the people of Austria had been decreed, it had been agreed that the constitution was to be regarded as a scrap of paper, it had been decided with full conscience and without a sham of modesty to run rampant over all that was law and justice in Austria." Using the rhetoric of Mark Anthony ("I will not discuss . . ." "I have no time to list . . .") Fritz catalogued the sins of the government and the illegality of the acts committed under the umbrella authority of Paragraph Fourteen of the constitution.

Where the lawyers had failed, Fritz was not likely to succeed, but his rhetoric had a fervor lacking in the dry constitutional arguments of the lawyers. For Fritz the question of the competence of the court went beyond the narrow issue of law to a matter of conscience:

> Gentlemen! You will say to me and have already said: That is an imperial edict and we, the court, have no possibility of testing it since an imperial edict carries "provisional power of law." But I have a rather broader interpretation of this question than the defense counsel. I believe that every man, as a citizen, must ask himself whether he can take part in an undertaking which he—from his own knowledge of the law —knows to be against the constitution, which he knows to be breaking the law.

As individuals, Fritz went on, the judges surely knew that this tribunal was unconstitutional. Yet, in the security of the deliberation chamber, they collectively decided to confer upon themselves the right to judge the case and the right to mete out the sentence of death which would surely follow in this case.

Fritz admitted that he had no choice but to accommodate himself to the force of the armed police who brought him to trial. If he resisted, the court could and would send more police. But he would not concede the court a shred of legitimacy: "I will declare at the outset that I do not see an institution of law in this court, that I see not an organ of justice, but rather an organ of an illegal government."

This attack on the court prompted the first of many interruptions and admonitions by the President of the court. Over and over during Fritz's long speech, whenever he began to single out individuals or specific institutions, von Heidt would politely but firmly punctuate the proceedings with a warning: "From now on I must ask you to moderate yourself . . ." or ". . . that is a personal attack, which is not in order, and which is not necessary to your defense. You know the limits exactly, you realize exactly as well the moment when you have crossed them." To the surprise of almost everyone in the courtroom, the limits were extremely generous. Several times von Heidt assured Fritz that he would not "limit his freedom of speech." He kept his word.

Von Heidt was in the difficult position of presiding at two simultaneous trials. The first was the case against Friedrich Adler for murder, a simple and straightforward case in which the facts were scarcely contested. The second was the volatile case that Fritz was building against the government, a case decidedly beyond the competence of the court as a tribunal, but one that nonetheless presented a difficult choice for the President of the court. And in the latter Fritz was presenting his case to the grand jury of the galleries and the street, which was subject to every persuasive trick of rhetoric. Fritz had only to hint, to insinuate, and the crowd would know what he was driving at. At the same time there was no one to "answer" the charges he made, and no way in which von Heidt could instruct the "jury" to disregard various allegations as being "inadmissible evidence," unless he were to forbid Fritz from testifying. Yet if von Heidt were to do this, it would appear to the public that justice was not being done; in fact, it would appear to prove everything Fritz was arguing about the state of justice in Austria.

Von Heidt chose to be lenient. Only when Fritz strayed so far from the facts of the case that no connection at all was apparent, or when the tone and direction of Fritz's rhetoric seemed to expand beyond the courtroom, would von Heidt admonish him. The warnings were simple reminders: "Speak here, to the court, not out the windows!" or "You have gone too far . . ." After each admonition Fritz would return to the attack, qualifying his remarks just enough to circumvent the limits von Heidt had set. Usually he had already made his point, whether by accusation or insinuation ("I need hardly go into the present record of . . ."). It was rarely necessary to press the argument.

Step by step Fritz turned the government case around,

picking up threads of the indictment to weave his own indictment of the government of Austria. The indictment had said that murder as a political means could not be discussed in an orderly society. Austria, he demonstrated, was not an orderly society. Thus: ". . . there was an absolute justification for my deed, in my eyes, as a citizen. The ministries had torn the constitution to shreds, had abandoned it in order to take over the law in Austria. There remained no other way but the way of force."

Did a citizen have the right to commit an act of force?

> . . . every citizen not only has the right to force, according to my beliefs, he has the duty to stand up at the moment when the last resorts of the constitution fail, when there is no parliament, when all the guarantees of law which we have known have been set aside. Only a people who have completely gone to the dogs, who have lost all consciousness of citizenship, would let this befall them. It cannot therefore be a question of rights; it is a duty. It can only be asked— and this is the most important matter I will discuss here— whether it [the act of force] serves the desired end . . .

As he spoke Fritz stalked back and forth across the front of the courtroom, waving his papers or an outstretched finger at the bench or the empty jury box to make his emphatic points. Until censured he would direct his remarks to the windows or the audience, which followed him with rapt attention. By mid-afternoon the crowd in the street had grown large enough to alarm the police.

The indictment asserted that because of his prolonged residence abroad Fritz had "lost that natural feeling of being part of a Fatherland, with which every man is born," in short, that he was an "anti-patrict."

Indeed, Fritz answered, he was not a patriot. Nor was anyone else in Austria—until the outbreak of the war. The uniqueness of Austria as a state, its strength and its weakness, was that it had always been a multinational state, where the often mutually exclusive demands of the different nationalities had to be balanced to preserve the political unity of the whole. When the Social Democrats had refused to become involved in the contest of the nationalities they were sarcastically branded "Imperial and Royal Social Democrats" by the fervent German, Czech, Italian, and Polish nationalists. Only the dynasty and the bureaucrats had supported the state as a whole, and they had always met determined opposition from the nationalities at every juncture, especially when "patriotism" had been used as the justification for some act or other.

It was the war, and the imperialistic schemes of world, or at least European domination that had inspired the new patriotism, Fritz argued. It was not a patriotism of national defense, but a fervent chauvinism which government propagandists had manufactured to "test" the loyalties of subject peoples. Before the war, nationalities, in accord with the idea of the multinational state, were encouraged to exercise and enjoy certain freedoms. When war came the only freedom was to die for Austria, to wage an endless and murderous war for the benefit of the great industrial interests who would try to build a super-empire "from Berlin to Bagdad."

If this is what is meant by patriotism, Fritz continued, he was not a patriot and would never call himself a patriot.

I do not say that I am enthusiastic about being Austrian. Rather, I consider it a fate which one must bear. It is all the more a fate when Austria has a Count Stürgkh and a mass of officials who declare: It cannot be otherwise, Austria is a multinational state, doomed to live under absolutism. I will tell you the plain truth: To live forever in an absolutist state is no enticing thought for a civilized man.

Only von Heidt's periodic interruptions and an hour break for lunch broke up Fritz's speech. And after more than three hours on his feet, neither his vigor nor his voice seemed to weaken.

The prosecution had asserted that Fritz was politically isolated, without followers even in his own party; that his views were so ridiculous that he was completely alone; and finally, that this isolation prompted his desperate act. Fritz conceded that when the indictment was drawn up, six months before the trial, the first contention might have been right. His views then were the views of a silenced minority, and to advocate internationalism, to protest absolutism, to question the violations of the constitution, to talk of revolution in a country where freedom of speech did not exist —all this was to speak to deaf ears. But what had happened since? he asked. What had happened since those fateful bullets were fired in October?

For one, Fritz answered, his internationalism was no longer an isolated position. Now, even the Foreign Minister seemed to share his view, and even as he spoke the leaders of the Social Democratic party, at the behest of the Foreign Ministry, were preparing to leave for Stockholm to attend an international conference.

Our party comrades go to Stockholm not because they have remained internationalists throughout the war, not because they have remained true to the idea of the International; rather, the Chairmen of the Executive Committees of the pro-government socialist parties in Germany and Austria are going to Stockholm today as the *commis voyageurs* of the Foreign Office. Gentlemen! The minority in Austria, which has become tiny and resigned in this land, where men are allowed no freedom of speech . . . will not be represented in Stockholm. However, that there will be talk of the Austrian minority in Stockholm will be guaranteed by your sentence. The true greetings from Austria to the Stockholm conference and, at the same time, the true enlightenment about Austria will be the death sentence which you . . .

FRITZ

Fritz had gone too far. "Do not speak to the windows," von Heidt interrupted. "That has nothing to do with the explanation of your deed."

Fritz dropped the argument. He had made his point, there were other tacks to take. At the time of the assassination he had shouted "Down with tyranny! We want peace!" No one, apparently, had heard him, for in the pretrial testimony none of the witnesses recalled hearing those words. However, Fritz went on,

> . . . the shots they heard . . . I wanted to demonstrate for a peace without reparations or annexations. If I had said that seven months ago in this room, I would have been labeled a fool. Today I cannot be ignored so easily, because peace without reparations or annexations is quickly becoming an item of business in all political circles.

The third point about his isolation was simple. On October 21 one could hear almost nothing about the constitution or about violations of the constitution by the Stürgkh government. Now parliament was reconvened for May 30.

Fritz's final remarks on the question of his isolation were the most subtle and far-reaching. *"All my life I have been a revolutionary,"* he proclaimed, "and I have always viewed day-to-day politics as a means to the revolution and never *revolution* as a phrase of day-to-day politics. . . . seven months ago, in the majority of the public I would have been laughed at as a man foolish enough to speak of revolution in the midst of a war." And yet, he went on, the Russian revolution is being celebrated in newspapers of every political persuasion. "To be sure, as it has always been in Austria, even before the war, they are excited about freedom—abroad. The *Neue Freie Presse* and every other liberal paper is all for Democracy, Freedom, and the Rights of Man in France or anywhere abroad." No one was really discussing revolution for Austria yet, he conceded, "but the concept of revolutionary tactics is again on the daily agenda." That alone justified his deed.

Before he went too far, Fritz dropped the subject of his alleged isolation to move to another area of the indictment, the characterization of the milieu that had shaped his political values. The problem, he explained rather solicitously, was that his values were so foreign to the court that they could perhaps never understand him. It was like Copernicus or Galileo trying to argue that the earth was not at the center of the universe.

> In the beginning, people said: Anyone who explains that the "immovable" earth moves is a madman. As the Copernicans adamantly stood by their convictions, they were accused of attacking the most sacred of traditions—or as the State Prosecutor would put it, the "natural feelings with which every man is born." Thus Galileo was called before the court of the Inquisition, which followed exactly the rituals which this court executes [Von Heidt, interrupting: "Must that be so?"], and tried.

Two hundred years later, Fritz continued, the Copernican viewpoint was universally accepted, and no one could even understand the old Ptolemaic version. Now, in the age of relativity, men know that depending upon the viewpoint, both explanations were valid. From the earth it does indeed appear that the sun and stars move, while from the sun it would be the earth that appeared to move. (This was the same basic argument he had used in his first successful scientific article, the critique of Ostwald which had earned the praise of Ernst Mach.)

The views of Copernicus and Ptolemy, Fritz argued, were as different as those of the court and his own. And if the court would understand him, he beseeched, they must understand the world "not as usual, from the *basis of struggles between peoples* . . . but from the *basis of the struggle between classes*." Carefully and precisely Fritz elaborated the basic ideas of his Marxism, summing up the difference between his view and that of the judges in a single choice:

FRITZ

. . . just as one cannot stand at the same time both on the earth and on the sun, as one must choose between those two viewpoints, so too one cannot maintain at the same time the *standpoint of national unity of the different classes* and the standpoint of the *international unity* of a single class. There too one must choose.

Thus, Fritz pointed out, for someone of his views war between Austria and Russia, or between Germany and England, was senseless slaughter. He was not a defeatist, he was not in favor of a victory of Russia or England over Austria or Germany. To him there was little significance in the choice of whether England or Germany was to rule the world. The only possible benefit of the war between nations was that it might awaken thousands or hundreds of thousands of people to the truth about the imperialist absurdity of bourgeois wars. The futility of wars of conquest might accentuate the consciousness of the proletariat which was paying for the war in sweat, tears, and blood.

The same antinomy between national unity and international solidarity, he explained, was at the core of his break with the Social Democratic party. He had always stood by the concept of the international solidarity of the working class; he had always believed in a revolutionary class struggle with the ruling classes in all states; and those positions had been the viewpoint of the Social Democrats in all countries before the war. But with the coming of the war, the leaders of the Social Democratic parties had given up their internationalism to rally to the defense of their own states, to take up a position of unity with all of the other classes within Austria in order to make war against the fellow workers of other nations. With another of his history lectures, Fritz showed how the party had violated its own antiwar resolutions and how the positions the party had taken and rationalized were signs of the cowardice and hypocrisy of the leadership of the party. Before the war, he recalled, the meetings of the Social Democrats used to end with the shout, "Long Live the International Revolutionary Social Democracy!" After almost three years of war, during which the party had uttered not a single word to protest the aggression policies of the government, the party had not only lost its revolutionary direction, it had become an organ of tacit support for the government.

> I have become convinced in the years of the war [Fritz said] that a revolution in Austria certainly could take place only against the leadership of the [Social Democratic] party, that the Executive Committee of the party has actually become an organ to suppress the revolutionary movement.

So far had the leaders turned from the idea of revolution, he explained, that Karl Renner wrote articles in 1916 calling all discussion of revolution "putsch and hullabaloo." The party leaders had convinced themselves that the war, which might result in a greater Austria, was in fact the revolution for which the Social Democrats had been waiting and working. When Social Democrats had turned to the service of absolutism and wars of annexation, Fritz said, there was no choice for him but to split with the party and somehow to demonstrate the falseness of the party's politics.

This was why he had assassinated Count Stürgkh. Not, as the State Prosecutor asserted, because he was a lonely outcast in the party, not because he had deluded himself into thinking that his act would somehow prompt a massive uprising of the people of Austria. Only if he could demonstrate the effectiveness of action, Fritz said, could he negate and obliterate the false excuses that the party had given throughout the war. "We cannot risk it," the party leadership had argued when the idea of revolution was mentioned. "Violent action is impossible, violent action cannot be." Since he fired those shots, those excuses will no longer stand. "They will no longer believe their excuses," he concluded, "and that was my goal, that was the goal for which I have staked my life . . ."

FRITZ

After another one-hour break, at three o'clock, Fritz picked up again where he had left off, on the subject of individual acts and the effectiveness of an individual act as a revolutionary tactic. Speaking to the assertions of the indictment, he argued that he did not want to be a hero through his act. It was not the deed itself that deserved attention, but the consequences of the deed, the proof that even in Austria things could change.

After a harsh exchange with von Heidt, during which the President accused him of trying to incite agitation in the courtroom, Fritz told the long story of how in the course of the war he had tried to tell the truth about the Austrian war government and had met with the determined opposition of the censors, which was to be expected, and of his own party, which was not expected. From his position as party Secretary, he related, he had been able to see how censorship functioned in Austria. He had seen how men were interned or jailed or even executed for printing lines like "I didn't raise my boy to be a soldier." He told of political trials, where twenty-six death sentences and prison terms totaling nine hundred years had been handed down. He told of journalists who had been interned after summary proceedings because they had written mild criticisms of the government, or soldiers who had been shot for a casual quip in a letter home.

But those [Fritz continued] are only individual cases, which have only in their entirety brought me to this position. The most important foundation for all these things and situations is that for two and one-half years no one in Austria has known who ruled; no authorities admitted that they ruled. If you went to a minister with a grievance the answer was: "That is certainly a matter for my department, but go to Stürgkh, he has all these matters under hand, we cannot intervene." If you went to Stürgkh, he would say, "That is a matter for the military." It was a completely opaque system of competences and incompetences.

234

Fritz explained how Stürgkh had built up his own position, how although he too had been a pawn at the beginning of the war, by the fall of 1916 he so controlled the reins of power that he could not only forbid any discussion of the question of parliament but could even forbid parliamentary leaders from seeing the Emperor. Stürgkh, he said,

> . . . was not a man of the politics of *fortwursteln*. . . . He was a man, who with clear intent and conscience wanted to transform Austria into an absolutist state, and who with a clear course and a steady hand steered for that goal. . . . He was an opponent whom one had to notice, and with whom one had to battle relentlessly . . .

After a final warning by von Heidt that his testimony should be confined to the period up to the assassination and not venture into the future, Fritz quickly sketched his final break with the party—explaining such events as the sale of the bread factory which the indictment had not mentioned. Then he concluded:

> One can never know for sure, of course, what effect an act has had, since there is no way to compare with what might have happened otherwise. But I can say on the whole that I have never regretted this deed, and that I have always been convinced that it was a useful act, that I have accomplished all that an individual could accomplish. That is very little, the act of any individual is a small achievement, but I believe that I have accomplished all that one can accomplish with his life, and I am content to have used my life in this way.

With interruptions the speech had lasted a little more than six hours.

18

Austria *v.* Friedrich Adler

Von Heidt began the questioning of the accused. Because he was determined to guarantee the fairest possible trial in the explosive circumstances, or perhaps because he had begun to take a personal interest in the case of the fanatically sincere man who stood before him, von Heidt asked questions that seemed slanted to build a case for the defense. He was scrupulous in the unprecedented courtesy he extended to Fritz, whom he always addressed by his full title, Herr Doctor Adler.

Fritz parried every question that had no political value, and when he did answer a question, such as a query about his impressions of his father's criminal record, he would turn his answer into an attack on the court or a critique of Austria:

The sentences which were given to my father made a very strong impression on me. The last political trial that took place before a special tribunal in Vienna [before the war] was against my father, when he was exactly as old as I am now, that is in 1889. . . . Since then my convictions about special tribunals have remained the same. I have gotten to know this building very well, and I walk now in the same court where my father walked.

Von Heidt was probably amazed that an accused man would go so far out of his way to secure his own conviction.

Von Heidt asked whether Fritz had any thoughts about his family which might have dissuaded him from the assassination. Fritz shook his head in the midst of the question, then answered:

I am being asked whether the thought of my family was not an inhibition. During the interrogation I put an answer to that very succinctly in a letter to my father, which—I believe —has been introduced in evidence.* I told him that it was perhaps a moot question whether the assassination was historically expedient, but that the idea that historical deeds can only be performed by childless orphans was for me not a matter for discussion. It is a fact that in war, in which I too live, every man, when he falls in the field, is ripped away from his family, and the whole family is brought into misfortune, ground down under the wheels of fate. It is the same in the struggle that the Social Democrats must wage. To me that was always self-evident. Never have I thought that my father had done us an injustice—the idea was completely foreign to me, and it has only occurred to me with this question that he in fact sacrificed his fortune to the party. For me that was always self-evident . . .

State Prosecutor Höpler, who followed the President of the court in the questioning, did not share von Heidt's sympathies for the accused. His task was to prove Fritz guilty of a treasonous and premeditated murder, and every question he asked was intended

---

* He probably meant the long letter to his mother, which was later introduced as evidence by Harpner.

to prove the heinous assertions of the indictment about Fritz's politics and motives. He began with questions about Fritz's views of the idea of mobilizing the proletariat against the war, apparently in an effort to prove subtly what Fritz would have readily admitted—that he was a revolutionary. Fritz would carefully explain the different remarks Höpler quoted from the pretrial interrogation, replacing them in the contexts from which Höpler had plucked them, and using the opportunity to amplify theoretical views that he had not articulated in his six-hour speech.

When that tack failed, Höpler drove at Fritz's alleged heroics: "In the interrogation you said that it occurred to you that your deed would not remain a local incident."

Fritz answered: "Yes, I hoped that the world would speak of what happened in Austria; I wanted it to be impossible for things to be hushed up . . ." With that introduction Fritz launched another attack on the censorship in Austria, and Höpler, realizing he was getting nowhere, turned the questioning over to Harpner, the defense counsel.

Harpner began almost apologetically: "I beg you, Herr Accused, not to think immediately that I have the intention of setting you up as insane. I will make clear now, that will not be the case. You can answer me with the same openness as you would answer anyone else." From these opening remarks it is hard to believe that this is the defense counsel questioning the accused.

Harpner continued: "You have said that in the deed, the thought of your father, mother, wife, and children played no role whatsoever, since you were of the belief that a person must above all fulfill his duty and that private interests cannot play any role. But one thing you could tell me: Have you loved your father?"

Fritz answered:

I have had the closest relationship with my father that I could have with anyone. I can perhaps express it this way— we have often spoken of this, and I have written it in many letters from Zurich—that I not only feel this way because he is my father, but also because he is the most exemplary man of the party. Because he is such an exemplary man, he has been my best friend. I stand as close to him as to my wife. With regard to my ideals and my political convictions, both are the closest people to me.

Harpner tried many of the same questions which von Heidt had asked, whether Fritz had qualms before he fired the shots, or incidents in his youth: "You have told about a theater production which you saw at the age of ten, namely a performance of *William Tell*. Since then you have thought it was justified to kill an Austrian overseer."

It was not even a question, but Fritz answered patiently: "I have related in the interrogation when I was questioned about murder that the first theatrical production which I ever saw was *Tell*, and that since then I have never doubted that one could kill an Austrian overseer and that it could be morally justifiable."

It was one of the ironies of the trial that the questions of the defense counsel seemed to echo those of the prosecutor. Höpler had tried to show that Fritz was trying to revolutionize the masses, that he was a dangerous subversive. Harpner asked many of the same questions to try to show that Fritz was a deluded idealist. What neither of them understood, seemingly, was that Fritz was not at all interested in the trial of Friedrich Adler for murder, except where he could use the opportunity of that trial to indict the war crimes of the Austrian government and the Social Democratic party. After hours of questioning the accused, the court knew nothing more about the case against Friedrich Adler than they could have read in the briefs and the indictment in front of them. Indeed, the only revelation of Fritz's testimony was the bizarre workings of a trial in which the accused had turned prosecutor, the judges were trying to build a case for the defense, and the defense counsel was forced to treat his own client as a hostile witness.

Von Heidt then called up the other witnesses, beginning with the headwaiter at the Hotel Meissl & Schadn and Baron Franz von Aeherenthal, who had been sitting at Count Stürgkh's table at the time of the assassination. The testimony of both men on the assassination and the moments afterward agreed exactly with the version given in the indictment.

Then von Heidt called the witness for whom many in the courtroom had been waiting: "If you please, Herr Doctor Victor Adler."

The room was very quiet as Victor walked slowly to the witness stand. Old and ill, he hunched over as he walked. This was the man who for thirty years had led the socialist movement in Austria, the leader of the largest party in the empire, whose brilliant speeches had inspired praise even from his enemies. This was also the man whose son was on trial for the murder of the Prime Minister of Austria.

"You are the father of the accused?" asked von Heidt.

"Yes."

"It is my duty to inform you that you have the right to refuse to testify."

"I testified in the pretrial hearings, and I will testify now," Victor answered. "I am also ready to swear an oath."

Von Heidt began by asking about Fritz's psychological history.

Victor answered: "My son comes from a marriage and has a father who has much mental illness in his family. He was always a healthy but rather weak child and—I mention only those things which would be interesting for the court—from the beginning, from his youth I have had the fear that his nerves were not strong enough." Victor continued through the history of Fritz's schooling, emphasizing the fact that he had always tried to fight Fritz's tendency to study only "purely theoretical things." He told about the extraordinary success of Fritz's career in Switzerland, and the concentration which Fritz had put into everything he did. ". . . I ask to be excused if I praise the accused too much," he said, "but he is my son."

Always, Victor related, Fritz was almost fanatic in his concentration on his theoretical studies. He never drank, not even a glass of beer, he never smoked, he never joined student clubs. Even his friends were drawn only from the people with whom he could pursue his theoretical interests in all-night discussions. Nothing could distract him from his two passions—theoretical studies and the labor movement.

As he spoke of Fritz's psychological state, Victor's eyes welled up with tears. It is impossible to say whether he actually believed that Fritz had suffered a nervous breakdown, or whether he was only offering the idea to try to save the life of his son. For whatever reason it was a shattering experience for a father to have to relate that "as a father and as a physician the danger of a nervous breakdown seemed ever closer." He went on to tell how Fritz had abandoned physics for politics, how he had come to Vienna and worked far harder than any man should (". . . it was in his being—any work which needed to be done he did . . . day or night"). Predictably, Victor continued, Fritz's nerves were soon exhausted with the work, and the overload manifested itself in the form of repeated depressions and a heart condition. "I have no medical opinion to offer about this heart condition . . . but in any case the severe heart attacks always came in a very intimate connection with his nervous conditions."

When he came to the history of the outbreak of the war, Victor related the story of the conflicts father and son had gone through:

What the war was for the whole world, I need not tell the court, that you all know; but may it please the court to consider what the war was for us especially. I speak here not

as a member of the party, but as a man, who loved his son . . .
and who through the war suffered agonies so formative, so
personal, that I should say I saw my life itself before me.

Tears streamed down his face as he told of the effects of Fritz's
political and intellectual isolation within the party—how Fritz had
suffered more repeated depressions because of his conflicts with
others in the party.

As Victor gave his version of the war years, he ventured
tepid attacks against the government. Speaking of the period before the assassination, he said: "The air in Austria was unbearable." There was no parliament, no restraints upon a government
that had usurped the powers of every ministry, that had built
barriers around itself. He compared the situation unfavorably with
Russia, and while he was careful to indicate the futility of Fritz's
deed he pointed out the futility of being a true socialist under
those conditions.

Von Heidt asked if Victor had noticed any special nervousness in the period of the assassination itself.

> *Victor:* My son is a cool man. He expresses his ex-
> citement in a certain taciturnity and consternation, I would
> say. . . . In the last weeks, when we had party discussions, he
> was [aroused]; the agitated nature in both of us was aroused,
> unusually aroused.
>
> *Von Heidt:* Your political relationship to your son,
> then, was actually clouded by the political controversy?
>
> *Victor:* He was and is the most loved of people to
> me. What haven't we said to one another! But I have never
> taken a political opponent as a personal enemy. Why should
> I suddenly break with my best friend, just because he is of
> different opinions than I am?

Von Heidt asked a few more questions, specifics about the
possible future of Fritz's relationship with the party, before Associate Justice Ehrenreich took over: "Your son has characterized

himself as careful, sober, and cool. Is he perhaps more passionate and impulsive than he says?"

Victor: He is a sober, cool man, by his true nature he is a mathematician, and not a political man. Sober and cool, but if a mathematician draws his line, he believes in that line. He considers himself cool and sober; he is however consumed with inner passions without knowing it, and with the best of wills he tries to squelch it without being in a position to control himself. . . .

Ehrenreich: Would you say that he was especially ambitious? Had he ever said that he wanted to play a role in the party?

Victor: In no way. He always undertook anonymous work, ten times as much as anyone else knew. . . . [Victor and Ehrenreich sparred for a while with the words ambition and vanity, until Ehrenreich turned the witness over to Harpner.]

For Harpner, Victor was a friendly witness. They had probably rehearsed the questions a dozen times before the trial.

Harpner: . . . Had he ever done anything like that before?

Victor: Never! Never! Not only nothing like that, he was the most considerate child that I have ever come across, considerate toward his brothers and sisters—his sister who unfortunately is so ill, he watched over her like the apple of his eye—toward me and toward his mother he was the most considerate son and if he now . . . [Rehearsed or not, Victor was weeping as he spoke.] I can only say this, I would never have believed that such an excess of the mathematical was possible.

Harpner: One more question, Herr Doctor: I have inferred from the testimony that in the period before the assassination—I mean the months of September and October

—your son by chance concentrated the following functions in his own work. I ask you because you . . .

Victor: I was his boss.

Harpner (continuing): . . . as his boss must have known. According to the testimony, he was at that time party Secretary, and indeed, during the absense of Skaret, who worked with him, in September he was the only party Secretary. Then he edited *Kampf,* when it appeared, by himself, because Doctor Bauer was a prisoner of war.

Victor: Since Doctor Bauer was drafted, my son has edited *Kampf.*

Harpner: Then, according to the testimony, he gave lectures in various party assemblies.

Victor: Several times each week!

Harpner: Is it true that when you were in Nauheim— when was that?

Victor: Every year from the middle of July to the end of August or the beginning of September.

Harpner: . . . during this period he also took care of your correspondence?

Victor: He did everything, day and night.

Harpner: In your opinion, was he overworked?

Victor: He was very overworked. I do not know what the doctor might deduce from this, but it was impossible to wrest a single item of work away from him.

Harpner: He had taken on everything by himself?

Victor: He had taken on everything by himself.

After Victor's testimony, the court called Engelbert Pernerstorfer and Friedrich Austerlitz. Although each of them had been through sharp altercations with Fritz in the course of the war, both testified pretty much as Victor would have wanted.

Pernerstorfer: I am only a layman. I have no expertise in these things and my opinion would have no authority, but for me it is obvious that in carrying out this deed he could not have been in full capacity of his senses. Instead he must have been overcome by some kind of hallucinations.

Austerlitz: I cannot say he was agitated; I mean, everyone measures the excitement of someone else according to his own reactions. When I am excited I become very impassioned, I speak very strongly and I raise my voice. This was not the case. Instead I had the impression that something was wrong with the man. I can say that I had the impression that he suffered from some affliction, that something foreign was in him. Disturbed is not the right term.

The testimony of Pernerstorfer and Austerlitz, Harpner's introduction of two character references (from the Physics Society in Zurich and from a Professor Zanger of the Zurich Institute for Forensic Medicine), and the testimony of Ferdinand Skaret, which confirmed details of the conference the night before the assassination and Fritz's behavior on the morning of the assassination, lasted until nine o'clock in the evening, when President von Heidt recessed the proceedings until nine fifteen the following morning.

19

"The Proceeding Is Closed"

The crowds in the street before the doors of the court-house were opened on the second morning of the trial were even larger than on the first day. Outside, and before the judges trooped in, in the courtroom itself, the talk was of Fritz's six-hour speech. Nothing he had said was a singular or shocking revelation about the situation in Austria, but no one had ever put all of the evidence together before. No one had spoken in one breath of the policy of repression, the deprivations and hardships, and the futility of the war. Even in the censored reports of the newspapers Fritz's statements were the strongest total criticism of the war government in Austria since the outbreak of hostilities. For people who had only the beginning of another summer offensive and another hungry year to look forward to, there was much to talk about.

The second day of proceedings began with the reading of the depositions of twelve people who had been in the dining room of the Hotel Meissl & Schadn at the time of the assassination. All agreed in every detail with the facts presented in the indictment.

When the testimony had been read into the record, Fritz again pointed out that he in no way challenged any of the facts, the the indictment was correct even in the smallest details concerning the assassination itself. Yet, because the process of justice requires certain rituals, the court went on to question Fritz on those details. It was certainly the best way to confine the proceedings to the case of Friedrich Adler and to avoid a repetition of the long speech of the day before.

For the first time since the trial began, the testimony sounded like a typical criminal proceeding.

> *Von Heidt:* . . . is this the weapon you used for the assassination?
>
> *Fritz:* Yes.
>
> *Von Heidt:* When and where did you acquire this weapon?
>
> *Fritz:* I bought it in Zurich, at Easter 1915.
>
> *Von Heidt:* That is, at the time when you first . . .
>
> *Fritz:* When I first thought of an assassination.
>
> *Von Heidt:* Did you previously ever use a weapon?
>
> *Fritz:* I had never even held a weapon before.
>
> *Von Heidt:* Did you experiment with the gun?
>
> *Fritz:* I bought the gun in Zurich because I knew that automatic pistols were illegal in Austria and because I knew that it was a light and convenient gun and I had the opportunity to buy it. I was afraid that I might be conspicuous in a gun shop in Austria and that someone might recognize me. Since I was in Zurich and had the opportunity, I bought the gun and in the shop I had someone show me the workings, as is normally done. I am fairly handy with mechanical devices, and while I was there I fired three or four shots into a target.

If the judges did not have a transcript of pretrial testimony before them, the questions and answers might have been very revealing. As it was, they were no more than ritual, adding nothing to what the court already knew.

After Fritz was questioned on the details of the assassination, various other evidence was introduced. The rules of procedure require that any evidence that might be cited in closing pleas be included in the record of the trial. At the behest of the prosecution and the defense, the following items were read into the record: the results of the autopsy performed on Count Stürgkh, an affidavit of a ballistics expert confirming that the gun Fritz identified was in fact the gun that had fired the fatal bullets, the medical histories of several relatives of the accused, and the first letters Fritz had written to Kathia and Emma from his jail cell. It was not until the depositions of Karl Seitz, Wilhelm Ellenbogen, and Max Winter (who had testified on the party Executive Committee meeting of the night before the assassination) were introduced that Fritz made any objection. Their testimony included the damning description of how Fritz had been branded a "party traitor" at that meeting, and various comments about his "agitated state" during the meeting.

Fritz objected to the testimony in a long statement, admitting that he had been called a "party traitor," but challenging the characterizations that Seitz, Ellenbogen, and Winter had made of his mental state: "In short, it seems as though my mental capacity at that moment is being brought into question." In order to explain the situation correctly, Fritz said, he would have to explain the politics of the issues in question, lest they be misunderstood by the court.

> *Von Heidt:* In what sense do you believe they would be misunderstood?
> *Fritz:* That quite certainly my defense counsel will try to make a connection between this and the psychiatric testimony.
> *Harpner:* Impossible!
> *Von Heidt:* The gentlemen have testified about the

agitation they noted in you. I will not hinder you from testifying. However, since I see no connection with the deed or with the motives for that deed, it will be superfluous for you to speak of other individuals. It is out of the question that what has been read would be considered in the connection which you have suggested.

Harpner: The excitement on the afternoon had nothing to do with your psychiatric state. I will not make that contention.

Von Heidt: The question involved party details, which are not relevant here.

Fritz: I am forced, since the testimony of my witnesses was read into the record.

Von Heidt: Why? Since you are correct that if this meeting is the subject of testimony, you have the right to reply formally, I will not forbid you from testifying. But you must concentrate yourself, and make your point in a few sentences and clarify the situation . . .

Fritz had won. Again he was able to shift the trial from his own case to the political issues of Austria and the party, to the justification for his deed. He pressed the point:

Good. I believe I must say, however, that in fact the matter, if it is to be brought up, was significant in the state of my mind, and I would like to clarify exactly how that is so. For me the matter is a very deep one. I would like not to be stifled in clarifying this, since this is the last time I will ever have to speak. In fact, it concerns the following question. Already in 1915 the Executive Committee of the party had passed a resolution which said that members of parliament from the Social Democratic party should not be exempted from military service, that the party would not intercede on their behalf, and that Social Democratic delegates to the parliament had the duty to serve. Representative Seitz, who was a firm advocate of this viewpoint, argued that in taking this position the party was guarding its purity. . . . In a later session the resolution was revoked. Then a whole series of members of parliament were exempted from military service. The revocation of the resolution made a tremendous impression on me. I was appalled that men, who in word and speech were for the war, would then personally shirk serving in the war. This was the heart of the matter for me. I took the position: They are patriots, they are of a view which I did not accept—Good! But they must fully accept their views. They should not be for something in word and then personally shirk their duty. If they want war, they above all must join up. That was my position. Moreover, I took the same position with regard to my colleagues, the Left in the party, who were against the war from theoretical convictions —that they too should not be exempted from service, because it is beneath contempt to differentiate in such matters. If a people as a whole must go, then every individual has the duty to go. Thus I took no steps to hinder my own induction when it was time for me to go. And I see that my friend, the committeeman for the fifteenth district, Wistrazil, who was against the war, is now dead; the committeeman for the fifth district, who was against the war, is now dead; the son of labor union Secretary Huebner, who said that he would not shoot, is dead. Many who were against the war have fallen, while those who spoke and wrote in favor of the war have not gone. For me, as a member of the party, that was an insult to my honor. . . . Then it was I—I must speak of it—who in that meeting was called a "party traitor," and it was I . . .

Von Heidt interrupted: "On that matter you will not speak any further."

Fritz had made his point. The actions of the party and the very concept of patriotism in Austria were before the court and the grand jury of the gallery and the street. He had succeeded in contrasting his own absolute integrity with the hypocrisy and cowardice of the party leaders.

One other piece of evidence was introduced, a deposition by a Herr Albert, who had known Fritz in Switzerland and who described speeches Fritz had made condemning anarchism. His testimony had been introduced by Harpner to show that the assassination went against Fritz's most basic political values and was therefore the act of a man who, at least temporarily, had lost control of his senses.

Fritz objected:

> I would like to say just one word about the episodes in Switzerland: namely, that it is completely correct that I protested energetically when violent action was being considered, because there, the basic assumption was, as the State Prosecutor would have it, that there was "an orderly society." That was my struggle with the anarchists and the syndicalists, who said: The time will come when the bourgeoisie can no longer help and will turn against the workers; then we must turn to force. I answered: That is correct, but always *it must be the ruling class which starts with the force*. That was my theory. And I have remained true to that theory. I have advocated nothing in Switzerland which I have not advocated here. The difference is in the countries.

Fritz stopped before he was cut off by von Heidt. After a day and a half, he had learned the rules and limits.

In American and British courts, psychiatric testimony can be introduced by both the prosecution and the defense. Each side presents expert witnesses, which the other side usually tries to discredit or challenge by cross-examination or counter-testimony. The court then rules on the competence or incompetence, sanity or insanity of the defendant according to the prescribed rule of criminal insanity.

In European courts psychiatric testimony is usually entrusted to a special commission appointed by the court to investigate the matter and present its findings. The defense or the prosecution may take exception to the findings of this commission, and they often do. They may also present additional expert testimony to counteract or reinforce the findings of the commission. Usually though, the testimony of the court-appointed experts is very persuasive on the outcome of the case.

In Fritz's case the panel from the University of Vienna had spent six months interviewing the defendant and collating their findings. Before their testimony was read, von Heidt introduced a deposition by Professor Dr. Ludwig Braun, the physician who had treated Fritz for his heart condition since 1911. The deposition, which had been introduced at Fritz's behest, made the point that Fritz's heart condition, while it may have contributed to his depressed state at times, was a pure and simple affliction of the heart and not a product of any nervous disease. After the deposition was read, Fritz explained that the depression that accompanied his heart attacks was really caused by the thought that he might have to give up some of his political activities, and had no other significance. It was not, as the defense might argue, a psychiatric phenomenon.

The court recorder then read the report of the psychiatric commission. Their complete report, totaling sixty pages of material, went far beyond the purely psychological questions of the case to discuss the "validity" of Fritz's avowed motives. Even the twenty-one-page formal opinion read in the courtroom discussed the values of the accused as well as his psychiatric state:

> . . . even with all the damning criticism, we find nothing illusory in the motivation of the deed, and nothing which is not fully comprehensible from the given character of the accused and the given circumstances.
> . . . We must also recognize that the extraordinary

agitation of Adler in the last period [before the assassination] was not a cause of the deed, but a consequence of the decision to carry out the deed.

. . . He is, however, a fanatic, for whom the cause which he holds to be correct cannot be influenced by conventional considerations, and for whom the end, to which he has dedicated his life, sanctified all means.

. . . It is certain that such a fanatic, a man who is totally ruled by such a life goal, is quite distinct psychologically from the standard of normality. It is also certain, quite apart from the influence of circumstances, that Adler's severe psychopathological exhaustion was a factor in the makeup of his psychic identity. The fanatic and the madman are branches of the same stem. One must be careful, however, to place both in the proper social estimation and also in the correct sense of accountability. . . . Thus there are fanatics who have been capable of great cultural works. And from the ethical standpoint, Adler's deed is less objectionable, for example, than that of a man who to soothe his wounded love kills another in cold blood . . .

In conclusion the report pointed out Fritz's psycho-pathological heredity, his obsessive (fanatic) character, and his cyclothymic personality, which subjected him to repeated periods of depression. Nevertheless, the report ended, the assassination was committed in a manner and in circumstances that were perfectly comprehensible from the personality of the defendant, and not under the influence of an extreme psychic state. Fritz was not criminally insane.

Before the final pleas of the lawyers, von Heidt read out Fritz's previous criminal record, significant only by its very brevity —two minor convictions for violations of the press censorship. Then von Heidt said: "If there is no further evidence to be introduced, I declare the proceedings of evidence closed. The prosecutor may speak."*

Höpler's task was to represent the interests of the state, as he made clear in his opening remarks:

> May it please the court!
>
> The proceedings of this trial have called before us clear memories of an event which caused a legitimate sensation not only in our own country but also in the whole world, and which, for the many who hold the weal and woe of our state dear in their hearts, released great sorrow. In the difficult times through which we have lived and in which we still live, the question of whether the murder of Prime Minister Count Stürgkh has exposed us to new dangers, or whether our enemies . . . can use this event to build up the hopes of our inner weakness which they cherish, cannot be rejected. Even if these considerations should suddenly vanish, because it can so easily be established that it was the *individual act of an individual*, it would be no credit to the accused, who not only foresaw the danger to which the state would be subjected, but reflected upon it, indeed—I should say—*held it as his aim*.

As he spoke the crowd in the street, realizing that the trial was nearing its end, began to push its way into the courtroom. The chaos and commotion was soon loud enough to drown out Höpler's words.

"Quiet, I beg!" said von Heidt. "The guards shall see to it that the doors are not continuously opened and closed. No one else may enter the room. It is already too full."

Höpler went on with the details of the assassination. What-

---

* In American and British courts, where the burden of proof is on the prosecution, it is customary for the defense to proceed to summation first. In the inquest procedure of European courts, the accused is in effect presumed guilty, the burden of proof is on the defense, and it is the prosecutor who summarizes his case first.

ever the motives, he argued, the facts bespoke premeditated murder: "In a constitutional state, if a murder is proved, it is irrelevant to the question of guilt whether the murder spring from questions of jealousy, revenge, unrequited love, or perhaps political situations." Yet, he conceded, he would have to discuss the motives of the accused, even though he could scarcely bring himself to answer those arguments:

> I would not do so for this reason, because I could perhaps not control the indignation which I feel as an Austrian when I think of the torrent of blind, raging hatred which the accused poured out on Austria yesterday . . . in a time when, I believe, even the blackest pessimist should take pride in our course through these three terrible years, a course which has been led, from the lowest to the highest, in a true fulfillment of duty and self-sacrifice.

Because, as he saw it, Fritz's speech "was heard more by a tribunal of the people than in the courtroom, and would not stand the probe of legal questioning," Höpler agreed, at the peril of exploding his own indignation, to answer several of Fritz's arguments—in effect to serve as a defense counsel for the government of Austria.

Fritz had attacked the policy of mass execution and internment in the Galician provinces. Höpler answered with rhetorical questions:

> Does the defendant know nothing of the difficulties under which our troops had to fight in the early days of the war in Galicia? Has he heard nothing of the fact that Russian Tsarism flooded our country with spies who betrayed our troops so that hundreds and thousands were lost?

Fritz had questioned the policies of the Stürgkh government. Such questioning was irrelevant and inappropriate, answered Höpler. Speaking of the court, he said:

We must not arrogate to ourselves the right of representing the people, we must not transpose ourselves into the study like historical researchers, because we lack the means to deliver a sure verdict on the policies of Count Stürgkh, because the fundamental principles and assumptions upon which policies are built are wanting in this room.

Using the word *Fanatismus* which had been repeated throughout the psychiatric report, Höpler drew a sketch of Fritz's psychiatric development. Even before the outbreak of the war, he argued, "the child had already abandoned the world of ideas which was strange to him, which yielded him no understanding, which only confused, agitated, and infuriated the child." Lacking the "natural feeling of protection of his own herd in time of danger," Fritz at the outbreak of the war attacked even his own party colleagues, until he was completely alone in the world of his ridiculous ideas. Many of the phrases Höpler used in his summation were drawn verbatim from the indictment.

His final point dealt with Fritz's vanity and heroics, so clearly illustrated by the words which the court had used to censure the accused's speech: "Do not speak out the windows!" The speech, like the deed itself, or like the accused opening the back curtains of the automobile in the hope that the crowd might see him as he was driven from the scene of the crime, was intended to draw attention to a man who was a total failure in his life. And yet the psychiatric testimony showed that there was nothing insane in the motivations of the accused, nothing that could not be explained by his pathetic and confused personality. Therefore, Höpler concluded, the court had no choice but to render "a verdict of guilty and the appropriate sentence."

There had been no histrionics in Höpler's summation; there was no applause afterward. It was the same case he presented in the indictment at the opening of the trial, a simple case of premeditated murder made even more horrendous by the treasonous motives of the accused. The facts of the case supported him completely.

Harpner's defense plea was more complicated. He had presented little evidence in the trial, and as he recognized, the case was heavily against him.

He made his dilemma clear at the outset: "The defense is in the difficult position of fighting on several fronts: the first is the prosecution; the second appears to be—I say appears to be—the medical testimony; the third, the most distressing, is the client himself."

What Harpner hoped to prove, he assured Fritz and the court alike, was not that the assassination was the act of a madman, but that the accused "according to the word and spirit of the law, could not be legally responsible for what he had done." And this, he said, he would show by using the same evidence the prosecutor had picked into tiny pieces to show the responsibility of the accused.

Because his case was weak and sketchy, Harpner could not present a linear and logical argument. Instead he had to hop from point to point, picking at loose ends and using his extraordinary skill as a trial lawyer to weave a persuasive case from these loose threads. For facts he substituted the arguments of emotional rhetoric—a technique better suited to the jury trials in which he had established his legal reputation. The six seasoned judges on the tribunal were not likely to be overly persuaded by a rhetoric they had all heard too many times before.

With what right do I, a man who knows the law, take amiss what Doctor Adler has already proclaimed from the witness stand [Harpner asked]? With what right do I expect from this court that which I might not even expect from a jury—*the acquittal of a confessed killer? Yet I expect just that, I plead for it, I wish for it, and I would welcome it. I* will show you why. My motives go much deeper than the superficial: he has murdered—Paragraph one hundred thirty-four—sentence of death! They go much deeper, but I will plead as a jurist, as a moralist, and as a citizen—always at the hand of the law.

To justify this plea, Harpner tried to work with the meager material of the psychiatric testimony. It was an excellent piece of work, he conceded, but he reminded the court that it was they, not the psychiatrists, who had to render the final verdict. "The testimony says: Court, I present what I have found and what can be said from the standpoint of science. You must decide if it is sufficient to find the accused guilty, or if it leads to his acquittal."

Harpner read a few of the more ambiguous passages in the psychiatric testimony, then tried to present the situation in the mind of the assassin:

I will not forget today that a victim fell in the deed of the accused, as ultimately no feeling man would ignore the fact that someone was killed. But the accused killed without regard for the person, he had no regard for himself, nor for the father whom he loved more than anyone, for his dearly beloved mother, for the wife, of whom he wrote that she is the one who always understands him, and no thought of his children, of whom he wrote that they would understand his deed when they grew up. Not from brutality, but out of other motives . . . he killed, and all that he loved, he killed as well. Thus can the medical testimony say: "He had consideration for no one, because in this deed he was a fanatic."

The crisis for the accused, Harpner argued, was that he lived in a state where no avenue of protest or change was open.

He wanted to help—the fanatic—he wanted to influence. But how? He had the right to influence through the press—but there was none. . . . He or his party could participate in parliamentary activity—there was none, the parliament did not meet. Assemblies, the traditional right of every citizen—there were none . . .

Was this not enough to drive any dedicated man to rage? ". . . we all know: rage makes a man half-crazy. Frustrated rage will lead to an explosion even in the healthiest man." What then would happen to a man who was compulsive, who was obsessed with an idealistic rage against the state?

There were but two choices left to the accused in his frustrated rage, argued Harpner: exile or murder. For us, for the father of the accused who sits in this court, it would have been far better if he had chosen exile. But he loved Austria too much to leave. That left only one choice—murder!

The key to the case, said Harpner, was the word which the prosecutor had also picked up—*Fanatismus*.

The fanatic is far from a normal man. The normal man goes to see *Tell*, sees Tell shoot down the overseer, is inspired by this act of freedom, applauds, then goes to a pub for a beer. The normal man thinks no more of Tell or of the overseer. . . . The fanatic does what the accused did: He keeps thinking of Tell, of how he killed the overseer.

Even after he leaves the theater, he is obsessed with the idea, with the moral righteousness of what happened on the stage.

It is the same, Harpner continued, when the normal man and the fanatic view the situation in Austria during the war.

The normal man holds speeches about freedom, the normal man hangs the powers of Paragraph Fourteen on the lamp post with his words—the fanatic takes the whole question much more seriously. The normal man can speak one way as a member of parliament and another way as a minister, the fanatic insists on being absolutely true to what he holds as right . . .

Step by step, Harpner hypothesized how a fanatic would resolve the impossible enigma of immutable rage against an immovable state. Frustrated on every side by the callous reaction of the world, unable to write or speak the truth, he feels like "the dog whom the lord has whipped." And yet he says to himself: "I will not be a dog, I will not be a slave, I will be a free citizen of this state." From that conclusion it is but a few steps to taking up the gun he once bought, and at the exact psychological moment when he is most frustrated, striking out for that which he believes.

Harpner's final argument was to call attention to what the "psychosis of war" would do to a man like Fritz.

In these dreadful times, which have been upon us for years, the cleverest men, it is said, are driven mad. We see whole mounds of corpses pile up and we are supposed to remain sensible men. We see a centuries-old culture destroyed and we, sensible men and not fanatics, often feel the innermost foundations of our senses tremble. Imagine this man, this pacifist, who has dreamed of peace for all mankind and who sees that in this mankind a struggle rages of which no one knows whether it leads to betterment or destruction. He, with his predisposition, with his thoughts, sees all of that. I will forego all of the nomenclature, but I maintain that under these circumstances this man cannot be made legally responsible for this act. As a jurist and as a man, as a free citizen of this state who speaks to free citizens of this state, I beseech you for acquittal.

During the summations of the prosecution and the defense, Fritz sat nervously at the defense table, periodically shaking his head or jotting down a note for himself.

When Harpner finished, von Heidt asked Fritz: "Herr Accused, do you wish the final word?"

Fritz requested and was granted a five-minute pause before he spoke. The court recessed at six o'clock.

FRITZ

Unlike the two lawyers, Fritz did not have to draw a careful legal argument in his closing remarks. His final words, like the case against Austria that he had presented on the first day of the trial, were directed to the grand jury of the galleries and in the street. It was for the lawyers and the court to decide the case against Friedrich Adler; Fritz would take no part in their squabbles. What he cared about was the case against Austria, and that case could only be decided by the people.

After the recess Fritz took up his now-familiar sheaf of papers and began. It was a melodramatic moment, and he exploited it fully.

". . . in the moment when *I speak for the last time in my life*," he began, "I cannot allow myself to fall into the polemics or to answer the arguments which have been used by one side or the other."

Only because some of what the prosecutor had argued was relevant to his true motives, Fritz said, would he speak to the charges which had been made. The prosecution had argued that he was an anti-patriot and that his anti-patriotic ideas and his vanity were behind the assassination. Why then, Fritz asked, did he not accept offers to go to Germany or Switzerland and work with the socialist movements there? Those offers were a chance to escape Austria and to work with enormous audiences. He answered: "The tragedy, of which I am the focus, is grounded in this, that I could not tear myself loose from the Austrian Social Democracy." He had freely criticized his colleagues and their paper, the *Arbeiter-Zeitung*, indeed, had criticized them perhaps more sharply than anyone else. Why?

. . . because the *Arbeiter-Zeitung*, which was the work of my father, which I have loved, in which I have read every column, which was my daily bread—until the time when I was brought here and for the first time in my life I was forbidden it . . . because what had been *dearest* to me was disgraced . . .

262

The prosecution had argued that the court and its officers were not qualified to discuss or to decide the validity of government policies or whether or not they were constitutional. Fritz answered: "He, the State Prosecutor, who is supposed to be an attorney of this state, steps up here and says: I am not competent to know whether this state should or should not have a constitution. What is necessary for the state only a Count Stürgkh can know." There was no need to say more on that question, Fritz continued, for the chasm that lay between this view and the view of democracy would never be bridged.

Was his deed a historical act? There was much that could be argued, Fritz said, waving the sheaf of papers. One example sufficed:

In the last article which I read in the *Arbeiter-Zeitung*, on the twentieth of October, the day before the assassination, it was stated that Count Stürgkh reigns in the clouds and can be reached by no one. Then came the turning point, and five days later articles begin to appear in the *Arbeiter-Zeitung*: "A New Spirit," "A New Era," "A New Regime," read the titles. An entire series, each day a new article.

Fritz continued:

The real reason I want to speak is that I must explain that the question of murder, for me, has always been a *real moral* question. . . . I have always believed that the violent killing of men was inhuman, and that it is because we live in an Age of Barbarism that we are reduced to killing men. I completely agree with my colleagues who argue: *War is inhuman.* And I will not deny: *Revolution is also inhuman.* As long as it is necessary for men to kill one another, instead of rising together in the world with their minds, so long will we live in a world of barbarism, of inhumanity. . . . We must remain clear about this and we must orient ourselves accordingly—we still live in barbarism and we must direct our-

263

selves in all questions in order to break out of this barbarism. Surely we want a new society, a society without murder and violence, but we must use every means to work for that new society. Thus, gentlemen, just as you are convinced—and the prosecutor has said it so forcefully—that the sons of our country—and it is not only sons, but unfortunately also fathers, old men of fifty years—must stand out in the battle trenches, must give up their lives and extinguish other lives, just as these men stake their entire beings for what you see as right, just as they not only allow killing, but kill, just so, I say, must you understand that we must stake our lives for our goal, to break out of the society of barbarism in which we live. And if one consents to this, then one must also consent to revolution . . .

Speaking of Christianity, "not as it is represented by those who disgrace Christianity," but the true Christianity of Tolstoy, the Christianity that says men should never kill, not in war and not in revolution, Fritz admitted that in his youth he had been influenced by these teachings and by the idea that all men should be as Christ, turning the other cheek to violence. But, he continued,

. . . when one comes to the historical realization that man cannot and should not be a true Christ in the Age of Barbarism, in the Age of Inhumanity, in the Age of *Unkultur*, in which we live, then there is only this alternative standpoint: If we must really kill and be killed, then *murder cannot be a privilege of the rulers*, we must also be ready to resort to force. If it is true that the Age of Humanity has still not come, then we should at least employ force only in the service of the idea of humanity . . .

As Fritz spoke, his rhetoric gathered momentum and power. He was in complete control of the courtroom. The audience of the galleries and the street hung on his every word:

I have heard the war justified, and I have understood the arguments which justified the war.

As they marched through Belgium and an innocent people fell as victims, as women and children were killed, they said: Necessity knows no commandments, it is war, there was no alternative.

As the *Lusitania* sank, and a mass of innocent civilians met their deaths, again they said: It is war, there was no alternative.

Men must be hanged, they say, even at the peril of hanging innocent men, because as the prosecutor has said, the spies must be controlled. It is war, it is necessity, they say to justify it.

We live in a time when battlefields are covered with hundreds of thousands of dead, when tens of thousands of men lie beneath the sea. It is war, it is necessity, they say to justify it.

But if one man should fall, a man who has destroyed the constitution in Austria, who has trampled the laws of Austria into the ground, if the one man who is most guilty for these horrors should fall, then suddenly they confront me and say: Human life is sacred. Then suddenly they remember the fifth commandment: Thou Shalt Not Kill!

Gentlemen, this contradiction I cannot understand, and you may say what you will, I shall never understand it . . .

I know what the verdict will be, I have never had any doubts. I shall leave this room in the spirit of our old hymn, which for me was never empty words, but a living reality. Today they live for me more than ever before:

Nicht zählen wir die Feinde, nicht der Gefahren all;
Marsch, marsch, und wär's zum Tod;
*Denn unsere Fahn' ist rot!**

---

* We count not the enemies, nor the dangers all;
March, march, even until we are dead;
For our flag is red!

FRITZ

I do not know what will happen, whether I shall die soon or eventually be condemned to vegetate forever. But if you would be serious in the deliberation you are making, I have only one wish—that I can hold my nerves and senses together until the last moment, as I have held them together until now, so that just once the words of the poet, which were dedicated to a much greater revolutionary deed, will be said by me:

Auf den Lippen den Trotz und den zuckended Hohn,
Noch im Sterben rufend: die Rebellion!
So ist er mit Ehren erlegen.

But to all whom I love and whose love has been my joy, to all my friends and colleagues in the struggle, in all parts of the world, I recall in parting, as a consolation, the deep and pure truth of the Easter grave:

Nicht alle sind tot, die begraben sind,
Denn sie töten den Geist nicht, ihr Brüder!*

The judges deliberated in their chambers for just seventeen minutes before returning to the courtroom to announce their verdict.

Von Heidt read:

In the name of His Majesty the Emperor, the Imperial-Royal Court of Assize, as special tribunal, in general ses-

---

* The lines here and just above are from the "Abschiedswort" of Ferdinand Freiligrath (1810–1876):

His lips spoke defiance and scathing scorn,
Dying he still called out: Rebellion!
So was he struck down with honor.

Not all are dead who are entombed,
For you cannot kill the spirit, ye brethren!

sion on the indictment of the Imperial-Royal State Prosecutor, finds:

Doctor Friedrich Adler *is guilty* of firing four pistol shots at Doctor Karl Count Stürgkh, on the twenty-first of October, in Vienna, with the intention of killing him, and in such a manner that his death resulted.

Doctor Friedrich Adler has therefore committed murder according to Paragraph one hundred thirty-four and is sentenced to death according to Paragraph one hundred thirty-six as well as to a fine equivalent to the cost of the criminal proceedings according to Paragraph three hundred eighty-nine of the penal code.

Speaking without a text, von Heidt explained briefly how the court had reached its decision on the basis of the confession of the accused, the testimony of the witnesses, and the psychiatric testimony certifying that the accused was not insane at the time of the crime. No other verdict was possible if the court was to show a proper and decent respect not only for the law of the land but also for the integrity and sincerity of Fritz's act.

Finally von Heidt said: "The accused has the legal right to enter a plea of annulment of the sentence, which must be entered within three days."

"We will reserve our decision," answered Harpner.

The guards were already escorting Fritz from the courtroom. In the doorway he turned to face the galleries and the windows. Then he shouted: *"Long Live the International Revolutionary Social Democracy!"*

Voices in the gallery and the street—first a few, then dozens—echoed Fritz's cry. "Long Live the International!" "Long Live Friedrich Adler!" they shouted, louder and louder, until von Heidt ordered the courtroom cleared and Fritz taken away.

At seven ten von Heidt banged his gavel once more: "The proceeding is closed."

FRITZ

The police were still dragging and pushing the crowd from the courtroom. By the time the demonstration was over eight persons had been arrested in the courtroom and six more in the street. Young Paul Lazarsfeld was one of them.

20

Nemesis

Like almost everyone else in Vienna, Prime Minister Clam-Martinic read the newspaper accounts of the first day of Fritz's trial on Saturday morning, May 19. That day he summoned a meeting of the Council of Ministers to ask whether the censors should allow the printing of remarks "made by the murderer of Count Stürgkh, which are obviously hostile to the state." The ministers met at the Hofburg, not far from the courthouse where the second day of the trial was in session. There was, as usual, little real discussion at the meeting. The Minister of Railroads said: "Doctor Friedrich Adler has used his position as the accused to say, in an unheard of way, things which are definitely hostile to the state; it is incomprehensible that the censor should allow publication of these highly questionable remarks." The Prime Minister seconded this view, pointing out that he had been outraged when he read the morning papers. At the end of the meeting he directed the Ministers of Justice and the Interior to see that the censors did something about the matter.

The censor acted quickly. In the Sunday papers the reports of the trial were so mutilated that the version of Fritz's final speech in the *Arbeiter-Zeitung* was punctuated by twenty large white spaces where the censors had striken material. There was no mention in the newspapers of the demonstrations at the trial and the arrests of fourteen people.

But even the ukase of the censors could not silence discussion of the trial. The editors of the *Neue Freie Presse*, traditionally reluctant to take any political position that might compromise the absolute neutrality of their urbane liberalism, wrote that they were "impressed with the seriousness" of Friedrich Adler. It was obvious where the sympathies of the *Arbeiter-Zeitung* lay. And the censors were powerless to stop the grapevine that had developed to carry news through three years of censored reports. Those who had been at the trial or in the street outside passed rumors and word-of-mouth reports until phrases of Fritz's speeches were heard in quiet discussions all over Vienna. Late Saturday night the ubiquitous Joseph Redlich noted in his diary: ". . . the defense speech of the condemned Friedrich Adler has made the deepest impression in Vienna."

The impressions of Vienna soon spread to other cities in the empire and to the troops in the field. In the munitions industries of several cities a long-threatened strike over the military control of civilian workers erupted at the time of the trial. When the strikers heard reports and rumors about the trial, phrases from Fritz's speeches and a demand for his release became part of their ultimatum. The strike was not mentioned in the Austrian newspapers.

By the end of the month even the closed frontiers and the battlelines of Central Europe could not contain the now fantastic stories of Fritz's speeches on peace and oppression. Weeks after the trial an early meeting of the Petrograd Soviet of Workers and Soldiers named Fritz an honorary member. Throughout Russia, streets, barracks, and regiments were named after him in salute to a fighter for peace whose proclamations seemed to echo the message of the Bolsheviks. Trotsky, then Chairman of the Soviet, referred to Fritz as his "comrade in ideas and friend." Other Russian revolutionaries, some of whom had never met Fritz, lavished paeans of praise on his antiwar efforts.

The rump of the Socialist International, busy organizing its first wartime conference in Stockholm only weeks after the trial, received telegrams—in the name of fourteen hundred Austrian, Hungarian, and German prisoners of war who labored in the coal fields of Siberia, and from the Free Lettish Army—protesting the sentencing of Friedrich Adler. No official position was taken at the Stockholm Conference, but gossip in the halls, especially from the leftist delegates of the Scandanavian countries and Holland, indicated how far away the speeches in the Vienna courthouse had been heard.

The Zimmerwald group, meeting again in September, were less tentative in their view of Fritz's deed. The agenda for the meeting listed Fritz on equal terms with the entry of the United States into the European war. A resolution equated his deed with the struggles of Karl Liebknecht and Rosa Luxemburg, who had been jailed in Germany for their antiwar activity. The conference also voted to send "warm brotherly greetings to the heroic undaunted fighter Friedrich Adler."

Fritz heard none of this commotion from his cell. He was still allowed no newspapers, and his only visitors were his parents and the lawyers, who seemed more concerned with the immediate consequences of his sentence and the appeal than with gathering reports on the impact of the trial. In fact, the only indication Fritz received that anyone had heard what he said in the courtroom was a short note which arrived the day after the trial:

Dear Honored Dr. Adler,

The woman who sat behind Count Stügkh in the dining room before the assassination, and to whom you were so noble, thanks you in her own name and in the name of her three children. In spite of your seriousness and deliberation, my presence must have caused you a difficult inner struggle. Right after the assassination, I said to the people who were congratulating me on my luck: "I do not believe that it was an 'accident' that the man apparently did not want to make an innocent woman the victim of his deed." From the reports in the newspapers, I see that I was right.

In your life, my thanks will play no role. I would forever reproach myself, however, if I were to neglect you. Please make no mention of this letter . . . as nothing lies further from me than the idea of creating a sensation.

Respectfully,

H. Z.

A few days after the trial Fritz was given a copy of the transcript (together with a bill for the cost of the judicial proceedings). With the help of Sigmund Popper, who checked various documents and corrected errors in the copy, Fritz worked to convert the transcript into a book, hoping that publication in Germany might give a still larger audience to his remarks. He remained quite oblivious to the efforts being made in his behalf.

Harpner's formal appeal was based on the argument that according to the constitution only a trial by jury could have decided the case against Friedrich Adler. In a closed session on July 24, the Supreme Court rejected the appeal, ordering that the sentence be carried out. That left only one recourse, a pardon by the Emperor, which Fritz refused to seek. But events in Austria soon caught up with the judicial proceedings.

Parliament was scheduled to reconvene, for the first time in three years, on May 30. The afternoon before, several thousand demonstrators, organized by a new group called the Revolutionary Socialists of Vienna, and with the support of the Association of Young Workers and the Social Democratic Women's Organization, paraded in front of the parliament building with signs and leaflets demanding an end to censorship and the military control of factories, and the freeing of Friedrich Adler. The demonstrations were disavowed by the Social Democratic party, but the size of the crowds convinced more than a few of the party leaders that the Social Democrats would have to make strenuous efforts to win back the numbers of workers who were growing disillusioned with the party line in the war.

The parliamentary session opened, amid torrid heat, with impressive ceremony and much fanfare. Many deputies wore military uniforms, and at the beginning of the session wreathes were placed on the seats of the four members who had been killed in the war. Yet even before the Emperor made his elaborate opening address from the throne, arguments broke out among the deputies. The militant Czechs were outraged because deputies who had been convicted for crimes of lese majesty during the war were not seated, and because an outspoken Bohemian German, Gustav Gross, had been selected as presiding officer. The German Nationalists were angry that parliament had been convened at all, and by the signs that a peace bloc might emerge in a coalition of the Czechs and the Social Democrats.

In his long speech Karl praised his predecessor for a passionate adherence to the principles of parliamentary government, assured the parliamentarians of his own faith in the constitution, then went on to list, as vaguely as possible, the tasks which faced the parliament—taking care to exclude the topics of constitutional reform and peace. Peace, Karl announced, was the duty of the Emperor, adding as a caution: "The true peace formula is only to be found in a mutual recognition of a valiant defense, and in establishing conditions whereby the future life of peoples may remain free from anger and vengeance, so that for generations to come the appeal to arms may be unnecessary."

When the formalities gave way to regular business, the Social Democrats introduced a motion calling for the retrial, before civilian courts, of all persons who had been convicted and sentenced for political crimes by exceptional tribunals. Despite the sarcastic cries of the Magyars and the German Nationalists ("Long Live High Treason!"), the motion passed with Czech and Social Democratic support. After approval by the House of Lords the bill would become law.

During the debates over the bill in the House of Lords, the Emperor invited several members of parliament to a special audience, where he asked about the bill. Engelbert Pernerstorfer attended the audience as a representative of the Social Democrats. He explained why the party was so anxious to have the sentences of various political prisoners reviewed, giving Fritz's case as an example.

"Yes, but what should one do?" asked the Emperor.

"Defer!" said Pernerstorfer. "Were he to be tried before a jury today, there would be a very different sentence than the one handed down by the exceptional tribunal." And, he explained, only if the House of Lords were to pass the new law would a retrial be possible, providing the opportunity for what the public would certainly consider a more "appropriate" sentence.

"That will happen," assured Karl. "And for me it is the best solution."

As he spoke the House of Lords rejected the bill.

The Emperor was interested enough in what Pernerstorfer and some of the Czech deputies had told him to ask to see the trial records of some of the more infamous cases. After perusing several, including the case of the clerk, Karl Langer, who had been sentenced to death for distributing translations of the poem "I Didn't Raise My Boy To Be a Soldier," Karl admitted that some of the trials were "really worse than the Spanish Inquisition." Discussions with representatives of the major parties finally convinced him to publish an imperial decree of amnesty for civilians who had been sentenced by exceptional tribunals. "I have chosen for this purpose the day on which my dearly beloved eldest son . . .

is keeping the feast of the patron saint of his name," the manifesto explained. "Thus the hand of a child who will be called one day to guide the destinies of my people leads those who have erred back to the Fatherland."

Those whose "errors" had led only to prison sentences were immediately released to take up their jobs. The imprisoned Czech deputies regained their seats in the parliament and there raised enough commotion to turn the sessions into harbingers of the good old days, as German Nationalists and Czech separatists threatened to throw tables at one another, backing up their threats with the familiar cacophony of vituperative shouts in half a dozen languages, flying inkwells, and the rest of the old routine. The Czechs even introduced a new variation on the old theme: When speakers of the opposition rose, the Czechs would march out en masse, leaving the speakers to address half-empty benches.

In tenor the sessions sounded little different from the sessions of the early spring of 1914, before Count Stürgkh prorogued the parliament. Yet there was a vast difference, for in 1914 the threats of the Czechs and the South Slavs were idle dreams; the most drastic solutions anyone posed in the halycon prewar years were federative structures in place of the centralization of Vienna. The Czechs and South Slavs who berated and threatened in 1917, however, were true separatists, backed up by the exile movements in London, Paris, and Washington, where men like Masaryk and Beneš carefully schemed the creation of new states. Vast numbers of Slav soldiers had already defected to the Russian side rather than shoot their "Slav brothers," and they were rapidly organizing into a new army which could exert direct pressure on the Habsburg forces.

Prime Minister Clam-Martinic tried to brush away the clamor for reform by sleight of hand, declaring that the various proposals were all mutually contradictory. "The program of my government," he declared, "is Austria—an Austria which has grown up through splendid historical development." What he would not admit was that it was Austria which was contradictory, that the empire was torn hopelessly by centrifugal nationalistic forces. In peacetime the forces were disruptive; in war they were likely to prove fatal.

Clam-Martinic lasted only until June 23, when he submitted his resignation to the Emperor. In his place Karl appointed another professional civil servant, his former tutor in administrative law, Baron Ernst von Seidler. The only accomplishments of the parliamentary session were a decree rescinding the martial law under which some areas of the empire were still governed, and a series of measures mitigating some of the censorship and political activities of the War Surveillance Office.

The imperial amnesty was not as generous with the subjects under death sentences as with those in term imprisonment. The terms of the amnesty overturned the death sentences, but remitted those cases to the Supreme Court for re-sentencing. In Fritz's case the court commuted the sentence to eighteen years' imprisonment in the fortress of Stein on the Danube.

Fritz was seemingly oblivious to the outcome of the appeals procedure. Indeed, although he had heard rumors about the harshness of Stein ("Men who are on bread and water here are reduced to water without bread there," he wrote in a letter from the city jail), he was actually looking forward to the move. With the sentence settled he would no longer be disturbed from his scientific work by the constant coming and going of lawyers and psychiatrists, or by the necessity of planning for a trial. Allowed to elect either regular imprisonment or solitary confinement, which as the harsher punishment would shorten his sentence, he choose solitary, guaranteeing the isolation and quiet he treasured.

The sentence was formally handed down on September 6, and on October 12, 1917, Fritz was taken to the fortress, forty-nine miles up the Danube from Vienna. As a political prisoner he was permitted to wear his own clothes in prison, and while there was no heat for the long winter, Emma somehow found enough blankets and warm clothing to make the situation tolerable. Through letters and the smuggled correspondence, which Sophie Lazarsfeld handled, he could keep in touch with political developments in Austria and abroad. The guards at Stein were all adamantly anti-Habsburg. Either because they just liked Fritz, or because the trial and the ill fortunes of Austria had convinced them that the political future might somehow rest with this strange prisoner, they were remarkably lenient in allowing Sophie to carry on an extensive smuggling operation. For his scientific work Fritz requested long lists of books and articles, which Sophie would obtain from the library or from secondhand bookstores. At one time she even got noncirculating books from the Imperial and Royal Library by confiding in an anti-Habsburg priest from Croatia who had special borrowing privileges. Officially forbidden journals and newspapers could easily be smuggled in while the guards willingly turned their backs.

In July 1917, before he left the city jail, Fritz had finished editing the transcript of his trial. It was smuggled to Paul Cassirer, a Social Democratic publisher in Berlin, but it could not be issued until the winter of 1918–1919, by which time it was more interesting to historians than to the antiwar effort. The same fate befell a collection of Fritz's wartime writings and speeches which a sympathizer named Robert Danneberg edited. The books with an introduction by Karl Kautsky, was finally published at the end of 1918.

At Stein, in the peace and quiet of his harsh monastic seclusion, Fritz set to work on his critique of Einstein. Eighteen years allowed plenty of time for a relaxed work pace, but Fritz, forever impatient, worked as though an imminent deadline loomed. While he waited for Sophie to get some of the books and articles he needed, he spent his time reviewing and summarizing his earlier work in a short, somewhat adulatory biographical study entitled *Ernst Machs Überwindung des mechanischen Materialismus*. It was written for a general audience, which to Fritz meant those who were familiar with differential and integral calculus, mechanics, and various philosophical and mathematical assumptions of a Newtonian world-view. Before the volume was published in 1918, Fritz went back to the work which began with his insight into the Foucault pendulum problem, and which he thought was the basis of a decisive critique of Einstein's relativity theory. By September 1918 he had finished, and in October copies of the study (*Ortzeit, Systemzeit, Zonenzeit—Eine Untersuchung über die Lorentzsche und Einsteinsche Kinematik*) were typed by Paul Lazarsfeld, printed, and sent out to colleagues and friends.

Fritz was relatively happy in prison. He got on well with the guards, thrived on the peace and quiet, and seemed immune to the hardships of cold and poor food. Each week he was allowed two visitors, and the regular visits of Victor and Emma or of Sophie and her children were the perfect interludes in his studies. With Paul and Elizabeth, Fritz would discuss their schoolwork or books they had read. He convinced Paul that mathematics was a good foundation for any future studies. In turn Paul helped Fritz by typing the smuggled manuscripts, and little Elizabeth would make embroidered book covers and other presents for him.

Kathia returned to Zurich after the trial. The restrictions on travel that were later imposed made it extremely difficult for her to return to Vienna.

Since further discussions of the assassination and the trial led nowhere, Victor and Fritz agreed not to disagree anymore. Instead they used the visits for pleasantries and for political discussions of the changing situation in Vienna. Father and son still had immense respect for one another as political thinkers, and the leniency of the guards permitted discussions that would have been broken up on the streets of Vienna. Emma, like Kathia, never forgave or forgot. In time, she learned not to cry during the visits.

21

The Last Waltz

By the summer of 1917 Fritz seemed to be the only man in Austria who enjoyed peace, quiet, and a kind of security. In May, during the days of Fritz's trial, German and Austrian statesmen had met at Kreuznach to discuss a wide-ranging agenda of war aims. For two days the diplomats labored over an enormous map of Europe, parceling and redistributing vast areas of territory that were occupied by the armies of the Central Powers, or that the Germans assured would soon be occupied. The Austrians were wary of the more grandiose German schemes, but from their position of weakness there was little they could do to restrain the ambitious Germans. Reluctantly, Foreign Minister Czernin signed a new agreement about the future of the war and returned to report to his Emperor.

Karl publicly assured his allies that he would never seek a separate peace, but officials in Germany warned that, as usual, Austria was not to be trusted. The Germans were confident of victory (despite a peace resolution in the Reichstag which the Prime Minister had to deflect by saying that he accepted it "as I understand it"), and the German High Command resolved that Austrian tergiversation should not be allowed to weaken the war effort. Germans were shifted into Austrian divisions and even into smaller units; German officers began to issue commands with their inevitable, implacable, and for the Austrians, intolerable efficiency. When the Austrians balked, the Germans would subtly threaten that Austria too could be invaded, which was usually enough to persuade the diffident ally.

When grain and oil reserves from occupied Romania became available, the Germans deflected the material from the civilian population of Austria-Hungary to the troops in the field, arguing that food and fuel were needed for the new offensives. Austrians from the Emperor down protested that Austria could not hold out much longer, but to no avail. "God save us from our friends!" shrieked the prescient few.

By 1917 only one front remained where the Central Powers were without a single victory. Two years of fighting in Italy had not moved the front more than ten miles in either direction. During the summer of 1917 General Ludendorf, the German Commander in Chief, decided that there was no reason why Italy could not be annihilated by assault the way Russia, Romania, and Serbia had been. Six divisions of German troops were sent to join the Austrian forces on the Isonzo front, and in October the combined forces attacked the Italians in a dense fog. The Germans and Austrians advanced more then ten miles on the first day, and within three days the Italian lines were broken and in disarray. Only hasty reinforcement by British and French troops halted the German-Austrian advance at the Piave, and even so, three hundred thousand Italians were taken prisoner and an even larger number deserted.

The victory at Caporetto, on the "field of honor," should have bolstered lagging spirits in Vienna. But the victory had been won only with the direction, leadership, and manpower of the Germans, and to many it seemed one more confirmation of Austria's second-rate status. The newspaper headlines proclaimed the glory of the armies, but the people of the cities waited in the same endless lines for bread. Doubts were not assuaged but enhanced.

More than anyone else, the Social Democrats in 1917 began to question the program they had followed throughout the war. Although meetings of the party were quiet and orderly since the assassination, Fritz's trial and the subsequent demonstrations had drawn many followers to the Left minority. The majority of the party had done little to inspire a new following. They had gone to the Stockholm conference and met there with representatives of the Russian (Menshevik) party and with representatives of the other parties of the Central Powers. The English and French representatives were denied passports at the last minute, which made the conference a rather one-sided affair. Like the other groups there, the Austrian delegation came out for a peace without annexations or reparations. After much protocol and formalized debate the conference passed the usual resolutions which bound no one to anything. "Long live the international mass struggle against the war!" read the final pathetic manifesto.

In July 1917 Otto Bauer, who had been a prisoner of war in Siberia, came back to Vienna as part of an exchange of prisoners. He immediately assumed the leadership of the Left in the party, and with a flair for party politics that Fritz had never mastered, Bauer turned the opposition into a potent and influential force. In October, when the party convened its first official congress since the outbreak of the war (none of the previous all-party conferences had been elevated to the status of a congress) the Left was ready to mount a concerted campaign against the war. The main issues before the congress were the war and the question of constitutional reform in Austria. Debate centered between Renner, who advocated continuation of the old policies on war and reforms which would go only as far as sweeping away the historic

boundaries of the crown lands in favor of a federation of nationalities, each with a parliament and each represented in a central
parliament, and Bauer, who called for Fritz's stand of immediate
peace, and who questioned whether the monarchy should be preserved at all. In the end Renner's views won out, but not without
extended debate and a very vocal and evident opposition from the
Left. Instead of the overwhelming votes of the early years of the
war, the contest was now a close one.

There were more than a few references in the congress to
Fritz as a great fighter against absolutism and for peace, and at the
end a resolution was passed sending "brotherly greetings" to Fritz.
He had become a hero of the working class.

At the congress Victor Adler tried once again to justify the
prowar posture of the party. "If the house is on fire, the first thing
is to extinguish the flame," he said once again, but his arguments
convinced no one anymore, for while the majority in the party was
still hesitant about taking a stand in favor of revolution, the loyalty of the party had been broken since Fritz's trial. Rank and file,
in particular, had defected widely from the leadership, and it was
questionable if the party still commanded the respect and following of the working class of the empire.

The well-choreographed seizure of power by the Bolsheviks in November 1917 provided the first real test of the Austrian
Social Democratic party. The smoke had barely cleared from the
cannon of the cruiser *Aurora* when the new Soviet government
issued a manifesto calling upon the belligerent governments to lay
down their arms and begin negotiations for a "just and democratic
peace." When the Western cabinets, already as afraid of the Bolsheviks as they were of the Central Powers, indignantly spurned
the overture, Leon Trotsky, in his capacity as Foreign Commissar,
applied to the Central Powers for an immediate cease-fire and
negotiations for a peace without annexations or indemnities. As a

token of good intentions, Russian commanders were ordered to stop their troops from shooting, and soldiers were instructed to fraternize with Austrian and German troops in the trenches.

For war-weary Austria the chance to eliminate Russia from the war was the first optimistic news in years. "What a tremendous change!" Redlich confided to his diary. "Decaying Europe saved by the Communists. Peace may be arranged in a couple of weeks." Foreign Minister Czernin saw the situation in straight realpolitik: "Peace at the earliest possible moment is necessary for our salvation, and we cannot obtain peace until the Germans get to Paris—and they cannot get to Paris unless the Eastern front is free."

The cease-fire was quickly negotiated, with the German Major General Max Hoffmann, an expert on Eastern Europe, representing the Central Powers. He balked when the Bolshevik representatives demanded that no troops of the Central Powers be shunted west during the negotiations and that rival troops be permitted to fraternize during the negotiations, but finally yielded in the hope of hastening a permanent peace agreement.

When it came time for the actual negotiations, it was the Bolsheviks who procrastinated. Trotsky later explained the Bolshevik program:

> We began peace negotiations in the hope of arousing the workmen's parties of Germany and Austria-Hungary as well as those of the Entente countries. For this reason we were obliged to delay the negotiations as long as possible to give the European workmen time to understand the main fact of the Soviet Revolution and particularly its peace policy.

Lenin and Trotsky had remained faithful to their prewar stance and to the resolutions of the Zimmerwald movement. They intended all along to turn the war into a revolution, and the enthusiastic support their ideas had received in the Zimmerwald meetings and in the writings and speeches of vocal minorities in the

Central Powers were enough to convince them that the revolution would spread. "The disintegrating Habsburg monarchy," wrote Trotsky, "had long ago hung out a sign for an undertaker, not demanding any high qualifications of him." If only the masses in Austria and Germany followed the leadership of Friedrich Adler and Karl Liebknecht and Rosa Luxemburg, the Bolsheviks reasoned, the revolution would sweep across a ripe Europe.

The Bolshevik estimate was almost correct. When the peace negotiations began in December 1917 at the grim Polish town of Brest-Litovsk, Vienna was already blanketed with several feet of snow. The early winter had been more severe than usual, and with fuel supplies near zero and the rationed food supplies almost depleted, the population of Vienna and other cities of the empire was ready for peace, especially a peace that promised food and fuel. Fritz's trial had planted doubts in the minds of suffering Austrians everywhere, and the continuous stream of propaganda from the Bolsheviks, conveyed in the speeches of their negotiators at Brest-Litovsk and by the fraternizing soldiers, hammered away at the very questions Fritz had raised: Why fight this war? Who profits from your fighting? Why suffer starvation, maiming, and death? To make the munition makers wealthy? To move a meaningless frontier in an empty area of the steppes?

The company that gathered to work out the peace treaty at Brest-Litovsk was the most unusual collection of "diplomats" Europe had ever seen. Gone was the frock-coated, French-speaking fraternity of social equals, replaced by a cast of hard-boiled German generals and Austrian nobles, sitting across a long barren table from the diplomatically inexperienced but professionally dedicated revolutionaries. Both sides put their cards on the table at the first session. The Bolsheviks proposed that all armed forces should be withdrawn from foreign soil, and that the peoples of contested areas (Russian Poland, Lithuania, Courland) should determine their own political destinies. The Germans angrily rejected the offer, arguing that large sections of the former Tsarist empire could no longer be considered Russian soil. The contest quickly developed into an angry screaming battle between Trotsky's brilliant doctrinaire harangues and Hoffmann's cool but infuriating claims for huge hunks of Eastern Europe. By January 12 Hoffmann was so exasperated by the intransigence of the Bolsheviks that he slammed his fist on the table—the first signal that the talks had deadlocked.

The Austrians, forced to take a back seat in the negotiations, were the most anxious to conclude a treaty, even without any annexations. The *Arbeiter-Zeitung* fretted daily about the slow pace of the talks, and tried to hint that if a settlement were not to come soon, "a complete change of system would be necessary . . ." The censors deleted amplifying remarks. Czernin himself wrote the Emperor: "If this unprecedented state of affairs continues, we shall unquestionably be confronted with a great collapse and revolution." No news to the Emperor, who wrote back: "The whole fate of the monarchy and the dynasty depends upon peace being concluded as quickly as possible."

On the home front the worst winter in a decade hampered transport so severely that needed food and fuel supplies could not be moved at all. "We are faced with a catastrophe that will hit us in the next few weeks, unless we receive foreign help," wrote the Governor of Bohemia. "The situation is much worse in the crown lands; there starvation has already begun." "The people are suffering from hunger," reported the Archbishop of Cracow. "Bread rations have been cut down by half," wired the Governor of Trieste. "There is flour in Vienna only till next Monday," announced the Mayor.

By the middle of January mass rallies of workers were demanding an immediate peace settlement. "Without any warning or signal from the socialists," explained Victor Adler, "the idea had suddenly sprung up among the masses that if this hope vanishes, and there is nothing to eat, we have nothing to lose."

The final straw was an announcement, on January 14, that

bread rations for Austria would be cut. The next day the workers at the Daimler plant in Wiener Neustadt, an industrial suburb of Vienna, went on strike. Spontaneously the movement spread to locomotive and munitions plants, and from there to other industrial centers in the empire. By January 17 two hundred thousand workers were out on strike in the Vienna area alone, and while the walkout was less widespread in the Bohemian industrial areas, the empire was faced with a situation that had the makings of another Petrograd. Workers in the factories elected soviets on the Bolshevik model and rampaging groups attacked town halls and other symbols of government power. The printers were also out on strike, so that the only news in Vienna came from broadsides which the striking workmen agreed to print up. The demands of the strikers were included in each broadside:

1. Peace delegations elected by the people.
2. Immediate cease fire on all fronts.
3. All war controls and militarization of factories to be terminated immediately; all measures which limit the right of assembly or political freedom to be lifted.
4. *Friedrich Adler and all other political prisoners to be released immediately.*

Many of the leaflets also urged distrust of the Social Democratic leadership "who have betrayed you since the start of the war," and support of the Bolshevik cause.

The strike took the Social Democratic party by surprise. Many members of the Executive Committee had refused to consider the idea of revolution for so long that they were paralyzed when the momentum of the popular demonstrations caught on. But after a day of discussions, the Left faction of the party convinced even the stodgier committeemen that the Social Democrats would lose the last shreds of leadership if they were to abandon the movement instead of taking control. On January 16 the party leaders issued a manifesto in the *Arbeiter-Zeitung* declaring that the workers would not go on fighting against Russia "for the purpose of electing the Emperor of Austria King of Poland and of helping the King of Prussia to gain military and economic domination over Latvia and Lithuania."

Even as the party organized mass meetings in Vienna to coordinate the strike, the Habsburg army command mobilized to meet the situation. Several divisions of Bosnian, Romanian, and Ruthenian garrison troops, who could neither speak nor understand the German of the striking workers, and who had not been influenced by the propaganda of the fraternizing Bolshevik troops on the Eastern Front, were brought into Vienna. Plans were drawn up for a military dictatorship, should it prove necessary to maintain law and order.

The old Habsburg trick of pitting nationalities against one another, which had worked to put down the Revolution of 1848, worked again. Under the menacing threat of machine guns a delegation from the Social Democratic party negotiated a pledge from Czernin that peace would be arranged as soon as possible with the Bolsheviks, that food supplies would be expanded, and that military controls in the factories would be curtailed. Most of the Workers Councils approved the negotiated pledge, and the workers returned to their factories, only eight days after the strike had broken out. A small faction of Left radicals refused to accept the pledges, but even Otto Bauer recognized and explained that an overthrow of the regime would have brought an invasion by the Germans—a fate even worse than slow starvation.

The revolution had failed. Yet important lessons were learned. The week of revolutionary demonstrations showed how powerful and organized the working class of the empire could be. For anyone who still doubted, it showed that peace could not long be delayed. It woke the Social Democratic party to the responsibility of leading a mass movement with revolutionary inertia; and the reassertion of leadership by the party restored mass support to the leaders, leaving the Far Left as an isolated minority again.

Even more important, the revolutionary demonstrations of January were the first notes of the last waltz of Habsburg politics, notes which showed that the old one-two-three of Emperor-Army-Bureaucracy might break down as the tempo changed from the familiar *Blue Danube* to the mad whirl of *La Valse*.*

For Trotsky and the other Bolshevik negotiators at Brest-Litovsk, the outburst in Austria signified "the first recognition of our method of conducting peace negotiations, the first recognition we received from the proletariat of the Central Powers against the annexationist demands of German militarism." Sure that the disturbances would ultimately bloom into a full-scale revolution, Trotsky declared that the Bolsheviks would neither fight the Central Powers nor carry on the negotiations for an annexationist peace. In a huff his delegation left Brest, believing that this last blast of their trumpet would surely bring down the walls.

Meanwhile, the Ukrainians had declared their independence from Russia, and they quickly concluded a peace with Germany and Austria which pledged massive shipments of grain and other rawstuffs in exchange for manufactured goods. During the parleys the Red Army thrust into Kiev, and to guarantee the independence of the Ukraine the Germans attacked the Russian troops. Communiqués from the front called it a tactical move to protect supply lines into the Ukraine; in fact it was nothing less than the resumption of war on the Eastern Front, which provoked an enormous outcry in Austria. "Bleeding from a thousand wounds, Russia today menaces nobody," declared the *Arbeiter-Zeitung*. "What the German empire does is its own affair. Austria-Hungary can neither prevent nor resist it. But 90 percent of the Austrians say, 'Germany's new war against Russia is not and shall not be our war.'"

---

* Maurice Ravel wrote of *La Valse*: "I feel this work a kind of apotheosis of the Viennese Waltz, linked in my mind with the impression of a fantastic whirl of destiny."

As the German troops rapidly decimated Red Army units, Lenin finally persuaded his colleagues in the Bolshevik leadership that it was futile to continue the fight, and on February 24 the Soviet government capitulated. A treaty was signed some days later by a delegation from which Trotsky was conspicuously absent. The peace lopped off about one-third of the prewar land and population of Russia, more than half of the industrial facilities, and almost all of the coal mines. Reflecting back on the abortive January "revolution" in Austria in which he had put all his hopes, Trotsky mused, "We mistook the second month of pregnancy for the ninth." The *Arbeiter-Zeitung* dutifully condemned the draconian character of the treaty, but as the German and Austrian troops moved in to occupy the Ukraine, with its enormous reserves of coal and grain, hungry Austrians were too excited to worry seriously about the fate of Soviet Russia.

The fierce waltz of Habsburg politics did not stop for the formalities of the treaty. At the beginning of February a mutiny broke out among the sailors of the main naval squadron at Kotor on the Dalmatian coast. The sailors, driven to desperation by months of inactivity and by the daily injustice of eating black bread while the officers' dogs were fed beefsteak, deposed the officers on most of the ships of the line, hoisted the red flag, and appealed for support to the socialists in Vienna and Budapest. A loyal naval squadron from Pula quickly put down the mutiny (mainly because the naïve sailors had neglected to seize the radio transmission facilities). Only Victor Adler's threat that massive strikes in the munitions factories were still possible saved most of the mutineers from execution. In the next months there were scattered instances of other military disturbances. Hungarian, Slovene, Czech, and Serb battalions mutinied, refused service, or even murdered officers. Returning prisoners of war who brought Bolshevik ideas posed another threat to military discipline. Yet, on the whole, the armed forces maintained their stance. The real threat came on the home front, where the tentative first notes of

January built up in a slow crescendo of exhaustion from war and starvation.

It took time for the occupying forces to move into the Ukraine and other areas of Russia, and in the meantime the situation within Austria grew daily more desperate. By late spring the bread ration had been cut again. The daily food allowance consisted of three ounces of flour, one ounce of meat, one-quarter ounce of fat, two and one-half ounces of potatoes, and three-quarters of an ounce of jam. Even this ration could not be met with available supplies, and to make up the deficit food scientists worked frantically to produce fat substitutes from chestnuts and even from rats. Fuel shortages were so severe that heating became the luxury of those fortunate few who were able to take valuables out into the country to barter with the peasants for a basket of wood. Even well-known aristocrats did not hesitate to barter feminine dainties for grain and other foodstuffs. Soldiers who were released from service to work in the mines and other civilian industries found the horse meat and black bread at home so intolerable that many begged to reenlist.

The promise from the East kept people alive and hoping through this deprivation. Yet, as the months crept by, the promise was never fulfilled. Vast areas of the Ukraine were occupied, and Austrian administrative headquarters were established at Kiev and Odessa. But the constant bureaucratic delays of a quartermaster corps which seemed to be staffed with Schweiks, together with the fact that the Russian peasants were unwilling to grow and harvest crops that they knew were destined for Germany and Austria, kept shipments to a minimum. The coal mines mysteriously halved their production overnight, and the railway network in Russia was so wrecked by the war that shipments could seemingly never be routed in the direction of Austria. What little grain and fuel was gathered was taken by the German army, and with the exception of a ship which the wily Austrians commandeered on its way to

Germany, and a few paltry token shipments, almost nothing reached the civilian population of Austria.

To most Austrians the situation was incomprehensible. First there had been Hungary, rich with grain and coal and supposedly part of the monarchy—but little food or fuel came from Hungary. Then there was Romania, crushed in the difficult fighting of 1916 to supply grain and oil—but no grain or oil came from Romania. Now Great Russia was supposed to supply enough food and fuel to make up for three and one-half years of death and privation—and nothing came from Russia. It was hard to know whom to blame more, enemies or allies. Even more, it was hard to understand why, after peace had been concluded in the East and victories won on the Balkan and Italian fronts, the war had to be continued.

And yet the war went on. The Germans, flush with their victory over the Russians, massed troops from the Russian and Italian fronts for the final onslaught in the West against France, England, and now, the United States. After the German attack of March 1918 had begun, the Habsburg High Command, goaded on by the Germans, decided to strike afresh at Italy. Dreaming of a repetition of Caporetto, the generals set Venice and Padua as their immediate targets. Troops released from the Romanian and Russian theaters were concentrated on the Italian front. It was the first time in the war that the entire Habsburg forces had been assembled on a single front, without German support. Borrowing a page from Napoleon, Karl published a proclamation to remind his soldiers that beyond the Piave "Glory awaits you, and also honor, good food, abundant spoils—and peace."

Although many might question the priorities, there was no question that the empire needed glory, honor, food, spoils, and peace. But once again fortune was not with the Austrians. The ferocious attack in June met determined Italian resistance. The one column of Austrians that broke through the Italian lines was halted by torrential rains and unprecedented floods. After ten days of fighting Habsburg losses in killed, wounded, and missing exceeded one hundred forty thousand. No territory had been captured. Whatever scrap of dignity the Austrian military forces had once affected was now a sham. Although discipline miraculously held together in the armies, as a fighting force the Austro-Hungarian troops were too decimated and starved to matter any longer.

As if his military woes and the now widespread starvation were not troubles enough, spring brought Karl the unexpected harvest of the peace feelers he had sown the year before. Karl had not appraised his Foreign Minister of the exact nature of the secret peace proposals, especially the fact that he had offered to side with the French on the question of Alsace-Lorraine. The upshot was that a careless speech by Czernin alienated Clemenceau, who retaliated by publishing the Emperor's "Sixtus Letter" with the damning clauses about Alsace-Lorraine. The Emperor swore oaths that the letter was a forgery, but no amount of juggling by the propagandists could restore his credibility. Chauvinists blamed the Empress Zita and her Italian background, wags nicknamed the Emperor *Karl der Letzte*, and the Germans decided to tighten the alliance even further. The Austrians were forced to send four divisions to the Western Front, guaranteeing that Austria-Hungary could make no separate peace with the Entente. Under a scarcely veiled threat that Austria too could be invaded by Germany, Karl and Wilhelm personally renewed their alliance in a "summit" meeting at Spa. A few chauvinists in Austria managed to find praise for the new alliance; the *Arbeiter-Zeitung*, unhampered by the censors, called it "The Road to Hell."

22

Revolution

By the spring of 1918, the monarchy had long given up any hopes of victory. The fight was simply for survival, and in that struggle too the chances grew ever more slim as from every side the empire itself was called into question. In the foreign press analysis ranged from expert historical studies to the wretched doggerel of some of the English papers:

> But what is Austria? Is is fair
> To name among the nations
> Some Germans who have clutched the hair
> Of divers populations,
> And, having clutched, keep tugging there?

And even as the empire was threatened by enemies and allies alike from without, the centrifugal and hostile forces within began to tear at the structure, like vultures mauling a still-live but moribund body. "In the great world league of nations," warned the *Arbeiter-*

Zeitung, "there is no room for the old Austria; if Austria is to continue to exist, it must be changed into a union of free nations. . . ." When the parliamentary session of 1918 opened, a Czech delegate shouted out: "Long live democracy, long live the new, free Europe, long live the free Bohemian state, long live self-determination of peoples, which will end the present butchery and yield rich blessings to humanity." Free nations? Democracy? Self-determination of peoples?—such ideas were anathema to the very idea of the old Habsburg empire.

In April 1918 a Congress of Oppressed Nationalities met in Rome, attended by Czech, Yugoslav, Polish, and Romanian representatives who jointly proclaimed the right of self-determination, denounced the existence of the Habsburg government, and pledged an unending struggle against the Habsburgs. Czech, Polish, and Yugoslav legions already fought against the Habsburg troops in Russia, France, and Italy; and in Paris, London, and Washington the newly formed exile governments prepared to declare their independence from the Habsburgs. First Masaryk's Czechoslovak state, which had the special blessings of Woodrow Wilson, then the Polish and Yugoslav states, received recognition of their independence from the Entente powers. Only Hungary and German-Austria remained.

The Magyars of Hungary remained loyal to the crown, but only if the integrity of the historic crown lands could be preserved, which meant somehow denying the rights of the large Romanian, Croat, and Slovak minorities, who were busy organizing their own governments. Poor Karl, eager to cultivate his only loyal supporters, made desperate efforts to straighten out the tangle, but his flustered machinations led only to unpardonable faux pas. On one visit to Budapest he allowed the Austrian national anthem to be played in front of his residence, alienating all but his most blindly faithful Hungarian supporters. On another visit he appointed two prime ministers for Hungary in a single day, without telling either about the other. The politicians who dashed from Vienna to

Budapest and back succeeded only in tying more knots in what was already a hopeless tangle.

In German-Austria almost every week of the spring and summer brought fresh strikes and demonstrations. The Social Democratic party, by coordinating and sponsoring the strikes, grew daily more influential and stronger, until it was clear that in the inevitable change of regime the Social Democrats would be the leading force. They were the only party whose principles allowed, even compelled, plans to deal with the collapse of the monarchy. Not long after the January strikes the party formulated a new "nationality program" which recognized the rights of self-determination for the Czechs, Poles, and Yugoslavs, and claimed the same rights for the Germans of Austria. There were hints that the socialists favored joining up with a democratic Germany. In any case, the Social Democrats were through with the old monarchy. "There are three kinds of rats," said Victor Adler. "Some are clever and leave the ship before it sinks; others are honorable and remain although she sinks; the third kind are stupid, notice nothing at all, and go on board the ship. We are not going to be the third kind of rat."

The bourgeois parties either quit the ship, like the German Nationalists, who concluded that they had no choice but to side with the Social Democrats, or stayed on board to the end, like the Christian Socialists who with the Church stuck by the honorable "My Emperor, right or wrong!" Ministers resigned as fast as they could be appointed, beginning with Czernin, who left after the Sixtus Affair, and Prime Minister Seidler, who quit his "temporary" appointment after a year of frustrated efforts to force the parliament into action. Endless ministerial meetings and crown councils always came back to the same question—How to save the monarchy? If things continued, the strikes and the revolt of the subject nationalities would overturn the government in a matter of months. If troops were withdrawn from the front to put down the strikes the empire risked a massive invasion by the Italians, who were known to be assembling their troops for an attack. What to do? the rulers asked each other. For the first time it was too late to *fortwursteln*.

The final bars of the last waltz began in the middle of September, when French troops under General Franchet d'Esperey broke through the Bulgarian front. The Bulgarian army, even more demoralized and decimated than the Austro-Hungarian forces, melted away. The defeated troops marched on their own capital. On September 29 Bulgaria signed an armistice.

The same day General Ludendorf admitted that the final German offensive in the West had failed, that the German armies were defeated, and that there was no course open but to sue for peace. The shocking news of defeat, following on four years of promises of victories, brought down the German government and brought the cities to a state bordering on revolution.

When the collapse seemed imminent in Austria, "Lieutenant Berger" of the Left-Radical organization, came to Sophie Lazarsfeld with the plan that the railway workers could engineer Fritz's escape from Stein. Sophie's job was to clear the break with Fritz.

On her next visit Sophie told Fritz the plan. He listened with his usual patience, holding his head perfectly still and attentive as if he agreed with every word. Then the great head of hair shook back and forth.

"No," he said. "The Emperor has imprisoned me, the Emperor must set me free." There was no further talk of any escape.

The Emperor and his government were not so ready to discuss the end. Parliament reconvened on October 1, but the only concession to change that the new Prime Minister, Baron von Hussarek, would allow in his opening address was that a certain amount of federalization of the empire might prove necessary. From all sides speakers jumped up to answer him. A Czech deputy, Stanek, hurled out his defiance of the old order:

The turning point in this terrible war, which we Czechs did not want and which we fought against, has been passed. The war is approaching an end. The day of judgement is at hand. . . . The time is coming when all races must consider what their attitude is to be toward Austria and Hungary. And we? We have suffered most under the Austrian yoke. Not one drop of blood have we shed willingly for the Central Powers. Our co-nationals, however, as an indication of our willingness, are present in all the Entente armies. There we have shed blood gladly, there we have fought for an ideal, have done our part.

As he continued, the session broke into antics which exceeded even the traditional travesty of decorum. Some deputies applauded, others shouted "Treason!", the presiding officer clanged away at the gong to restore order, a briefcase flew across the room, an inkstand flew back. When order was finally restored the only remark the Prime Minister could summon up was: "After all, this House is here to deal with practical questions. The minority matters which I have just explained are a side issue."

Most of the Slav deputies left that night, never to return.

On October 3 the Social Democrats all but proclaimed a German-Austrian state:

We recognize the right of the Slav nations to form their own national states, but we protest sharply and forever against a subjection of German interests to these states. We demand that all German districts of Austria be united in a German-Austrian State which shall regulate its relations to the other nations of Austria and to Germany as it itself requires.

While the dismemberment went on, the Emperor and his tiny coterie of officials floated in a dream world. On October 12 the Emperor called representatives of the nationalities to his headquarters to discuss plans for the future structure of the empire. On October 16 he issued a manifesto, promising that each nation should have its own state within the federated empire. At the insistence of the Magyars, who threatened to cut off the last trickle of food into Austria, the manifesto contained a fatal clause: "The integrity of the provinces of the Holy Hungarian Crown is in no way affected." In effect, that clause invalidated the whole intent, but it did not really matter, for no one took notice of the manifesto except to remark that it came anywhere from six months to fifty years too late.

In planning for a new German-Austrian state, the Social Democrats insisted upon a clean break with all of the institutions of the old regime, including parliament, which they wanted to replace with a constituent assembly having the right to appoint a provisional government. The other parties balked at the demand that the new government would have to be a republic, but under the pressure of the crowds of workers who now surged through the streets, the German Nationalists and the Christian Socialists finally yielded. On October 21 a Provisional National Assembly of German Austria met to begin negotiations for the formation of a new government.

It was obvious that the republic could not be postponed for long. In fact, with the formation of new governments the old empire was dead—all that remained were the formalities of the abdication of the Emperor and the proclamation of the republic.

Crowds in the street could hardly wait for the abdication. Striking workers, joined by housewives and soldiers who were discharged at the front or who simply left the front (in a more orderly era it had been called desertion), rampaged through the streets of the city, tearing down the imperial eagles from the fronts of houses, stomping on the Habsburg standards wherever they found them. Soldiers tore the rosettes with the imperial initials from their uniforms and insisted that officers do the same. Bands of Left-Radical workers, some of whom were already calling themselves Communists, marched through Vienna shouting "Out with Friedrich Adler! Out with all political prisoners!"

Two officers climbed on a trolley stand to shout that a deputation should be sent to the government to call for the building of a new army. Another officer stood nearby holding up a portrait of a national guardsman in uniform. The crowd would have none of it. "We need no soldiers and no police!" they shouted back. "We have had enough of always being ruled! We are free men! Down with militarism!"

Having failed at everything else, poor Karl was left with the inglorious task of arranging an armistice, hopefully in time to use the remnants of his armies to restore order and somehow preserve the monarchy. Frantically he wired to different Entente capitals to arrange a cease-fire before the Italians should attack. Woodrow Wilson, speaking for the Entente, answered that a peace could be arranged in accord with the Fourteen Points, but that commitments to the Czechoslovaks and the Yugoslavs made them the final arbiters of any terms of peace. That answer was the death knell for the monarchy.

On October 23 Karl pathetically implored the Pope, in the name of humanity, to seek a pledge from the Italians not to attack. The next day, on the anniversary of the battle of Caporetto, General Diaz launched an enormous assault along the whole front. For five days the Austro-Hungarian forces miraculously held out —soldiers fighting and dying for an empire that had ceased to exist. Then rumors of what was happening at home reached the troops in the trenches, and the cry went up: "Home to protect our villages!" The retreat quickly turned to a rout. Units ceased to exist as soldiers who mistakenly thought an armistice had been concluded became part of the three hundred thousand prisoners taken by the Italians in the victory they were to call the Vittorio

Veneto. For the other Habsburg troops it was every man for himself, as soldiers threw down their guns and by train, truck, horse, or simply walking, they went home. Within days, the mainstay of the monarchy, the imperial armies, vanished.

With the last vestiges of authority collapsing, the Supreme Command, haunted by the specter of a Bolshevik upheaval, authorized subordinates to conclude an immediate armistice. The Italians, under the auspices of the Supreme War Council of the Entente, had already prepared an essentially military surrender, with terms as harsh as could be imagined. "There is one thing you have omitted," said Clemenceau when he read the document. "You have not demanded the Emperor's breeches." The agreement was signed on October 31 and went into effect on November 4.

As the generals signed the agreement at the Villa Giusti, near Padua, the Imperial Crown Council met in Schönbrunn Palace to discuss the terms of the surrender. Politicians and generals stared at one another and at the Emperor in absolute disbelief as everyone hesitated to discuss the inevitable.

Victor Adler, attending the meeting on behalf of the Provisional Assembly, said: "We did not make this war. Let the men who are responsible for the war reply to the armistice demands."

"Neither did I make the war," plainted poor Karl.

It took a minor state functionary named Maier to recall what almost everyone had forgotten: "I remember how wildly everyone demanded war when it started. The whole nation is guilty for the war."

"Tomorrow at eleven there will be a revolution. In case of rain the revolution will take place indoors." The anonymous placard on a Vienna kiosk was a remarkably accurate caricature of the denouement of Austria-Hungary.

In the classic pattern of revolutions, events are usually

decided on the barricades, where the forces of revolution square off against the forces of repression. If the forces that represent the old order can be disarmed or won over, the revolution is victorious. In Austria the forces of repression—the imperial armies—were so destroyed by four years of war that the revolution found no opposition at home, no need even to mount the barricades.

On October 30, the Provisional National Assembly for German-Austria met again, this time to nominate a Political Council to take power from the all-but-defunct imperial government. For the first time in Austrian history, Social Democrats were put in charge of state departments: Victor Adler was named Secretary for Foreign Affairs, with Otto Bauer as his deputy; Ferdinand Haunusch was named Secretary for Social Welfare; and Karl Renner was named Chancellor. The appointment of the Political Council was in fact the political revolution in Austria, although the proclamation of the republic was delayed in the hope that the Emperor would abdicate without the prodding that was so distasteful to the kindly revolutionaries. In the meantime, the newly nominated state secretaries shared the offices of the ministries with the Emperor's ministers. Because Karl and his ministers neither gave orders nor obstructed the actions of the new secretaries, the "dual power"—to use Trotsky's expression—functioned without a hitch.

At the first official meeting of the Political Council, on October 31, the Social Democratic members moved that all political prisoners be amnestied immediately. This had been one of the chief demands of the crowds in the streets, and the Social Democrats were eager to maintain the support of their constituency. The motion passed. Before it could be proclaimed, the old Council of Ministers rushed to preempt the Political Council, hoping that a popular measure would grant them some support in the streets. On the afternoon of All Saints Day, the Minister of Justice, Paul von Vitorelli, signed an amnesty for all political prisoners.

FRITZ

The next evening Gustav Harpner spoke at a Social Democratic rally: "I have a joyful announcement to make to you. At this moment, as I speak, Fritz Adler is free."

The announcement prompted a sustained standing ovation. When the news hit the streets it provoked loud demonstrations. ". . . there is no proletarian among us whose heart does not beat faster when he hears the name Friedrich Adler," read the lead in the *Arbeiter-Zeitung*. Through the assassination, and especially through the now well-publicized speeches in the trial, Fritz had become the hero of the working class. In the strikes and demonstrations that had constantly rumpled the order of Austria since the beginning of 1918, the Left faction of the Social Democratic party had constantly kept Fritz's name alive with their shouts and demands for his release. He was the only working-class leader—except perhaps for Otto Bauer—who was not tainted by some record of cooperation with the now thoroughly discredited war government. He had never supported the war, and as the Left reminded everyone, he had never "sold out the workers."

Among the bourgeois of Vienna, too, there were few hearts that did not beat faster at the name of Friedrich Adler. Since the trial, and especially after the first violence of January 1918, Fritz's name had become almost synonymous with Bolshevism. In their propaganda, the Russian revolutionaries had saluted Fritz as the true leader of the Austrian working class, and while he had never made any endorsement of Lenin and Trotsky, his views seemed to echo the Russians, whom the good burghers of Austria feared more than the victorious armies of Italy, England, and France. For thousands who feared that the imminent revolution could mean their status, their property, and perhaps their lives, Fritz Adler was the most notorious man in Austria.

Because he was afraid that Fritz's reception in Vienna might precipitate demonstrations that the Social Democrats could not control, Victor kept the details of Fritz's release secret. He went alone to meet Fritz at Stein, and told no one when or where they would come to Vienna.

Victor did not have his son to himself for long. Later that morning Victor and the other members of the Political Council met with the Emperor at Schönbrunn Palace. For Victor, whose heart condition had worsened appreciably, the broad steps of the palace were almost too much. Although he was escorted on each arm, he stumbled in the middle of the staircase and fell to his knees. The Empress came down to offer her arm. Victor, refusing all help, somehow found the strength to stagger up the rest of the steps alone.

While Victor met with the Emperor, Fritz hurried to the pension where Sophie was living. It had been arranged already that he would meet there with the leaders of the Left-Radical faction. The delegates, who represented the revolutionary social-ists who had wanted to seize power in January 1918 and many veterans who had returned from Russian prisoner-of-war camps, told Fritz that they wanted to form an Austrian Communist party, and that they wanted him to be the leader of the new party. The same day the Soviet Ambassador in Vienna, Christian Rakowsky, brought Fritz the formal greetings of the Soviet government, with the intimation that in Moscow there was hope that he would take the lead in a soviet revolution in Austria.

The Workers and Soldiers Councils had already reformed in Vienna and other industrial centers of German-Austria to dis-seminate news on the progress of the "revolution" and to solicit and organize the views of workers on the situation. They were already echoing the Russian model in their fervent shouts: "All power to the Workers and Soldiers Soviets!" One word from Fritz would have been enough to set off an attempt to seize power.

It was not until November 6 that Fritz finally addressed the Workers Council of Vienna. Ironically the room they had taken over for their meetings was the Jury Trial Room of the

FRITZ

Vienna courthouse, the room in which Fritz had been tried some nineteen months before. The workers greeted his appearance and his every word with thunderous applause.

"The Entente has won," he said. "The war has not ended as we would have wanted four years ago, through the rebellion of the international proletariat; unfortunately it has ended through the power of the weaponry of one of the warmaking powers." The problem now was to draw lessons from the past and to decide upon the future—the revolution.

He continued:

You know, colleagues, that there is a prescription—the Russian. It has been said: the soviet republic instead of the democratic republic. I will not debate the question here, hopefully I can do something about it in the near future. For now I will only say that both possibilities lie within the range of choice open to the proletariat. . . . I would have to study this question much more closely before I can give a definitive opinion.

The question for now, he went on, was the party itself. Reviewing the difficulties the party had suffered in the 1880s, when it was divided into bickering factions which the government had played off against one another, Fritz urged the importance of unity.

Thus, when men come and find, now is the moment to found a new party, then I say: Two years ago, it was perhaps the moment to discuss this matter, when the question was immediate and real. Today I believe we are beyond that point and we can *work within the party for the international revolutionary program of the Social Democracy.*

That point was greeted with the loudest applause of the speech, giving Fritz perhaps a truer inkling of the sentiment of the workers than the views of the group of leftists who were so anxious to declare themselves a Communist party to set the revolutionary seizure of power into motion.

The stormy applause certified Fritz's popularity. It did not settle the question of what direction the workers should follow in the future. Without Fritz's charisma the Left could not move. Yet Fritz, suddenly cautious, insisted upon studying and familiarizing himself with a situation with which he had lost all touch for more than two years. He would rely only on his own judgment. The mad whirl of politics in Vienna could not wait.

In the Political Council negotiations were in progress to work out the future form of the government of German-Austria. Potentially Fritz and his father were headed on another collision course as his father, in the capacity of Foreign Secretary, drew up many of the plans for what would be a democratic coalition government, a government in which the Social Democrats would be a majority but without absolute control. Only the fact that father and son were too busy even to meet kept them from another round of ferocious political arguments, which might have driven Fritz precipitously to a position farther to the left than his own perception of the scene would lead him.

In peace, as in war, the Austrians remained desperately dependent upon the guidance of Germany. It was not until the collapse of the German empire and the abdication of the Kaiser in favor of a Social Democratic government, on November 9, that the Political Council in Austria decided to go ahead with the plans for the proclamation of the Austrian Republic. By then the Social Democrats had concluded that Austria could not survive alone, and the planned proclamation of the republic was to include a clause proclaiming the unity of German-Austria with democratic Germany. November 11 was set as the day when the final details would be worked out, and another meeting of the Provisional National Assembly was scheduled for November 12 to ratify the program.

While his empire collapsed around him poor Karl sat almost alone in Schönbrunn Palace, Emperor of a fallen empire and Commander-in-Chief of armies and navies that had ceased to exist. On Karl's name day, November 5, Cardinal Piffl had celebrated mass in honor of the sovereign in St. Stephen's Cathedral— as if nothing were changed in Austria. But what Karl saw in the city was enough to convince him of the truth. Everywhere the Habsburg insignia and standards had been torn down and replaced with red flags, crowds sang the *Internationale* and workers' hymns instead of the imperial anthem, irregular bands of troops calling themselves People's Militia marched through the streets to the *Marseillaise*.

At noon on November 11, Karl penciled his signature to a letter of abdication:

> Since my accession to the throne, I have unceasingly tried to spare my nations the horror of war, for the outbreak of which I bear no responsibility. I have never hesitated to restore constitutional life, and I have opened the way for my nations to their independent political development. Since I am filled now, as before, by unchangeable love for all my nations, I will not place my person as an obstacle to their free evolution . . .

That evening, as the Emperor and his entourage left in a fleet of seven cars for the imperial hunting lodge at Ecksartsau, the city was filled with rumors. The deliberations of the Political Council, the Workers and Soldiers Councils, and the remnants of the imperial government had all gone on in varying degrees of secrecy, leaving the people in the streets to speculate on what would happen. The President of the Police heard that the Red Guard (a defense force the Left-Radicals had built up from cadres of former prisoners of war) was set to storm the parliament building. On a signal from their leader, Frey, they would seize and arrest the members of the Political Council and the government.

Then Friedrich Adler would proclaim the Soviet Republic of Austria.

The rumor was false.

On Sunday, November 10, Victor was getting ready to leave for the Foreign Ministry when he suffered another heart attack. After a morphine injection he fell into a half-sleep, from which he did not awaken until the next morning. Emma and Fritz sat by his bed through the night.

When Victor finally woke, his first words were to Fritz: "Did someone excuse me from the meeting?" Then: "What is happening in Germany?"

Fritz told his father about the formation of the Social Democratic government in Berlin. Victor murmured: "That is good. And the cease-fire—is it working?" He mumbled a few more incomprehensible phrases, then said, clearly, "Yes, I will not be going there anymore. They will have to excuse me."

Two minutes later he died.

23

Aftermath

The Austrian Republic was proclaimed from the steps of the parliament building on November 12, 1918. A general strike honored the occasion, and while the Provisional National Assembly ratified the necessary measures inside the building, a crowd of thousands outside cheered each messenger who brought reports of the proceedings.

In the following months and years the crowd would painfully learn the hardships that faced a small republic in Central Europe. Austria was cut off from the sea and from its regular industrial and agricultural supplies, surrounded by potentially hostile states, and at the mercy of the victor powers. Yet somehow the little republic survived, and the Social Democratic government was able to muddle through, despite continuing food and fuel shortages, an attempted Communist coup d'état in June 1919, and the harsh treaties imposed by the vindictive peacemakers who had gathered in Paris under the tutelage of Woodrow Wilson. Although chaos and privation were to continue for many years, the new government did manage to effect many important reforms of the economy, the bureaucracy, and the educational systems. Indeed, in the 1920s Austria was transformed from one of the most backward states in Europe into the first modern welfare state.

Early in 1919 the old leaders of the Second International decided to revive the defunct organization. A conference at Bern in February 1919 was attended by representatives of what had become the Right and Centrist factions of the socialist movements, those parties and splinter groups who had either supported the war all along, or who had broken with the warring governments but had refrained from leading revolutionary activity. The consensus of the new group was that the era of revolution had long passed. The proper course of all socialist parties, they decided, was to work for reforms within the existing government structures. Yet while the group had broken with the ideology of the old International, they had inherited its intolerance. One of their first acts, passed over the objections of a small group of Centrists who wanted to leave the road open for a reunification of the international movement, was a resolution on "Democracy and Dictatorship" which condemned the Bolsheviks and other revolutionary groups. Even before the resolution was voted, the Social Democratic government in Germany had put down a Spartacist (Communist) uprising, in the first of many instances of workers shedding the blood of workers.

One month after the Bern conference, a hastily summoned conference of leftist and revolutionary factions of labor movements gathered in Moscow to form the Third International under the patronage and direction of the Bolshevik government. As their first act they condemned the "social patriots" of the Second International, thereby ratifying the already irreconcilable split in the international socialist movement. The following years aggravated the break, and it was not long before the polite names of the early twenties escalated to the raucus epithet of "Social Fascists" which punctuated the political rhetoric of the pre-Hitler era.

His courtiers did not abandon the old titles, but for most of the world Karl had become Herr Habsburg. He spent four months at the Ecksartsau lodge. From his window there he could see the field where his thirteenth-century ancestors had fought the battle that ultimately led to the great fortunes of the dynasty. In time the reminder became too painful, and Karl left by train for Switzerland. People who were at the siding when the Emperor's train left Austria for the last time seemed not to know what gestures would be appropriate. Most looked at their feet in embarrassment.

Twice Karl returned from exile to set up plans for a restoration. The first time he traveled by ordinary train coach, using the passport of his gardner. "I have eaten nothing except salami and dry bread for two days," was his first statement on reaching Vienna. When negotiations proved fruitless he returned to Switzerland. The second return, by airplane, included a dramatic landing in the Burgenland between Vienna and the Hungarian frontier. The reception committee consisted of two small boys who seemed much more interested in the airplane than in the august passengers. When the royal party crossed into Hungary they were captured by a *Honved* regiment and placed in custody aboard a British destroyer anchored in the Danube at Budapest. Some of the more excitable Central European politicians suggested St. Helena as a suitable place of exile. The British were loathe to invite the comparison and took Karl to Madeira instead. There he died on All Fools Day 1922.

We are left with our hero.

For Fritz the end of the war and the revolution in Austria were the fulfillment of years of political dreams. It was for this that he had struggled with the censors and the party during the war, for this that he had been willing to sacrifice everything, for this that he had forced himself to a violent act which was repugnant to his very nature, for this that he had spent two years in prison. Yet the realization of those dreams was an anticlimax. There is a security in adversity; the peace and the revolution robbed Fritz of that security, forcing him to step into a politics for which he had little patience and talent. And unlike those heroes who are fortunate enough to be martyred at the moment of glory, it was Fritz's fate to live on for another forty years, watching his dream crushed again and again by the same old enemies.

After years of complete self-absorption, years in which he had relied upon his own judgments to the complete exclusion of the opinions and views of colleagues and enemies alike, Fritz was ill-prepared for the world of politics toward which events were rapidly thrusting him.

Even as he stepped into his father's shoes, Fritz was an outsider in Austrian politics, caught between the Social Democratic government, which included men like Karl Renner who would never forget the wartime antagonisms, and the more radical elements of the working class, the Communists, who wanted to seize power and proclaim the Soviet Republic. As the popular hero of the working class, Fritz was acclaimed Chairman of the Workers Council, which continued to function even after a new coalition government was elected.

Fritz thus inherited the thankless task of coördinating the interests and demands of the workers, as expressed in the Workers Council, with the new programs and policies of the government, many of which he did not wholly approve. Rationing laws and strict economic measures especially were rather unpopular with the workers, and since the Workers Council seems to have inherited the protocol and procedures of the Austrian parliament, it was a demanding task to persuade the workers into accepting various measures. Indeed, it was the kind of work on which Victor, the politician, would have thrived, and for which Fritz, the theoretician, had little patience.

Fritz's biggest problem was the Communists, with their unrelenting demands for the seizure of power by the Workers Council, especially after the proclamation of the Soviet Republics in Munich and Budapest in March 1919. Fritz was convinced that in the tiny Austrian Republic, which was still occupied by Entente forces and dependent upon daily shipments of supplies from potentially hostile neighbors, the seizure of power would be suicidal. In less than a week a revolutionary government would be toppled by the occupying forces, with ultimate consequences in an even harsher peace treaty and an imposed government that would be very antipathetic to working-class demands. After long acrimonious arguments, his views finally prevailed in the Workers Council, but his support of what had gradually become an unpopular position ultimately cost him his commanding role as a working-class hero. "Popularity," he said, "is capital which has only to be employed for this purpose to be consumed."

In the International, too, Fritz was trapped between the old Right and the new Left. In January 1919 Lenin and Trotsky invited Fritz to be the Honorary Secretary of the new Third International. He turned them down to attend the Bern conference, where he unsuccessfully led the fight against the purge of the Bolsheviks. His stand alienated him from both groups. He became an outspoken minority in the renewed Second International, and his refusal to accept the entreaties of the Third International earned him a permanent election to the new list of traitors to the working class which was being compiled in Moscow. In time Fritz became so discouraged by the antagonism between the two factions of the international movement that he quit the Second International in protest. That was in 1920.

It thus took only a little more than one year for Fritz to tumble from a charismatic zenith in the International and in the Austrian party to his old and familiar position of isolation. Once again the absolute intransigence of his integrity, his unwillingness even to discuss what he called principle or to consider a compromise of policy, had left him without influence or a position from which to operate in the formative years of postwar Europe.

In 1921 Fritz tried to reunite the International by forming a new international organization in Vienna. The new group, dubbed "the Second and a Half International" by political wags, was promptly rejected by both sides. To the Second International Fritz and his new colleagues were guilty of factionalism, a socialist crime for which he had already established a certain notoriety during the war. To Lenin and the other leaders in Moscow, the Second and a Half International, like the Second International, was nothing but a renegade band of counterrevolutionary traitors.

When the mediation effort failed, Fritz went back to the Second International, which had by now changed its name to the Socialist Workers International to escape the opprobrium of wartime memories. Fritz and the English trade-union leader Tom Shaw were elected Co-Secretaries of the International in 1923.

For the next seventeen years Fritz worked at the tedious and menial labors of the International Bureau, work not unlike what he had done when he first worked for the Austrian Social Democratic party in 1911. He coordinated the correspondence of the various parties, arranged trade-union conferences, held discussions and forums on the status of reforms in the European states, and traveled throughout Europe to speak on various topics. His scientific pursuits, which ended with the lukewarm reception given his last work,* were not the only personal sacrifice of these years.

---

* After he received a copy of the *Ortzeit, Systemzeit, Zonenzeit* study, Einstein wrote unequivocally that it was based upon a grave error. (Einstein is on record as being of the opinion that the writings of Engels did not have "any special interest either from the point of view of

When the bureau moved from London to Zurich and later to Brussels, Fritz followed, leaving old friends from Vienna, like Sophie, to the vagaries of letters and the occasional fleeting meetings of his speaking tours.

After 1921 Fritz could no longer afford to support his family in Switzerland. Kathia reluctantly moved first to Vienna, then wherever the activities of the bureau took them, but the years of separation and the effect of Fritz's friendship with Sophie could never be repaired. Home life became a series of bitter and rancorous disputes which left Fritz resentful and frustrated. Yet he could no more leave Kathia than he could have left the Austrian Social Democratic party, even in the worst of times; once made, an oath of fidelity was too absolute to break.

Although he had become the Grand Old Man of the International, Fritz remained always a man of an earlier generation, a man who endlessly dreamed of the era when the great International had the potential of standing up against war and oppression by the sheer strength of its numbers. The 1920s and 1930s were the era of the League of Nations, an era when men looked to the international organization of states for the stability and peace that the Socialist International had not been able to guarantee in 1914. Men like Fritz, who still dreamed of the old days, seemed strangely out of place. When Fritz addressed an audience in France after the Popular Front government came to power, Leon Blum gave him a glowing introduction. In the middle of Fritz's speech Blum murmured to a colleague: "He shoots better than he speaks."

Especially after the attempted coups d'état in Austria and Germany in 1919 and the following years, Fritz grew more and more antagonistic toward the implacable and procrustean tactics of the Communists. He spoke out repeatedly against the excesses

present-day physics or from that of the history of physics.") Fritz went ahead with the publication of the work, but discontinued any further studies of epistemology.

315

of Stalinist policy, especially the purges, and from his work with the reformist International he gained a reputation as a firm anti-revolutionary, even among the non-Communist working-class parties. His repeated insistence that he was neither against any particular party, nor against revolution, but in favor of whatever policy was appropriate to the situation, was generally ignored. And when he visited Spain during the Civil War, his qualified disapproval of the Popular Front left behind feelings of incomprehension and hostility. "He disapproved of Madrid [the center of Communist strength] in offensive silence," remarked Arturo Barea after Fritz concluded an unimpressive tour.

When the other leaders of the International refused to take a strong and active stand against Hitler, even after the occupation of Czechoslovakia and the *Anschluss* with Austria, Fritz quit the International again in protest. "There can be no doubt," he wrote, "that the attempt to renew the International, to which I have dedicated my work, is wrecked; that the tendencies which in 1914 led to the worst defeats of the international labor movement, have again menacingly appeared."

At the outbreak of the Second World War, Fritz fled Brussels for New York, via France and Portugal, with the aid of a special "danger visa" obtained through the intervention of the American Federation of Labor. In New York he founded the Labor Aid Project, which used funds from the American labor unions to place emigré workers from Europe into jobs. He also worked with the Austrian Labor Committee, a group that was planning for the future of Austrian labor after the war.

In 1946, at the age of sixty-seven, Fritz returned to Europe to live in Zurich with his daughter. Kathia remained in New York for some years with their son, Felix. Two wars, each of which had destroyed the hopes and dreams of a generation of Europeans, left Fritz too disillusioned for a return to politics. Instead he turned to the quiet security of scholarship, beginning by collecting the papers and documents needed to write a biography of his father.

In 1954 he published a brilliantly annotated edition of Victor Adler's correspondence with Karl Kautsky and August Bebel. Fritz kept working on the various documents for the biography, transcribing and editing manuscripts and letters and collecting data from people who had known and worked with Victor, but as his strength faded he seemed to know that he would never finish the biography.

He died on January 2, 1960, at the age of eighty-one. In his original testament he had specified that his body be donated to the Zurich Anatomical Institute. After a long and bitter fight with Kathia he had given in to her wishes and withdrew the bequest. His remains were cremated and interred in a tomb with the remains of his father and other leaders of the Austrian Social Democratic party in the Central Cemetery in Vienna.

No monument was ever built for Fritz, and although many suitable lines could be found in his writings, there is no epitaph on his tomb.

Notes and Sources

After Fritz's death his private papers were collected at the Adler-Archiv (Verein für Geschichte der Arbeiterbewegung) of the Vienna Arbeiterkammer. Other significant papers and documents relating to his life have found their way into the archives of the Internationaal Instituut voor Sociale Geschiedenis in Amsterdam. This study has been based in large measure upon these unpublished documents, supplemented with what I have been able to glean from Fritz's published works, the scant writings on his life, and the voluminous writings on socialism and the Habsburg monarchy.

In the chapter notes which follow I have cited only those sources, both published and unpublished, that have proved especially valuable in writing this book. I have noted wherever my use of a source has been controversial or novel. Full citations are given in the first mention of a source; subsequent citations are by author or short title.

FRITZ

Since they were based upon information released by the War Surveillance Office, the accounts of the assassination in all of the
Viennese newspapers were almost identical. Here, as elsewhere, I
have relied upon the *Neue Freie Presse* and the *Arbeiter-Zeitung*,
because their coverage was usually fuller than that in the other
papers, and because their editorial biases are predictable.

CHAPTERS 2 AND 3

Three editions of the judicial proceedings against Friedrich Adler
have been published, all under the title *Vor dem Ausnahmegericht*. The first edition (Berlin, 1919) included only the transcript
of the trial, which Fritz had edited to exclude much of the medical
testimony and parts of Harpner's defense plea that referred to the
medical testimony. In the next edition (Jena, 1923) Fritz restored
the deleted material, and added other important documents, including the transcript of his pretrial interrogation, the letter of
resignation from the party which he had written in 1914, the
manifesto of December 3, 1915, and his postwar speech to the
Workers Council. The most recent edition of *Vor dem Ausnahmegericht* (Vienna, 1966) includes only the trial transcript.

Other material on Fritz's youth and his father's early involvement with the labor movement is from unpublished letters,
manuscripts, and memoirs in the Adler-Archiv. I have used much
of the unpublished material on the youth of Victor Adler in my
doctoral dissertation, "Victor Adler: the Making of a Socialist"
(Harvard University, 1968), which includes a lengthy biblio-
graphical essay on the Adler family and the early days of the labor
movement in Austria.

Stefan Grossmann's reminiscences of Fritz are in his auto-
biography, *Ich war begeistert* (Berlin, 1931), which is titled
rather more accurately than he may have intended. Grossmann
also wrote a play about the assassination and the trial, *Die beiden*

Adler (Vienna, 1931). It is not very successful either as history or as drama.

CHAPTER 4

Fritz describes much of his development as a scientist in the introduction to *Ernst Machs Uberwindung des mechanischen Materialismus* (Vienna, 1918). Fritz's letters to Kautsky are in the Kautsky Archive of the Internationaal Instituut voor Sociale Geschiedenis. Victor's correspondence with Kautsky and many other important socialist leaders has been published in Friedrich Adler, ed., *Victor Adlers Briefwechsel mit Karl Kautsky und August Bebel* (Vienna, 1954). Extracts from some of these letters and part of the unpublished correspondence of Victor and Fritz are cited in Julius Braunthal, *Victor und Friedrich Adler* (Vienna, 1965), an "official" biography by a man who knew both father and son well.

CHAPTER 5

The important documents on the development of the Social Democratic party in Austria are quoted at length in Ludwig Brügel, *Geschichte der österreichischen Sozialdemokratie*, 5 vols. (Vienna, 1922–1925). Volume 5 is the most important for the period of Fritz's involvement with the party.

CHAPTER 6

There are useful bibliographies on almost every aspect of the Habsburg monarchy in texts such as Arthur J. May, *Habsburg Monarchy, 1867–1914* (Cambridge, 1965) and the difficult but indispensable R. A. Kann, *The Multinational Empire . . . 1848–1918*, 2 vols. (New York, 1950). But no text is a substitute for a close reading of the incredible documents published in the *Reichsgesetzblatt*, the official Gazette, or for the memoirs of the many intellectuals and politicians who watched the monarchy through critical if jaundiced eyes. I have tried to balance the observations of insiders like Conrad von Hötzendorf, *Aus meiner Dienstzeit*, 5 vols. (Vienna, 1921–1925) against Josef Redlich's incisive observations of the great and near-great in his diaries, *Schicksalsjahre Österreichs: Das Tagebuch Josef Redlich*, F. Fellner, ed., 2 vols. (Graz and Cologne, 1953), and the brilliant autobiographies of Leon Trotsky, *My Life* (New York, 1960), and Stefan Zweig, *The World of Yesterday* (Lincoln, Nebraska, 1964). Yet neither the documents nor the memoirs seem to capture the spirit of the monarchy as well as the two novels I have quoted on the epigraph: Jaroslav Hašek, *The Good Soldier Schweik*, and Robert Musil, *The Man Without Qualities*.

CHAPTERS 7 AND 8

An excellent bibliography of published and unpublished materials on the Second International appears in Georges Haupt, *La deuxième internationale, 1889–1914* (Paris, 1964). The theoretical and tactical struggles of the socialists are chronicled, in the words of the leaders, in *Victor Adlers Briefwechsel*. Reactions to the threat of war and the Brussels meeting are reported in Fritz's own testimony, and in Angelica Balabanova, *My Life as a Rebel* (New York, 1938). Georges Haupt, *Le congrès manqué* (Paris, 1965) is a thorough study of the last terrible year of the International, based on all of the available published materials and on the unpublished archives of the Bureau of the Socialist International in Antwerp.

CHAPTERS 9 AND 10

See the notes to Chapter 6. In addition, I have relied heavily upon Arthur J. May, *The Passing of the Habsburg Monarchy, 1914-1918*, 2 vols. (Philadelphia, 1966) and Z. A. B. Zeman, *The Break-up of the Habsburg Empire 1914-1918* (London, 1961). Josef Redlich, *Österreichische Regierung und Verwaltung im Weltkriege* (Vienna, 1925), is an important analysis of the incredible workings of the Stürgkh System. Here again, though, imaginative literature is most successful in describing the alternating hopes and despairs of Austria at war. Many of the memoirs, especially Trotsky and Zweig, capture the enthusiasm of the outbreak of the war, but no other work chronicles the rise and fall of the Austrian spirit as does Karl Kraus, *Die Letzen Tage der Menschheit*, an untranslatable satire in the form of a five-act play intended for performance over ten successive evenings.

CHAPTERS 11 AND 12

Fritz describes his tribulations in the pretrial interrogation. The letter of resignation and the Manifesto to the Internationals are included with the transcript of the interrogation in *Vor dem Ausnahmegericht* (1923). Fritz's wartime speeches and writings are collected in *Die Erneuerung der Internationale*, Robert Danneberg, ed. (Vienna, 1918). Victor's and Emma's views are in letters in *Victor Adlers Briefwechsel*. The important party documents are in Brügel, *Geschichte* and Rudolf Neck, *Arbeiterschaft und Staat im Ersten Weltkrieg 1914–1918* (Vienna, 1964). The collapse of the International and the efforts of the Zimmerwald Commission are described and documented in Merle Fainsod, *International Socialism and the World War* (New York, 1969) and in Horst Lademacher, *Die Zimmerwalder Bewegung* (The Hague, 1967), as well as in the memoirs of participants such as Angelica Balabanova and Trotsky. Fritz's own contacts with the Zimmerwald movement are documented in letters in the Robert Grimm Archive of the Internationaal Instituut voor Sociale Geschiedenis.

CHAPTERS 13 AND 14

Fritz described almost everything that led up to the assassination in the pretrial interrogation. I have added some material on the Executive Committee meeting of October 20, 1916, and the events of the morning of October 21, from the trial transcript. There is no evidence that Fritz thought about the passages from

Marx's *Theses on Feuerbach* at this time, but Fritz referred to the *Theses* in several speeches and articles, which inspired me to the poetic liberty of supposing his thoughts.

CHAPTER 15

Victor's reactions are described in the unpublished memoirs of Emma Adler, Max Winter, and Wilhelm Ellenbogen in the Adler-Archiv. Fritz describes the interrogation procedure and his reactions in the foreward to *Vor dem Ausnahmegericht* (1923). Kathia's letter to Victor and Emma, and one of Fritz's descriptions of his discovery are in Rudolf Neck, *Arbeiterschaft*. Fritz's letters to Kathia and Emma are included in the transcript of the trial. Victor's defense work is described in *Victor Adler's Briefwechsel*, and Fritz's experiences in jail are described in letters to his parents in the Adler-Archiv. One of these letters was published in the *Neue Freie Presse*, May 19, 1917. Philip Frank's appraisal of the discovery is in his *Einstein, his Life and Times* (New York, 1947). The postcard from Einstein is in the Adler-Archiv, and was published in *Archiv* (Mitteilungsblatt des Vereins für Geschichte der Arbeiterbewegung), vol. 2 (1967).

CHAPTER 16

See the notes to chapters 9 and 10, and the memoirs of Ottokar Czernin, *Im Weltkriege* (Berlin, 1919).

CHAPTERS 17, 18, AND 19

The only complete edition of the trial transcript is in *Vor dem Ausnahmegericht* (1923). Details on the crowds and the staging of the courtroom drama are from the *Neue Freie Presse* and the *Arbeiter-Zeitung*.

CHAPTER 20

The letter from "H. Z." is in *Archiv*, vol. 2 (1967). Fritz describes his prison experiences in letters to Louise Kautsky in the

Kautsky Family Archive of the Internationaal Instituut voor Sociale Geschiedenis.

CHAPTERS 21 AND 22

The breakup of the monarchy has attracted more attention than any other aspect of its history. I have relied mainly on the materials cited in the notes to chapters 9 and 10, together with Otto Bauer's hastily composed but brilliant study, *Die österreichische Revolution* (Vienna, 1923). There are some useful documents in Brügel, *Geschichte*, and in Rudolf Neck, ed., *Österreich im Jahre 1918* (Vienna, 1968).

CHAPTER 23

The halting start of the Austrian Republic is described at close hand by the British consul in C. A. Macartney, *The Social Revolution in Austria* (Cambridge, 1926). Stefan Zweig was a witness to Karl's departure from Austria and described it in *The World of Yesterday*. Herr Habsburg's wretched finale is recounted in Tomás von Erlödy, *Habsburg's Weg von Wilhelm zu Briand, Die Memoiren des Grafen Tomás von Erlödy* (Zurich, 1931). Fritz's later life is recounted in Braunthal, *Victor und Friedrich Adler*, and documented in the enormous collection of letters and papers in the Adler-Archiv, the product of almost forty years of thankless and inglorious labor. The remark of Arturo Barea is in his *The Clash* (London, 1946), and the remark of Leon Blum was told me by a witness who wishes to remain anonymous.

The many friends and colleagues who have offered advice and criticism, and the many librarians and archivists in Europe and the United States whose helpfulness I have shamelessly exploited, will hopefully forgive me if I do not thank them all by name. Yet I cannot forego a special word of gratitude to a few individuals without whose aid this book could never have been

FRITZ

written: Mej. Marie Hunink of the Internationaal Instituut voor Sociale Geschiedenis and Frau Dr. Wanda Lanzer of the Adler-Archiv located, identified, and deciphered dozens of manuscripts, documents, and letters. Mrs. Sophie Lazarsfeld and Professor Paul Lazarsfeld patiently shared their memoirs and memories, and graciously allowed me access to the unpublished Adler correspondence that they have placed in the Adler-Archive. And finally, my wife, Heather, not only supplied invaluable legal advice and criticism, but for more than two years put up with the pratings of an intense young man with a bushy mustache and gold-rimmed glasses.

Yonkers, New York
October 1970

326

Index